Connected

From Godfather to God-the-Father

J. Alden Hall

choose now
PUBLISHING

J. Alden Hall

Published by Choose NOW Publishing,
300 N. Maplewood Drive
Rantoul, Illinois, 61866
www.choosenowpublishing.com.
Our mission is to provide issue-driven resources for families.

Printed in the United States of America.

Acknowledgements

Just like my life wasn't a solitary adventure, writing about it took the inspiration, consolation, and encouragement of many. So I would like to extend my heartfelt and eternal thanks to several people.

First and foremost I thank God who gave me His Son. The good news in this book is all about you. May you get all the glory.

And, in no particular order:

To Nicole O'Dell, and her team at Choose NOW Publishing, I thank you for your hard work in taking this manuscript and giving it the breath of life. Your ministry heart is refreshing.

To the members and staff of the three churches I have been a member of since my release from prison: North Peachtree Baptist, I'm still amazed by how you accepted this baby-Christian ex-con. First Redeemer, it was a joy and an honor to be part of your birth. I love whom you've chosen as your new pastor! Sugar Hill Church, your servant's heart is what the Church is all about.

To the ministries I have been honored to serve. May God continue to bless you as you follow His will.

To Bruce Wilkinson, Bill Phillips, Jim Kinney, and the other teachers, mentors, and advisors who have helped me on my Christian walk. Your inspiration and counsel has been invaluable.

To Ane Mulligan and the sweet ladies of the Seedwriter's group. This book would still be but a thought without you all. Your help, encouragement, and smiles continue to warm my heart.

To my family, I pray that your lives are daily filled with joy that only comes from God. Where I have failed you, please accept my sincere apology. Where I have not, give the credit to The One who changed me.

To my wife's mother Blanche. Your acceptance and prayers for me were only surpassed by your walk. I wish you were still here to read this, but I can't wait to visit your marvelous mansion in heaven.

Finally, to my wife Judy. Your passion for Christ and your family is a wonder to behold. Thank you for putting up with my many faults and for never giving up on me – I love you more than you will ever know!

Foreword

The story of Jim Hall's life is a testimony of the supernatural, life-changing grace of The Lord Jesus Christ. This book chronicles the story of one man who got caught up in the enticing bondage of the mob with all the allure of money, power, and control. But we rejoice to see the darkness of the underworld dispelled by the glorious light of the Gospel of Jesus Christ.

No one's sins stretch beyond the loving reach of the grace and mercy of the Lord Jesus Christ. This truth shines through the life of Jim Hall. You will be captivated by the transparent and truthful story of how he went from having every worldly thing with the mob, yet had no peace.

Convicted, imprisoned, and then pardoned in life and for eternity, J. Alden Hall experiences the transforming power of salvation as he begins to understand his true purpose.

It was around this time, about twenty-five years ago, our paths crossed in an Atlanta church. There I found a spirit-filled man and his loving wife faithfully serving in the church. The joy of the Lord radiated from their lives. Since those days I have observed how Jim Hall has been used in several Christian leadership positions. And in these roles he has served with even more zeal and commitment than he exhibited in his former life. God truly redeemed all the enemy tried to do through Jim Hall's life.

This book is a true testament of how wonderful and free is the grace of our Heavenly Father.

Dr. Richard Harris
Ambassador-at-large and former
President of the North American Mission Board

5

I've gathered memories from a life only God could have salvaged. I've done my best to recreate events, locales, and conversations as accurately as possible. While all the incidents are true to my memory, some names and identifying details have been changed to protect the privacy of some and the safety of others.

~ J. Alden Hall

Part One

What if faith, not fear, was your default reaction to threats? If you could hover a fear magnet over your heart and extract every last shaving of dread, insecurity, or doubt, what would remain? Envision a day, just one day, where you could trust more and fear less.

– Max Lucado

Chapter 1
That Day

"There is always one moment in childhood when the door opens and lets the future in."
Graham Greene, The Power and the Glory

Bad choices are sometimes birthed before we make them. Like all babies, I came into the world free, made in the image of God. However, I lived much of my life as a prisoner of my selfishness and greed...and eventually of the federal penitentiary system.

My incarceration, birthed in fear and overflowing with wrong decisions, began on a summer morning in 1954, which I refer to as *That Day.*

I was seven.

The rooster screamed for my eyes to open. I'd never seen this bird or even knew who owned it, but always welcomed its voice on weekends. I ran to the window to confirm what I already knew. Sunshine. Warmth. And lots of both. I tossed on my clothes and bolted to the kitchen. Saturday. Dad would have a great breakfast waiting. Maybe even his famous chocolate-chip pancakes. Famous to me, anyway. We'd eat together, and then I'd be free.

Mom's trained voice sang a Doris Day tune as I grabbed my usual chair at the table. I flopped on a seat and rolled up the flapjack.

"Bobo, use your fork and make sure to chew each bite at least thirty times."

"But, Mom, they're pancakes." Who counted someone's chews, anyway?

From the stove Dad smiled, "Bobo, if you don't chew your food, your poots will smell."

"D-a-a-d!" Thank heaven there were no cute girls around. Parents could be so embarrassing. Times like that, I wished he'd call me by my given name Jim. James would do, too. But no one ever did.

It was like any Saturday in the small Michigan town where we'd moved two years before. With Dad gone all week at his job as Chicago pastry chef, weekends were special. But nothing could keep a young boy in the house on such a beautiful day. I gobbled up he last of my food and gulped my OJ. I was so out of there.

Dad rinsed the plates, and Mom tucked a carton of juice in my pack as I blew through the kitchen in search of my shoes.

"Bye, Mom! Bye, Dad!" I called to the open window as I threw one leg over my bicycle seat and turned in the direction of anywhere.

That day, my ride took me up a super high hill— challenging for a boy whose feet barely touched the pedals. At the top, I stopped to rest and sip from a carton of orange juice. I peered down the hill I'd just climbed.

My gaze stretched to the right beyond the rows of houses that dotted the ground directly below.

"Wait a sec." I searched for the streetlamp on the corner of my road and then counted five houses over. I peered closer at what I was sure was my driveway. Four squad cars. What on earth were four cruisers doing in front of my house? That could mean nothing but trouble.

My juice sprayed across my shin as I dropped it to the ground. I sailed down the hill I'd just powered my way up and then pumped my short legs as hard as I could to keep my momentum. What I'd give that moment for a bike with gears.

I maneuvered my bike past one brown and three black squad cars parked on the street...waiting. Biking slowly up the driveway, I passed a dark, unmarked vehicle with a small blue bubble thing on the roof above the driver's door.

I hoisted my leg over and jumped, my still-moving bike sailed on rider-less, and then dumped onto the grass. I ran hard, right into the arms of a huge cowboy.

"Whoa, where you think you going?" The man was massive. His brown uniform, beige cowboy hat, and holstered gun reminded me of an unmasked Lone Ranger.

"You belong here young man?"

I stared up at his huge head, certain he could swallow me whole if he chose. No words came.

"Is this your house?"

I think I nodded.

"What's your name?"

"Bobo."

"Okay, Bobo," I sensed the smile in his voice though none appeared on his face. "Why don't you wait here with me until everyone's finished inside?" The man knelt on one knee. Even bent over, he seemed colossal. His immense fingers softly squeezed my shoulder. I'd never seen anything like it. His thumb was bigger than my whole hand.

"Is that your bike?"

Would he get mad if I didn't talk? But no matter how hard I tried, I couldn't get the words to leave my mouth.

"It's sure a pretty one." He seemed like a nice man, but I stayed frozen in place. Giants can be very tricky.

The front door flew open and two policemen darted out. Shouting something I couldn't understand, they sprinted around to the back of my house. Why were they holding guns? Something bad happened in my house.

My muscles strained toward the front door. I had to get in there. I had to know. But once I knew, there'd be no going back. Maybe not knowing was better.

The hulk beside me rose and joined the other officers in a huddle like they do at football games. In less than a minute, they all, expect the big one, rushed to their cars and sped off with sirens shrieking and blue lights flashing.

The beast offered me an open hand.

I froze. I couldn't touch that guy. What if he was bad?

He nodded. "It's okay. I'm not going to hurt you."

Something told me he was telling the truth, so I reached for his hand, grateful for the contact. How could such thick fingers be so gentle? We headed to the door where my mother stood.

"Thank you, Sheriff." She peeled my hand from his, my grip tighter than I'd realized.

"That's all right, Billie, I'm sure it'll all work out." He offered my mom a sympathetic smile.

He strode to his car and opened the door, but stopped. He lumbered to my bike and lifted it off the ground like it was a feather. He took a handkerchief from his pocket and wiped my bicycle clean, then wheeled it into the garage just like my dad would have done.

Where was Dad?

Tears streamed down the sheriff's face. What did that mean? Giants weren't supposed to cry.

I glanced at Mom. Dark circles had appeared under her bloodshot eyes and her uncombed hair looked a bit crazy.

I had to know. "Where's Dad?"

"Later ... we have to talk."

Maybe I could find him myself. I marched to the kitchen where a medley of coffee cups and ashtrays littered the table and the window ledge. One lay shattered on the floor. I collected the chunks of white porcelain of Dad's last Father's Day gift. The spilled coffee blended with the caramel linoleum floor.

I placed the broken fragments on the table and headed to the living room.

I heard voices outside. Was that shouting? Had Dad come back? I peeked through the heavy drapes. The cars that had sped off minutes before were back.

"Mommy, where's Daddy, and what are the police doing here?"

She paced the living room and whispered into the phone. "Madge, could you please keep the kids tonight, maybe tomorrow too? No, Bobo will stay with me. Thanks, I'll explain everything tomorrow." Mom hung up the phone and tapped on the red plastic and chrome kitchen chair. Obediently, I sat down. She took a seat across from me and pulled a long, shaky draw from her cigarette. "Bobo, let's talk."

That's the second time she said this. It seemed strange because only adults "talked." Her fingers massaged her temples so hard I thought her eyes might pop out. "I don't know how to explain this to you, to anyone ... even to myself."

"Bobo, the police say your dad is someone else, not who we think." She tried to use the sleeves of her light blue robe to wipe her tears, but it was no use, there were too many.

"But, how can Daddy not be Daddy?"

"No, he's your dad. It's just that..." She drew in another puff. "I just don't know..." Her sobs took over.

I put my arms around her and held her. Our tears mingled as she clung to me. But why was I crying? Nothing made sense.

She left the room and returned with a roll of toilet paper, took a handful for herself, and handed me the rest.

"He's your father, but they say he's someone different than we think. While you were out the sheriff arrived with some of his men and two FBI agents. They wanted to talk with your dad. I yelled for him. He came out of the kitchen carrying the baby."

She dropped her cigarette into a coffee cup to swim with the other butts, and shook another from the pack. Trembling hands worked at the lighter until she managed to light her next smoke. "The FBI said they had some reason to believe your dad was an escaped prisoner from the Missouri State Prison. They asked him to get dressed and come down to the local police station. About that time, a couple other police cars pulled up."

A sort of buzzing filled my brain.

Her whole body trembled. She used both hands to get the cigarette to her lips and then sucked on it like it was oxygen.

"Bob, the sheriff, who both your dad and I know, said this had to be some kind of mistake. He said the County gets a mistaken identity from the FBI pretty often. I offered to make some more coffee and your dad went into the bedroom to put some clothes on." Mom walked to the refrigerator, grabbed the orange juice and drank directly from the carton. She always told us to never do that, but when she handed it to me I took a long gulp. Some rules don't matter when a dad goes to jail.

"About the time Madge left with your brother and sister, and one of the FBI agents asked me to tell your dad he needed to get a move on. I went to the bedroom, but when I opened the door it was empty, and the window was open. Dad was gone."

"Gone? Gone where?"

"Your father ran away through the cornfields. He escaped from the police!"

Escaped? Where? Why? The room spun. I looked at the floor to make sure it was still there.

"Bobo, you've got to be brave." Mom clutched my hand.

I wanted to be strong like John Wayne and Gary Cooper in the movies, but fear begins with the unknown. I stared into her eyes. Surely she'd pull me into her arms and tell me it would be okay. She'd tell me that she'd take care of me ... of us.

Mom palmed her pack of smokes and stumbled to her bedroom. The door closed with a loud thud.

I paced the room. What had he done? When had he escaped? How did they find out? I clutched at my hair. Why hadn't he told us? Why had he run? The questions ... it was too much.

I ran to the bedroom door and knocked softly so it wouldn't startle her.

"Leave me alone! No more questions." Her wail sound far away, under a pillow maybe.

I stumbled away from the door. I'd leave her alone, but I was the one truly left alone.

The day passed in a blur as I waited for something to happen. For the police to come back with news. For Dad to come back through the window and tell me it was okay. Or take me with him. For me to wake up and discover it had all been a dream.

Night fell, and I needed escape. I crawled into bed begging my body to sleep. Maybe it was time to pray for real. Not the little-kid prayers I'd been saying since I was born, but the kind of prayers grown-ups prayed in church.

"God, please keep my daddy safe. Please bring him home. And please make my mom come to my room and kiss me goodnight." Her arms around me would help me get through the night.

The dark silence droned on and on. If God was real, then He wasn't listening to me.

Mom never came.

Chapter 2
Lives Intertwined

"One sinner destroys much good." Ecclesiastes 9:18

I pushed aside the green, plastic soldiers that blocked the face of my alarm clock. Nine-fifteen? I never slept this late. If the rooster didn't rouse me, my sister's hungry cries always did. Then it hit me. *Yesterday.*

I raced to the kitchen, but there was no sign of breakfast, or my mother. I knocked on her door. "Mom, are you in there?"

"Go away." Her muffled voice seemed to come from beneath a pillow again.

I tiptoed to the kitchen and emptied a box of Cheerios into a bowl. I added milk and headed to the living room. I fumbled with the dial on the television set. Not that there would be anything worth watching. Sunday mornings were for nothing but news or preachers. Didn't they know kids were home on Sunday mornings? Or maybe they thought kids should be in church.

I jumped at the slam of a car door and looked out the window. Dad?

No. The neighbors were dressed up and heading to their cars. Judging by the little white gloves and white hats on the girls, at least they were going to church.

"Stupid." I tried out the word Dad used to describe churchgoers. We were Catholics, whatever that meant. But it always seemed like Dad agreed with the Bing Crosby movies. "Church is full of nothing but hypocrites." A hypocrite sounded a lot like something I didn't want to be.

I gazed out the window. Hypocrite or not I'd have gone with my neighbors to church to get out of the house and away from reality.

I spooned the cereal to my mouth until nothing was left but warm milk, then set the bowl on the end table. I laid my arms on the windowsill and rested my chin on the top of my clasped hands. As the morning sun climbed, I watched friends ride their bikes up the same hill I'd topped yesterday.

What would happen if I went with them? Would Mom know? Or care? But she probably shouldn't be left alone. And what if she came out to comfort me and I'd already left. I stared at the closed door to her room. Could I will it to happen?

The rest of the day was like a foggy snapshot. Around noon I knocked on her door, but no answer. The rule had always been to never bother Mommy and Daddy if their door was closed, but this was different, right? I paced my fingers around the knob and gave it a slight twist. No luck.

I leaned against the locked door and slid to the carpet. I rested my head against the door and waited. The sun sank behind the trees and the room was cloaked in darkness. The door never opened.

***

Bacon?

I sat up and flung the covers off my body. The smell of bacon meant only one thing. Mom was cooking. She'd come out of her bedroom.

I scurried down the hall and slid into the kitchen. She sat at the dinette reading a newspaper. The smoke from her ashtray and her steaming coffee cup intertwined and rose as one. Her eyes locked with mine for a split second before they flitted off to focus on something else. Her face registered no flicker of emotion as she folded the paper and went to the stove, silent.

I followed her lead and sank into my usual chair. A thousand questions dying in my throat.

A typical Monday morning was chaotic and loud. The music from the radio would merge with my mother's voice as she sang along. Cindy, testing her own vocal chords, would cry with abandon while we ate. My younger brother and I would have to shout to be heard. I missed the disorder. Dad would sail into the room and swat Mom with a dishtowel. She'd cover her mouth and giggle.

"Mommy, is everything okay?"

She stood at the sink carefully washing a plate, wearing the same robe as she'd been wearing on Saturday when the cops were there. Her eyes stayed on the dirty dish. "You better be prepared to hear some bad things at school. Kids can be cruel." I stood at the door holding my lunch bag waiting for more. For comfort. Promises. Encouragement. Love. Something.

But that was it.

I imagined I was a covert CIA agent as I stealthily made my way into my seat, desperate to go unnoticed by my classmates and teacher. Oh no. The Monday morning report. What would I share about the weekend?

Bobby told the class why Jimmy Durante always said, "Goodnight Mrs. Calabash—wherever you are." Ruthie explained how to plant potatoes.

What would I share? I wiped my palms on my legs. Maybe I'd pretend I was sick and go to the nurse's office.

Angela stood, her chair scraping on the tile floor. "I saw police car lights and heard the sirens while I was watching Mickey Mouse. It was so scary. My dad read in the paper this morning that an escaped convict opened a window and ran away. And ..." she looked around the room for effect. "...they never found him." Angela raised her eyebrows as if tell them to draw their own conclusions about the criminal on the loose.

Was it possible she had no idea it was my dad?

She pointed right at me.

My stomach flip-flopped.

"It's Bobo's dad the police are looking for."

Her words aimed a beeline to my heart, and I cringed as the sting of something I didn't yet understand entered my life. I didn't know its name was shame, but it hurt.

The minutes ticked by like a time bomb set to go off at recess. When the bell rang, I trudged out to the schoolyard as if walking to my own execution. The kids had all morning to come up with some real zingers.

"Did your dad kill someone?"

"Did you kill someone?"

So far not the brightest questions ever. I squared my shoulders and waited for more of the onslaught.

"Are you going to go to jail too, Bobo?"

"Bobo the bad guy! Bobo the bad guy!"

Ah, yes. There it was.

I covered my ears to block out the merciless questions and taunts the kids pelted at me for the twenty-two minutes outside. Did the teachers really not see? Or didn't they care? Alone in my room, I'd have buried my head in my pillow and sobbed. But I wouldn't let those mean kids see me that way. I would fight. Defend my dad no matter what.

If only I were bigger.

But these were my friends. Or they had been. They had to see it wasn't my fault. It wasn't even Dad's fault.

"It's just a mistake. You wait and see." I pulled my knees to my chest and rocked back and forth on the bench. "You'll be sorry you acted such a fool."

Dad would come home soon and everything would be all right.

It had to be.

***

"Don't say anything, they have the phone bugged!" Mom hissed into the receiver and then slammed the phone onto the hook on the wall. She glanced at the front door as if expecting company.

Nothing made sense anymore.

She took a quivery draw on her cigarette. Ashes drifted to the floor and joined the scatterings of ashes from days of chain smoking.

Her eyebrows raised as sirens sounded from far away. She smoked on as the noise drew closer. Within minutes, police were charging into our house with guns drawn. One took my mother aside and screamed, "We can take you to jail! You're aiding and abetting an escaped con. Who just called?"

Mom tried to light another cigarette, but her hands trembled so violently she couldn't get the lighter to catch.

I ran into the kitchen and stood between her and the policeman. I took the lighter out of her hand and held up the blue flame.

She bent over and took a deep drag and held the smoke in her lungs as long as she could. After a few more puffs she seemed ready to answer the questions.

I planted my feet and remained a tiny buffer between her and the policeman. There was no way he'd hurt her on my watch.

"I don't know who called." She glared at the cop.

"Yes, you do." His hand rested on his holstered gun. Habit or threat?

"No, I really don't know. He hung up."

"If he hung up, how do you know it was a man?"

"I assumed so ... wouldn't you?" I'd never heard my mother's voice dripping with sarcasm in that way before. It was like she was someone else entirely.

My head felt like a volleyball for the twenty minutes they went back and forth with accusations and defenses.

"I didn't do anything wrong."

"You're interfering with an investigation."

"Prove it." Mom crossed her arms across her chest.

"Do you really think we don't have recordings of your phone calls?"

They were recording our calls? Who had I spoken to? Had I said anything that could get Dad in trouble?

Finally the police officer strode to the front door and motioned for his partner to follow him. He gave one last look at my mom. "Next time you go straight to jail."

***

A loud bang sounded from the living room. My eyes snapped open and tried to adjust to the darkness. What was that?

There it was again.

"Shh. You'll wake Bobo."

I edged my way through the pitch-black living room and heard a noise in the kitchen. I tiptoed to the kitchen door and opened it just a crack.

Dad!

This was it. My life would return to normal. I could go to school and tell everyone it was all just a mistake. Dad was home. I reached for the light switch. I had to see him. To know he wasn't hurt.

"Don't turn the lights on!"

"But, Dad. I want to—" For the first time in the whole ordeal, it hit me. My father was a fugitive. He was a criminal. Just like in the movies.

I could only make out the shadowy silhouette of my mom in my daddy's arms, but the sound of my mother's sobbing was unmistakable. Her despair filled the room. Maybe Dad shouldn't have come back there.

"Dad, I got a plan." I'd been thinking about this for a couple days.

He crossed the room and bent down to look me in the eye. "What would that be?"

"Well, they didn't look in the attic when they were searching for you. You could move up there. I'll bring you food and ..." Before I could finish my parents laughed uncontrollably. But I was dead serious.

Soon my mother's tears returned. "What are we going to do? What are we going to do?"

"I'll get word to you." Then he was gone. Disappeared out the window just like he had the last time I'd laid eyes on him. No hug? Not even a pat on the head? I lowered my head and closed my eyes. Tears welled behind my lids, but I refused to cry. Tears were for children. It was time for me to grow up.

Chapter 3
Midnight Move

"Security is not the absence of danger, but the presence of God, no matter what the danger."
The Daily Walk Bible

Within a couple weeks of my dad's disappearance, the teasing at school had slowed. Kenny was still an annoying little brother and Cindy was as cute as ever. My mother's smile never returned, but she didn't stay locked up in her room anymore. In some ways, life seemed to be heading back to some form of normalcy. If normal meant walking by squad cars parked across the street every day or talking in hushed whispers whenever Dad's name was mentioned.

I think the nights were the worse.

Before *That Day* Mom would come into my room at bedtime and we'd say the only prayer I knew. "Now I lay me down to sleep, I pray the Lord my soul to keep. If I should die before I wake, I pray the Lord my soul to take." I wasn't sure what a soul was, and really wasn't afraid I'd die during my sleep. But if I did, I wasn't sure I wanted anything taken–especially my soul. But the words made me feel good inside regardless.

Whenever I asked her about God, Mom always had the same reply. She'd sing, "Jesus loves you this I know, for the Bible tells me so..." She'd fumble her words and try to explain that Jesus was God. I believed her, although I couldn't figure out how that was possible or why it mattered.

Maybe it was the simplicity of my mother's prayers that assured me God cared about average people–even little kids like me. But, when the prayers stopped, did that mean God stopped caring? Was He punishing us for what Daddy did? Didn't He see it wasn't Mom's fault? And it definitely wasn't Kenny's or Cindy's. Maybe it was mine. Maybe I should have known what was going on and stopped it.

So, wishing for Mom to come sing and pray with me each night, I laid awake on my bed, fearful the police would smash our door down the moment my eyes slipped closed. Like sleep was the signal I'd given up.

I flopped over to my stomach and tried to drown the sounds of my own thoughts. Instead, I heard some faint whispering and then a dim moving light flashed under my closed door. I crept out of bed and carefully followed the sounds to the kitchen.

It was Mike, the friend who had hid my dad. He was holding a big box. Next to him my mother's arms were full with my sleeping sister. My bleary-eyed little brother was sitting on a chair looking up at them. "Shh, be quiet Bobo. Grab these boxes and help Mike carry them out to his car."

I deposited two small boxes of clothes and made my way around to the side of the house to my bike. I quietly pushed it toward the now full car.

"Bobo, there's no room for all of that." Mike shook his head and pointed at my bike. "Definitely not that."

"But..."

"No buts, son, we've got to take what's important."

Was he joking? To me, there was nothing more important. I loved my bike.

The car packed with bare necessities, my mother stood with her hand on the door handle and looked back at her house. She wept. "Mike, this was my dream. All I ever hoped for out of life was right there in that house." She sighed and climbed in.

Mike softly closed the door, slid into the driver's seat, and pulled away.

She never looked back.

The jam-packed back seat was a lonely place. Kenny and I sat like bookends for the cartons crammed between us. We rode in complete silence. Mike kept the lights off, and drove slowly and carefully.

I glanced at the boxes and a frightening reality hit me—this was all we had. Everything else was gone forever. Tears streamed down my cheeks as I turned to watch the dark outline of our home become smaller. The questions slurred together. "Where are we going? Will we come back?" Of course we wouldn't. Even I knew that.

"Bobo, be brave." It was the same command she'd given me *that day,* but this was different. This wasn't make-believe and it wasn't the movies. I wasn't John Wayne. I wasn't crying just because of fear, but because I knew my life had changed—and not for the better.

Kenny asked, "Where we going Momma?"

"To Chicago."

"Will Daddy be there?"

I sat up to hear.

"I don't know Kenny, I just don't know. Now go back to sleep."

He balled himself up and quickly drifted off.

How could he sleep? Oh, he was just a little boy and didn't know better. I was determined to stay awake, maybe forever.

I felt a nudge. "Bobo, you awake?" I rubbed my eyes and leaned forward to touch my mother's shoulder. "Yes."

"Try to not wake Kenny when we start carrying stuff from the car."

"Where are we?"

"We're home." Her voice was weary.

"Home?" Had we turned around and gone back while I was asleep? No, of course not, we were driving to Chicago.

Everything would be okay in Chicago. Right? I pictured a new bike with me peddling it around the nearby Lincoln Park. Then, my mind quickly latched onto the thought of the zoo, and its giraffes. Often, right before our bedtime prayers I'd ask my mother, "Tell me about the giraffes." She always smiled as she recited the story. She seemed to like it as much as I did.

"One day, when you were three, we were at the park. I was pushing you on a swing at the playground near the zoo. Kenny was with a neighbor, and Cindy wasn't born yet. I was just about to take you home when a man came up to me and said, 'Want to be on TV?'"

"TV?"

"I work for NBC and there's a live show-and-tell television program that's being filmed at the zoo. It's called *Zoo Parade*, and it stars Marlin Perkins. We're looking for some people to be part of the audience."

"Bobo, I didn't know if he was feeding me a line, but when he showed me his business card with the NBC logo I said, 'Sure, what'll I have to do?'"

"I followed him to a table set up outside a building next to the zoo where I signed some papers."

Every time I thought of my mother's story, I could hear the sounds and smell the odors of the zoo. As much as I craved for her to get to the giraffes, I never wanted her to skip anything.

"You held my hand when we were ushered into a dark room that smelled of sawdust. We sat down on some long boards lying on wooden crates. Before long, about two dozen other women with children joined us there."

"When the bright lights shot on, I could see we were in a barn with cameras on pedestals and microphones dangling in the air. A lot of the kids acted up, some were cried, but not you. You just sat there with your eyes wide with excitement."

"That first show they brought in hawks, an elephant, and some snakes. When the filming stopped, the man who invited us gave me a piece of paper that said we could come back. I bet they noticed how well you behaved. We became regular members of the audience and sometimes were on the show."

I always knew what was coming next, and it never failed to electrify me.

"And of course, there were the giraffes..." She loved to tease me, to hear me say, "Tell me. *Please* tell me!"

"One day Mr. Perkins walked up and asked, "'Is it okay if we feature your son on our program today?'"

"Doing what?"

"We'd like him to ride in on a giraffe. He's wearing a cute cowboy's outfit and we're putting a saddle on the giraffe. We thought it would look great."

"Will he be safe?"

"Sure, he'll be on one of the young ones, and there will be a trainer on the other side. There'll be a hand on him at all times."

"Bobo, that's how it all started. You did so well that day. They began each program that season with you riding out on a giraffe.

Often, when I felt I was drowning in worry and insecurity, I clung to this happy story like a life preserver. But as much as I wanted to, I never could remember the program or my rides.

The car bounced to a stop, and I reached my hand to the back of the seat in front of me. The streetlights cast a somber glow on a row of old dull apartments. Some had small shops on the ground floor with signs written in a language I couldn't read. There would be no giraffes here.

Mike and my mother opened their doors, my mother leaned over the front seat and stared into my eyes as if compelling maturity to bloom. "Bobo, watch your brother. We'll be right back."

In a few minutes Mike appeared with another man and they made several trips into one of the apartment buildings with boxes. Soon, Mike lifted the still sleeping Kenny.

The stranger said, "You stay with the car until we get all the boxes up."

In a few short trips they were done, so I followed them. As I climbed the three flights of stairs I noticed a strangely familiar smell. It seemed to ooze from the walls. It smelled like, well, I wasn't supposed to use this word, but the only thing that came to my mind to describe it was *pee*.

When I walked through the door where the last stack of boxes had just disappeared, the stench fused with the odor of garlic, beer, and cigarettes.

I clutched my stomach. How long would we have to endure that smell? I stepped in a bit farther. The door from the entryway opened directly into a small kitchen dimly lit by a lone light bulb hanging from a frayed electrical cord.

"You going to come in or are you waiting for more moths to follow you?" A plump lady pulled the tie tighter around her faded yellow bathrobe and ushered me into the apartment.

"Bobo, this is my sister Agnes, your aunt. And that," she pointed to the stranger who'd joined Mike to carry boxes, "is your Uncle Sheryl. They've been nice enough to let us stay with them for a while."

A while. That didn't sound permanent. Thank goodness. I took a quick inventory of our new home. There was no wall separating the small kitchen from the living room. To the right were two doors.

Before I could ask where they led, my aunt said, "The first door is where Sheryl and I sleep, and your cousins Shirley Ann and Dickey are asleep in the other room."

I had to force my jaw to stay put when all it wanted to do was drop open in shock. *Where do we stay?*

Mom patted my arm. "You'll like it here. It's in an area called Little Italy and it's near Maxwell Street."

Was that supposed to mean something to me? My aunt walked into the living room and turned a lamp on. "Billie, I got our old baby bed in the corner for Cindy, and made up the couch for you."

I looked at my brother. Nope he wasn't invisible, so I assumed I wasn't as well. "What about us?"

"Over there." My aunt pointed next to the baby bed. "I've done fixed you boys up with some blankets on the floor. It'll be just like camping."

Camping? I looked around and saw no tents. But what point was there in complaining? "Great, I love to camp."

30

"Mommy, where do I sit?" Kenny tugged on the hem of her skirt.

Cindy's wails kicked up to a decibel I'd never thought humanly possible.

"Does this child always screech like this?" My aunt scowled.

"How long are they going to stay with us?" Shirley Ann spoke loud enough to be heard over Cindy's cries.

Looking like a kettle ready to blow, my uncle silently sat at the end of the table.

I perched on my mother's couch/bed in our living/bedroom. It seemed wise to stay out of range. I tried to watch the pandemonium with the same distance one might watch an episode of The Honeymooners, but that distance was hard to fake. After all, it was my life.

After my uncle left for work, and Cindy seemed at peace, my mother turned to me. "Bobo, come and eat."

More than food, I wanted answers. "How long will we be here?" I whispered so Aunt Agnes wouldn't hear and think me ungrateful.

My mother faced the stove—no answer.

"Where's Daddy?" I knew she heard me, but her failure to reply told me it was time to shut up. I ate my bacon and eggs in silence. "What about school?"

"I'll work on that today. It may take a few days."

It was the first good news since we'd arrived. I wasn't ready to face new kids. I looked around the cramped apartment. "Can I watch TV?" It was directly in front of the sofa bed.

"Sure, go ahead." My aunt replied. I slowly turned the knob. Maybe Zoo Parade would be on so I could watch the giraffes and dream of a time I couldn't even remember.

Chapter 4
Cover Story

"We've all heard the story of Pinocchio. You better watch out baby. Your nose is starting to grow." –Kathy Murray, One Lie Leads to Another

Aunt Agnes' apartment was as drab and dreary as the flat itself. The soap operas on TV went well with the smells, and by eleven o'clock, I couldn't take it anymore. Mom had to do something about this. I worked up my best puppy-dog face and then crept into the kitchen where she sat at the table with her sister.

"There's nothing to do. I'm bored." I repeated a mantra I'd been whining since I was four. Maybe we'd go to the park or, even better, apartment hunting.

"Why don't you go outside and check out your new neighborhood?" Mom never looked at my sad face.

Alone? Even better. I quickly ran to where we slept and grabbed my shoes.

"Better write the address down, in case you get lost."

I looked at a piece of mail on the side table near the doorway and ripped off the address label. That would do.

I ran down the nasty steps holding my breath. I exhaled as I pushed through the old wooden door and exited onto a cement stoop gasping for fresh air to fill my lungs. What I saw when I looked into the new world before me stopped me in my tracks.

Cars and buses filled the street with sounds and smoke. A storeowner wiped at a window—what he could reach between the iron bars, anyway. Delivery trucks double-parked and angry fists fluttered from open car windows. People dodged left and right, evading each other on the tiny sidewalks. No one cared one whit about what anyone else was doing. It was busy, bossy, and beautiful–I loved it.

My legs came alive, and I skipped down the front stairs. I took a left and started my newest adventure.

I merged with the swarm of commuters like a bird joining a formation. Amazing how no one stepped on me without ever seeming to notice me. There were people of different colors, some speaking languages I'd never heard before, and others wearing clothes made of colorful sheets. I recognized a couple Chinese men, or at least they looked like what I'd seen in the movies. I wiped the shock off my face before I drew attention.

As I moved down the street, the air changed with the smells of Italian restaurants mingled with Chinese cuisine–and sewage near one area. Soon I breathed in an enchanting scent that seemed to float on notes of music. Wait. The music was real. I could make out the faint sound of a saxophone and a clarinet. I looked up at the street sign where I stood. Halsted. But the sounds and smells seemed to be traveling from the road to my left–Maxwell Street.

As I stepped off of Halsted and onto Maxwell Street my world transformed. Before me stood a wall of people. The street and sidewalks were one. Shops, all with their doors open, extended out onto the sidewalk, display tables piled high with merchandise. Musicians played their tunes near overturned hats at their feet. Next to them lay blankets crammed with clothes, radios, even tires–all for sale.

The street welcomed no vehicles. Instead, there was a kaleidoscope of carts stuffed with socks, watches, shoes, and food. Peddlers loudly hawked their wares to the throngs. At the end of the street, white smoke levitated from Polish sausage and Italian beef stands. How had such a place existed on the same planet as the hill I rode up and down each day?

Could I go in? Would I be safe among the crowds? What if I got trampled? I shook my head. No way I was hanging back from the heaven in front of me. Life was too short to miss an opportunity like that. Look at what happened to Dad. Did he know such a place existed? What I would give to have just one afternoon to show him what I'd found.

It took me an hour to cover the first block. I passed a store with small Styrofoam heads all covered with different colored hair. The sign on its window read, "Hair direct from China." How strange. I stopped and watched a blind man playing a guitar. I crissed and I crossed from one side of the street to the other. That way I wouldn't miss anything–like the arguing couple just beyond the juggler.

My heart beat wildly as I realized my whole world had changed. And maybe there was something good to come out of it.

During our stay with my aunt these streets became my personal playground. Other little boys might have looked for swings and slides, but not me. My idea of playing was walking and soaking up everything I saw, heard, and smelled. I made up stories about the beggars, even made friends with some of them. I daydreamed about playing an instrument on the corner one day.

It wasn't long before I knew every nook and cranny of Maxwell Street. One day I stopped near the two shops with the same names, "Mark Levinson & Sons," directly across from each other.

"Hey Pete." I called out to the bongo player nearby. "What's up with the two stores with the same name?"

He slowed his tapping to a rhythmical mantra. "Ah, yes. Good ol' Mark Levinson had two sons, though the letter S is faded. When he died and left his store to his two sons–" He banged the drum and a puff of street dust blew up as he shrugged his shoulder. "They fought ... as brothers do ... and decided sharing wasn't for them. Neither would let go of his share, so they set up their own shops." He squinted across the street and shook his head. "So this is what we got."

I sat on my usual curb and waited for the bickering to begin.

Mark Jr. poked his head out the shop's front door. "Five socks, three dollars!"

Across the street, his brother waved his hand in disgust. "For three dollars I'll give you five socks, without holes!" Each time a prospect slowed the two brothers went to work. Seemed each was more worried about people not buying from their brother than about actually making a sale himself.

"Buy from him and get moth-eaten socks."

"Moths won't even eat his paper socks."

Back and forth went the banter. Sometimes they would yell at each other with their fists waving in the air. No movie could be more original and exciting. And best of all, that day I learned two new words: Yutz and Putz. Who cared what they meant?

Six months after I discovered Maxwell Street, Dad showed up.

***

I sat on the curb watching the sock-sellers movie, my tummy rumbling.

"Bobo!"

What was that?

"Bobo, over here!"

I peeked around bookseller's cart and saw him. Dad!

I ran to him, wanting to jump into his arms, but the furtive glances and dark shadows over his eyes held me back. He was scared.

Dad held out his hand and offered me one of the greatest presents I ever received—a Chicago hot dog! I'd smelled them every day for six months. I'd heard people talk about them. But until I actually sank my teeth into that soft, steamed bun dotted with poppy seed, felt my teeth pierce the sharp onions, and let the tangy relish mingle with the mustard fill my mouth—no way I'd have known what I'd been missing. I chewed slowly, wanting to savor every bite.

But my Dad. He'd be leaving wouldn't he? Would I ever see him again? The hot dog sank into my guy with a thud.

"How'd you find me?"

"I followed you from school."

We sat on the curb and he bit a large hunk from his dog. I took tiny nibbles from mine to prolong the minutes. I told him about the sock peddlers and all the other neat things I found. He told me he had a job at a bakery on the north side of town and he lived in a small room above it.

"I'm glad you like it here." Dad smiled with a face full of regret and grief.

If he thought I liked it, maybe he wouldn't take us away with him. "I don't like it that much. Can we go home again?"

Dad finished off his hot dog and reached in his pocket. He pulled out some crumpled napkins, gave some to me and wiped his fingers. He stood up, tossed the paper in a barrel, so I followed. No. He was going to disappear. I could sense him pulling away.

He handed me a folded envelope.

"Give this to your mom?"

I shoved it into my pocket. "Sure, but are we all going to be living together soon?"

"Can you keep a secret?" Dad glanced up one side of the street and down the other.

"Sure." I'd promise the moon for information.

He took my left hand in his and we started walking. "I'll be coming for you and the family soon, and we'll all be together again. But you can't tell anyone."

Really? "I won't tell a single soul. Not one word." My heart raced with excitement.

He crouched down on one knee and took my face in his meaty hands. It wasn't a soft gesture. It was more like a trainer might grab a dog's nose to get it to obey. "If a stranger shows up and starts asking you questions, you've got to promise me you won't tell them you've seen me."

"But I did see you." Even as I said it, I knew better. He squeezed my face a little harder.

"You didn't see me. If a stranger asks you anything about me, lie."

I cocked my head. No stranger ever asked me anything. Adults—except nuns, and they didn't count—ignored little kids, especially if they weren't causing any trouble. Why would anyone ask me anything?

But more confusing, I'd just been ordered to lie–by my dad. That wasn't right. Dad had always said to tell the truth no matter what. I mean, I was no stranger to lying like any boy, but wasn't that bad?

What had changed?

But if I questioned him, maybe he'd stop coming to see me. Maybe he'd never come back for us.

I gave a solemn nod. "I promise."

He smiled and held out a clenched fist. When he opened it a moment later, a shiny quarter lay gleaming on his palm. "Go ahead. Take it."

I grabbed it as fast I could. "Thanks, but when..."

He held a finger to his lips. "Now you head on home."

He turned and walked away. No hug. No, "I love you." But I hadn't really expected Dad to show emotion...it wasn't his way.

***

"Hi, are you Jim?"

I stopped kicking at the pebbles on the sidewalk and squinted into the sun at a man in a grey suit. The only ones who called me Jim were the teachers. "Yes sir."

"Well, I'm an old friend of your dad and mom." Wearing that fancy suit, he didn't look like any of my parent's friends. "I haven't seen your dad for a while, where's he been staying? Does he come by your apartment much?"

I wasn't quite eight, but my lie antenna blinked.

This was the stranger Dad had warned about. It was time to lie. I had lied before, but this was different. This was big and important. The nuns said God got mad at liars. But it's okay to lie if it's helping someone, right? And if I promised. "No, sir. I haven't seen my dad since we came to Chicago."

"Certainly you know where he is staying, don't you?"

What would the Bowery boys say? How would Mickey Rooney protect his dad and send the law on a wild goose chase? That was it!

"New York City!" I was a genius. That was about as far away as possible. Let them look there.

I then learned something that would prove true over and over. One lie turned into another.

"Where in New York City?"

What? There was a "where" in New York City?

Of course. Just like the Lincoln Park and Maxwell Street areas of Chicago, a city as big as New York had to have many neighborhoods. The only thing I knew about New York was from movies. Then, in a flash it came to me, the name flew from my lips.

"Chinatown!"

The man's face registered shock and then he laughed as he walked away. The laugh pierced through me as I realized I'd failed my dad.

Or maybe my dad failed me. Maybe that's what ate at my gut. My sense of right and wrong challenged. Fathers are smart, wise, and always truthful. I knew deep down lying was wrong, but how could it be if my father asked me to? And if he cared about me doing right, how could he have asked me to lie?

"As the twig is bent, so grows the tree," the nuns barked at us all the time. Well, that day, on Maxwell Street, the bending began.

Chapter 5
Schooldays

"... Grace is like water, then the church should be an ocean. It's not a museum for good people; it's a hospital for the broken." Jefferson Bethke, YouTube

A week after our move from Michigan, my mother announced, "Tomorrow you and Kenny start school."

Hiding out from the law and going to school just didn't seem compatible to me. I assumed I'd never go to school again. But as much as I enjoyed my Maxwell Street adventures in those early days, it would be nice to have some kids to play with.

"Bobo, you've got to be careful to not say anything about what happened or even where we used to live."

"What do I tell the teachers?"

"Don't worry, I've talked to them. You might want to avoid talking with kids about the past."

I didn't see a problem with that. Most second graders cared about playing and not about asking questions. No one would believe him anyway.

That morning the apartment was typical bedlam. A chorus of screams flooded the tiny space and squeezed the walls together.

"Where's my lunch?"

"Mommy, Dickey hit me!"

"Now, eat your food."

I ate my Corn Flakes and waited for Mom to get dressed. Hopefully the fluttering in my tummy would go away before school.

"Bobo, Kenny, come on." She wore a pretty blue dress, looked just like Liz Taylor in *Father of the Bride*. She reached for Kenny's hand and held it as we walked. She let me walk free, her other hand claimed by a cigarette.

Five blocks from the apartment, she stopped and pointed at the huge buildings across the street. "There's your school St. Anthony's."

I squinted at the massive church connected to a long, flat building. I let my eyes trail up the gray stones, past the tall spire that pointed to the sun. Instead of normal windows, it had smoky glass blocks I couldn't see through. What were they hiding in there that a kid couldn't see? Surely Mom would find out before she'd leave us there.

Be a man.

"Momma, I'll take Kenny now. You can go."

My mother smiled at my boldness. "No, I think it best I bring you to the principal first."

She crushed her cigarette with the sole of her shoe and took our hands. When we went through the massive double doors I was amazed at its size. It seemed huge, much bigger than my school in Michigan. It was eerie in its silence, and no one roamed the halls. I almost expected Vincent Price or Bela Lugosi to pop out of one of the closed doors.

"Where is everyone?" I asked my mother.

"They're at Mass. The principal thought it best you come in when no one else was around."

Mass? What's a Mass? Why did grownups say strange things like that but never explain it? Before I could ask about this Mass thing she stopped and knocked on a door. Its old wood had glass panes, but I was too short to peek through them. When it opened, I stared up. Was that a woman ... or something else?

Tall and dressed in black robes, with beads hanging off a belt, she wore a white cap with a strange long black babushka flowing down from it.

"Bobo, this is Sister Mary Patrick."

Okay, so a woman. But she was definitely not my sister. The lady held out her hand and I shook it. "Pleased to meet you Ma'am."

"So polite." The lady said with a smile. "Please call me Sister."

"Mrs. Hall, you may go now. I'll take it from here."

My mother walked away and then returned, stooped down, and pecked us both on a cheek. My first kiss since *That Day.* "Be good boys. Bobo, you get Kenny and come straight home after school." Then she was gone, and so went the sister-lady's smile. I never saw it again.

"Okay, young man," Her finger pointed like a weapon aimed at my face. "Let's get one thing straight right now. I don't want to ever hear the name Bobo again." She spat it like a dirty word. "Do you want to be called James or Jim?"

I'm sure my mouth hung open in shock.

"Jim should do." She motioned us to two seats in front of a huge desk.

Kenny's lower lip quivered for a moment before he clamped it between his teeth.

She moved to the other side and sat on a huge chair. Her seat so high it reminded me of the queen in Alice in Wonderland. I waited for the fateful words, "Off with their heads!" But thankfully they never came.

"Your mother told me about your little problem." The way she said it seemed dirty. "I'll do my best to keep it secret, but you two must never tell anyone about it. I won't allow anything to disrupt *my* school." She picked up a ruler and made it a weapon. "Do you boys understand?" She pointed the ruler at me.

I nodded.

Her aim then shifted to Kenny, but he just sat there looking confused. "Ma'am, Kenny really doesn't know–"

Whack! The ruler hit the desk. "Did I not tell you to call me Sister?"

Not a good time to ask her about this alleged kinship, so I said, "Sorry, Sister."

"That's better. You two boys be good, do your homework, and go to daily mass, and we'll be just fine."

I shouldn't ask, but my tongue moved faster than my brain. "What's mass?"

"You don't know what mass is? You do go to church don't you?" I knew what church was, but never had been in one.

"No, Sister." I murmured.

Her brow under the white of her cap crunched up. She stood and walked over to me. She crouched down and her big right hand took my jaw captive. "You are Catholic, aren't you?"

I wasn't sure what a Catholic is, but I sensed that my answer was important. "I'm not sure, Sister. I think so."

"Think so? What a way to raise a child." She released my face, turned to the desk and scribbled furiously on a small piece of paper.

"You bring this to your mother." She folded it in half, and then half again.

As soon as she looked away, I opened the note.

Mrs. Hall, please send the boys' baptism certificates.

She dropped Kenny off at a classroom first.

I peeked in and saw someone dressed like Sister talking to rows of little boys and girls. Looked safe enough.

We walked a bit farther down the hall to my classroom. Sister Mary Anthony ushered me through the door and nodded her head at another twin sister standing at the front.

"You'll be fine here. Any questions?"

Did I dare ask about the robes? Why did they wear them, were they heavy, and did they ever wear other clothes? It seemed like I should know, but I didn't want to give Sister another reason to get mad at my mother.

As I entered my classroom every eye turned on me. Because I wasn't dressed like them, or did they know something I didn't?

"Class this is Jim Hall, please welcome him." The lady dressed like the principal said.

"Hello Jim," the class called out in unison.

"I'm Sister Mary Margaret."

Oh no, another sister. And she's a Mary too! But at least she smiled.

The next day Mom gave me a note. "Bobo, give this to the principal."

I regret to inform you that my sons' baptism certificates were lost during our move.

Not calling my mom a liar, but I doubted it. I wasn't sure what baptism was, but if it had something to do with being a Catholic, I was pretty sure we weren't.

Sister Mary Anthony read my mother's message and grunted. "Why were you not in church this morning, and why aren't you wearing your uniforms?"

Didn't she know I was seven?

"Sister, I didn't know we had to go to church before school. What kind of uniform?"

She rolled her eyes and pointed at other students.

The kids were all dressed alike, sure. But what did she mean about uniforms? Soldiers and police wore uniforms, not little kids. But at that school the girls all wore white blouses with plaid skirts. And from Sister's tone, I assumed I'd soon be dressed in shades of blue, like all the other boys. A tie? To school? Yuck. But blending in with the others seemed like a good idea for someone hiding from the law.

She walked to a file cabinet, reached in, and gave me a paper. "Here, give this to your mother. It's the school policies. Now, off to class."

Two days later, wearing crisp new uniforms, Kenny and I walked up the cement steps of the church. The massive wooden doors took two hands to pull open.

I'd entered a world of riddles. Why was there a bowl of water at the door, and why were people putting their fingers in it? Why were they touching their heads and belly buttons before touching both shoulders? What's in those small closets with red lights above the doors? The mysteries shrouded the musty cathedral like a cloak.

Ushered into the students' pews by arms draped with black, I squeezed in next to my classmates. My eyes roamed the walls and every nook and cranny of the carvings. I wondered at the candles flickering below the feet of statues and the small fence across the front. What would they do if I wandered up to that big table and took a look in the gold box or read from the huge book? Something told me there would be trouble.

A strange calm settled over me. Peace and protection. I hadn't felt those things in a long time. I fought back tears. Where had that come from?

Everyone stood as a man in white and gold robes entered the fenced in area followed by two boys wearing black mini-robes topped with fluffy white tee shirts.

The man faced the audience, and spread his arms. *"In nomine Patris, et Filii, et Spiritus Sancti."*

"Amen."

How on earth did the people know what he said? And what language was that? The man sang and spoke in a weird voice and so did the people. I couldn't understand a thing. I knew a little Italian, but his language wasn't quite that. Though it was close.

I earned more than a few giggles not knowing when to stand, sit, or kneel on the tiny cushioned benches that folded down from the back of the pew in the row ahead. Then, people moved forward and lined up in front of the fence looking at the man in the robes. Class by class, most students joined the lines. Thankfully, not mine. What would I have done if I had to talk to that man? He'd know I was a Catholic fraud for sure.

The priest handed each person a small cracker from a big gold goblet. The people made that strange hand motion, ate the cracker, and then returned to kneel in their pew. They looked serious, almost sad. Before long the mass was over, I didn't know any more about it than when I walked in. It made even less sense to me.

Row by row the students filed into line and we walked to a cafeteria.

The classes sat together, but only the third graders and up were given anything to eat.

"How come they get hot chocolate and toast and we don't?" I asked a little girl from my class.

"Because they took communion."

"What's communion?"

"I don't know, we haven't had it in Catechism yet."

A new word, a new mystery. "What's Catechism?"

At least she didn't seem to mind that I asked. I would pelt her with questions until she stopped answering or ran away crying.

"Religion class. Next year we get to take communion when we reach the age of seasoning."

"Age of seasoning?" I had fleeting thoughts of salt and pepper on my body. Maybe that was what the crackers were about. But if the older kids already had a snack, and a seasoned one at that, why did they get another while we got nothing?

"My mama says that's when we're old enough to sin." I guess her mama didn't know even seven-year olds could lie.

Chapter 6
Moving On

*"When I'm worried and I can't sleep, I count my
blessings instead of sheep." Irving Berlin*

Jack Scott, Jack Scottini, Joe Boronski, and *Jimmy
Allen.* Those were some of the pseudonyms my dad gave
me when he returned. Dad said it was a small price to
pay to be together. To me, it was more lying. It grew
easier though.

Kenny, on the other hand, didn't like it one bit. "But
I'm Kenny." He said through misty eyes.

Whenever Dad heard him, he'd get mad. "You dumb
kid. Do like your brother. It's just a name."

My mother would surround him like a hen protecting
her young. "Kenny, pretend it's a game. For a while just
say your name is John." Or Bob, Joseph, Anthony or any
other name our parents decided to assign him.

J-A-C-K S-C-O-T-T, Jack, Jack, Jack Scott. I had a
trusty memorization process so I'd know it forward and
backward in every combination. Name changes were all
part of being on the run. I knew that as much as the next
television watcher. It was like playing a part in a movie.
But with each name change came a new school, and I
hated that part.

After Dad returned, the first few moves were exciting.
Relocation was a new start. Who knew what could
happen? To a little boy with a wild imagination, the
possibilities were endless. But I soon realized that losing
friends was harder than making them, and, after a while, I
gave up expecting things to get better. What was the point?

Each change of apartments meant new schools and teachers. Sometimes a really good school with a great teacher, but this always made me more melancholy than happy. I'd soon have to leave again. It was my way of life. It was all I knew.

"Momma, can't I just go back to school one more time to say goodbye to–" With the substitution of names, I'd repeat this chant every time my parents announced a new move.

"Bobo, you know you can't." Mom never tried to explain why not. I knew better than to ask my dad. But, really, I just knew.

At first the name changes and outlaw life were appealing and dramatic, but they set in motion a life-long desire for close friends. I was afraid to get too close to anyone. The loss was too great every time I had to leave.

After four schools in ten months, we lived on the third floor of a Chicago apartment building over the dividing line. No longer in an Italian neighborhood, but neither a black nor Hispanic one. In this case, Puerto Rican.

The last day at school before summer break, we walked in the door and my dad made his announcement.

"Pack up. We're moving."

It had happened so often, no one grumbled. But that time, Dad's voice didn't give off the steely wall it normally did. It held an element of surprise. "Just wait until you see your new home, you'll love it." He actually smiled.

"What's my new name?" My current name was Diego, but I'd often wondered what kind of Puerto Rican kid named Diego couldn't speak Spanish.

"You get to keep your name from now on."

Kenny sighed in relief.

Could I maybe pick a different one and then keep that one? Dare I ask?

We loaded into our old Pontiac and drove one hundred and seventy miles to Moline, Illinois. As we traveled, the promise "from now on" echoed in my mind. Maybe things would be good again, like they were in Michigan.

When we arrived in Moline my dad pointed out the new school. Trees and large fields of green grass surrounded the church and school. In Chicago, schoolyards were cement and what little grass you saw was blanketed with trash. Everything here looked so unsoiled. Fresh.

"Wow, it's really pretty. Look, it has a playground with swings." Kenny stuck his head out the window. Swings? No thanks. But that baseball field next to the school looked all right.

Our old car sputtered to a stop in front of a large white home with a white picket fence. Behind the house was a backyard with bushes, two huge oak trees, and a white garage. I looked down the elm lined street and saw similar homes, kids playing in the street, and smiling adults waving as they noticed their new neighbors. It looked just like the block Ozzie and Harriet lived on—at least the one on their TV show.

"We're home." My dad said.

Home? This can't be home. I bolted to the front door and anxiously waited for my dad to find the keys. "Hurry, hurry!"

"Calm down Bobo, I'll let you be the first one in." Dad smiled.

Was that going to be a regular thing there in the postcard house?

I rushed through the beveled glass door, and then froze. I stared at a miracle. My eyes traveled up the long stairway. Every happy family on television had a staircase. I turned around and looked through the still open door and could see my mom and dad clutching each other. Touching. Smiling. I almost cried.

The day couldn't have gotten any better. Then it did.

"Boys, follow me." Dad gestured up the stairs. "Kenny, the first room to the right is yours. Bobo, the one all the way back belongs to you."

"My own bedroom!" I scampered down the hallway to the bedroom door. Really? I cracked open the door a bit and peeked inside. Too dark. I slipped a hand in and felt along the wall to flip on the light.

The room was painted light blue and had a wrought-iron bed draped with a navy blue blanket. A branch of an apple tree seemed to almost reach in the room from the window across the bed. My bed.

"Bobo, come on down." My dad's voice still rang with excitement.

Would he get mad if I slid down the bannister? I certainly wasn't going to risk soiling his good mood. Bannister sliding could wait a day. I leaped two steps at a time and darted toward his voice. He was in the kitchen, drinking.

Uh, oh. I always had to be cautious when he opened the whiskey bottle. He looked at me with a smile that would make the Cheshire cat proud. "Follow me."

He walked to the back yard and stopped by the apple tree, and looked up.

"Your room is up there isn't it? Do you like it?"

"You bet I do."

"Well, I've got one more surprise you'll like."

He headed out the gate into an alley and opened the garage door. He stepped back and smiled.

"A bike!" My heart leaped at least a mile.

It was shiny, new and blue. But, something wasn't right. Oh no. A girl's bike.

"Dad, is that mine?" I had to tread carefully there. Dad didn't like to be questioned. And this wasn't the day to doubt his provision. But ... a girl's bike?

"Yes!" He looked so pleased that I thought he was going to hug me, something he never did.

"But, Dad, it's a girl's bike." I instantly knew I blew it.

His grin dissolved into a mouth spewing curse words. He picked up the bike and threw it. I thought he was going to destroy it.

"No, Dad." I ran to the bike and covered it with my tiny body. "I like it, I do. It'll be easier to pedal with no bar across the top." I sobbed.

That seemed to work.

"I knew that. That's why I got it for you." He strode back to the house and I followed at a safe distance. Once back in our new dining room, he lifted a bottle and poured its golden liquid into his empty glass.

"Damn kids, no appreciation." He took a big gulp, and refilled his glass. That was my cue to leave.

Chapter 7
Unanswered Prayer

"Disappointment is inevitable. But to become discouraged, there's a choice I make. God would never discourage me. He would always point me to himself, to trust him. Therefore, my discouragement is from Satan." Dr. Charles Stanley

No matter which school, there was always a daily mandatory mass. Toward the end of each service everyone went forward for communion, except those guilty of mortal sin—and me. My classmates would stand, sometimes push my little kneeling body aside, and make their way to the line to receive Christ's body and blood... or so they said it was.

I'd slink back in the pew, feeling everyone's eyes on me. A non-Catholic was forbidden the sacrament, but most people didn't know I wasn't a Catholic. It was like I wore a sign proclaiming, *I am going to Hell!*

Like everywhere else we lived, my mother rose on the first weekday after we settled in Moline and went to St. Mary's to enroll us in school where she met the parish priest. "He's so nice. And he's coming here for lunch next Sunday to bless our house!" Her face was red, and her eyes seemed twice their normal size. I couldn't remember the last time I'd seen her that enthused.

She bent down to pick up some papers on the floor, then noticed some of Kenny's toy soldiers scattered about. "I will need to get the house in order, and you kids will need to be at your best when we all go to church. Bobo, go clean up your room."

All go to church? Did she really say all, like in Dad too? She went to church with us on Christmas, but usually it was just me and Kenny.

"How you going to get Dad to go?"

"I'm not sure, but he's going." Mom set her jaw.

This I had to see.

That Sunday my mother carried Cindy into church, and Kenny and I followed close behind. A few steps behind us, looking very much like he was going to a dentist, my dad followed. I watched as he reluctantly took his place in the pew. He struggled with following all the ups, downs, and kneeling movements, but at least he tried.

I glanced at Mom. She stared straight ahead. Not gloating, not judging. Just making all the right Catholic moves—where did she learn that stuff anyway? And she had this manner of deferring to my dad that let him keep his pride. As though it was his idea to come to church ... and wear a suit. She wielded more power over him than I ever realized.

We rushed out of there before the last "Amen" because we had lunch to prepare. We didn't ever have company, let alone someone like a priest. What would we talk about? How should I act?

We walked into the house and the fragrance of a roast, chicken, and pasta mingled with the wonderful aroma of freshly baked bread. What made this meal even more remarkable was my dad was cooking it, except for the pasta. Mom was the only one who touched spaghetti in our house.

Kenny and I were set to the task of cleaning up anything out of place that morning while Mom and Dad attended to preparations in the kitchen.

We all froze when we heard one swift knock at the door.

Mom broke the silence by bustling into the foyer wiping her hands on her apron. She plastered a smile on her face as she opened the door.

All business, the priest stepped into the house. After he said the nice stuff everyone expected, he draped a long white cloth over his shoulder. He then took what looked like a big microphone out of his bag. He walked around the house reciting some Latin while he pointed and shook the microphone. Water shot out of its tiny holes, which must be the holy water from the fountains at church. Hmm. That would bless our house? And what would that do for us?

What happened next probably shouldn't have bothered me, but it did.

"Want a stogie, Father?" My father asked.

Oh no, not one of his stinky cigars.

"Sure."

The priest was going to smoke a nasty cigar? Something felt wrong about that.

My dad headed for the kitchen and opened the upper left side cabinet.

Oh no. Dad's going for the booze!

The priest surprised me again by letting my dad pour him a stiff drink. The adults stayed in the kitchen most of the afternoon while Kenny and I watched TV.

"Bobo, come say goodbye to the father."

When I entered the kitchen the priest slurred and slapped the Formica table where he sat. "Boy, I've got some g-good n-news-s-s." He hiccupped.

"You and your mother are going—" His eyes were beet red, and his face so purple I was sure he was either going to pass out or explode.

"Did you hear me b-boy?" Hiccup. "You'll be baptized next week."

"Does this mean I can go to communion?"

"Yes-s-s, both you and your," hiccup, "mama." The priest tried to rise from the chair, but slid right to the floor.

I was too shocked to move. Neither Mom nor Dad made a move or even acknowledged it happened.

Father used the seat of the chair to help him to his feet. He brushed his pants off as though nothing was wrong. "Yep, next week will be your first communion."

My mother turned from the sink where she was elbow deep in Palmolive and said, "Not just us, Bobo." At that moment she looked beautiful. The red dress and white-and-black apron fit her body perfectly and she was wearing makeup. But it was her smile that gave her an angelic aura. "So will your dad."

"What will Dad do?" I asked.

"Because he was baptized as a baby, he won't need to be again. But, he will receive communion with us." She stood tall and looked at my dad who sat with fuzzy drunken eyes staring down at his shoes.

"He's going to confession right after we're baptized."

Hah. Dad would never do that. Not in a million years. Then again, Mom had superpowers when it came to him. I'd better bring a snack in my pocket. If Dad went into that confession booth, he'd be in there for a while.

That Saturday Mom and I stood side-by-side and were sprinkled with water to become official Catholics. And as Mom had promised, Dad headed right for the confessional booth when we were done. We sat in our pew and waited. I patted my pocket to ensure my cookie was still there if I needed it. Kenny fidgeted, and Cindy slept in Mom's arms.

After about an hour he came out with a red face and slumped shoulders. What had he told the priest? Then again, it had only been an hour. What had he left out?

Should I have felt different now that I was baptized? At least no one would think I was a sinner destined for Hell now. But if that were true, wouldn't I feel something? If there had been some big spiritual change, wouldn't I at least notice? Maybe if the priest hadn't been drunk ... but could I blame him, really? It was supposed to be about God. Maybe none of it was real. But at least I could take communion.

I could just add that lie onto the others. What difference would it make? Until the day the lies took on the form of our Christmas tree when Dad and I stole it.

Chapter 8
Learning New Tricks

*"We need to constantly remind our children that
lying is not as much deceiving others
as it is being deceived ourselves."*
Scott Williams, Learning (Not) To Lie

On Christmas Eve my dad picked out a red scarf, knotted it, and then faced me for approval.

"Perfect." I couldn't tell him it looked funny. Memories of my complaint about the girly bike were still fresh.

"Bobo, wear your red sweater. You and your momma are going to midnight mass after we get the tree. You want wear to red at Christmas."

"Aw, man." I hated that itchy sweater.

Mom helped me with my coat and gloves. "Be a good boy, and do what your father tells you." She knew I would. But did she know what he'd ask of me that night?

"Okay, boy. Let's go." Dad held the door open and let me step out into the cold night ahead of him.

I drew my coat lapels tight against the frigid air and gawked at the houses decorated with beautiful bright lights. Some blinked and others stared back as frozen as the snow around us. To this eight-year old boy, Christmas was a magical time when prayers were answered and miracles happened.

Sister Agnes told us we should all pray for a Christmas miracle. What miracle would I ask for? *Dear Lord, please let us stay here and have a normal life.* We turned the corner and my dad grabbed my hand.

"Quiet now, Bobo. We're almost there."

I could see the tree lot ahead, but its usually bright lights had all been blackened. "Dad, it's closed." I fought back the tears. They would do no good.

"Don't worry. I already paid. Let's pick a tree out." My dad tugged my arm, and we entered the lot. A streetlight gave a slight milky glow that seemed like a fog.

My dad moved stealthily with a hooked knife in his hand and some rope. Swaying shadows of the trees interrupted the light.

"This one looks good, doesn't it Bobo?"

I nodded, not so much in agreement as in fear. What was he doing?

He quickly took the rope and turned the tree repeatedly until its branches were all tied back.

"You grab the rope in front." My dad ordered as he lifted the trunk. He took a long look down the deserted street. "Let's go home."

I tried to lift the front end, but my gloved fingers slipped on the snow-covered branches and needles. I tried resting it on my forearms so I could at least keep it from scrapping the ground for the six-block march home.

Dad never complained about my speed or clumsiness. Instead, he whistled and then sang, "Rudolph the red-nosed reindeer, had a very shiny nose..."

He was happy, it was Christmas, and we had a new Christmas tree. But I didn't feel much like singing. I knew. Deep down, I knew. He hadn't paid for that tree, and there would be no Christmas miracle that year.

***

When I woke that first Saturday after Christmas, I went to the window and looked out. The clouds were gone, but they left behind four inches of shiny new snow. Any normal eight-year-old boy with a brand new sled would have been thrilled at the sight. But not me. Not that day.

Not the day I planned to rob a store.

Maybe I would be more like a man, like my dad, if I had the courage to steal something by myself. And, why not? If there was no God, who cared if I was good? And I'd already lied so much that nothing else could matter.

I moved away from the wintry view and peeked into Kenny's room. He was asleep. I dressed and headed downstairs. I opened the kitchen door, and the smoke from Mom's cigarettes choked me.

"What's for breakfast? I'm in a hurry. Can I eat now?" I coughed out the questions.

My mother, dressed in an old white cloth robe, set orange juice on the table. "You want eggs? Why are you in such a big hurry? I bet it's to ride your new sled down the hill before the other kids." She smiled. All was right in her maternal world.

"Yeah, that's it." I lied. Not the only lie I'd tell that day.

I quickly ate, put my coat on, and headed outside. I knew my mother might be looking out the window, so I grabbed the sled out of the garage and toted it past the kitchen window. Once out of sight, I hid it behind some bushes and started my long hike.

Wearing big black boots slowed me down. It took me much longer to get there than when I last cased the place. I chose it because of the distance from my neighborhood. No one would know me here. I saw it ahead.

Ted and Martha's. The large letters in red paint on a brown wooden sign hanging over the glass door welcomed me. The storefront's window had *Grocery and Butcher Shop* stenciled in white on it.

The store looked like many others in the days before the rise of large chains. The front of a brick home with the owner's living quarters in the rear.

The window fogged up as I peered in. *Now or never.* I pushed opened the door. A bell rang, and I saw the husband and wife talking behind the butcher counter. They ignored me as I walked over to the comic books lined up on a wall like a colorful stamp collection. I kept one eye on the couple as I flipped through *Tales from the Crypt.*

"Okay, I'm going to go finish the laundry." The woman exited through a door behind the cash register. Just then the bell announced another customer.

Perfect, a distraction.

A man dressed in a snowsuit walked in and walked straight to the meats. I couldn't hear what was being said, but the man was clearly ordering.

I watched the owner grab some sausage links. I knew it was time. I quickly moved to one knee and took a Baby Ruth from the row of candy near my boots and slipped it into my coat pocket and as I started to slip the comic under my shirt I heard the owner, "Young man, please come over here."

I looked around. "Me?" I whispered. The owner wasn't even looking at me. He was still wrapping the sausage.

"Yes, you. Come over to the register please." I slowly shuffled over to where he directed.

Did he see me? How could he? Was I caught? Can I get out of here? My heart beat wildly.

The moment the customer left the owner turned to me. "Well, young man. I think you have something that belongs to me."

Oh, no! He knew!

"No, sir, I don't think so." I stammered. The owner turned, opened the door behind him and yelled towards the back. "Honey, could you come up here?"

Escape. I eyed the door. I had to be faster than the old man.

"Don't even think about it." The man warned.

When the wife came in the man said, "Well, it looks like we have a culprit here."

I watched enough television. I was caught.

The shopkeeper walked around the counter and stood before me. He slowly reached into my left pocket and lifted out the candy.

I blurted out the best defense an eight-year old could fabricate, "How'd that get there? It must have fallen in."

I knew I was cooked the moment I said it.

"Why'd you take it son?" The lady said. She was about the size of my mother but a little older. She seemed nice, but her husband scared me.

The tears and the lies were on a parallel course, each rapidly falling. "I was hungry."

"Well dear, didn't you have breakfast this morning?"

"No." I whimpered. Maybe I could get some sympathy and they'd just let me go.

"Why not?"

"We're too poor." I knew that answer would lead to more questions, but I was desperately trying to lie my way out of trouble.

The man crossed his arms and shook his head. He wasn't having any of it. "What's your name?"

"Jack Scott."

"Where do you live?"

"New York City." It worked for me in the past.

"New York City? What are you doing here?"

"Visiting my aunt."

"What's her name and phone number?"

"Just Aunt Mary, and I don't know her number."

"Well, I don't believe–" Before he could say another word the wife stood in front of her husband and enveloped me with a tight hug.

"No more grilling, honey. Can't you see the boy's terrified?" She held out her left hand inviting me to hold it and come with her.

"If he's hungry, I'm going to do something about it."

Before long I had a huge plate of eggs and bacon in front of me. Although not at all hungry, I knew the wisest course was to clean my plate.

When I was leaving the wife gave me a small sack with a banana, chips and a candy bar. "Son, if you are ever hungry please don't steal. Stealing will only lead to future trouble."

"Yes, ma'am. Thank you." As I walked away I peeked into my bag of goodies. Hmm. Looked like lying did have its rewards. A little further from the store I turned around and made sure I was in the clear. I reached down my shirt and rescued the stolen comic.

***

"Kenny, you and Bobo wash up, your dad's taking you both to get some new shoes," my mother yelled from the kitchen.

I loved shoe shopping. I really didn't care about the shoes, but loved Buster Brown shoe stores. I knew the Buster Brown TV Show's slogan by heart, "I'm Buster Brown. I live in a shoe. That's my dog Tige, he lives there too." The show featured Froggy the Gremlin, a puppet who Smilin' Ed summoned with his, "Pluck your Magic Twanger, Froggy." Like magic, he'd appear in a burst of smoke saying, "Hi-ya kids, hi-ya, hi-ya."

"Come on Kenny, I teased my little brother as he slowly dressed, pluck your Magic Twanger and get a move on." He stared at me with a scowl as he carefully tied his shoelaces.

What delighted me wasn't getting new shoes, I'd be just as happy wearing my old ones until the bottoms fell off, it was the Buster Brown store. Not only did they have neat red rocking horses, but each store had an x-ray machine you placed your feet in to see if the shoes fit.

At each visit I'd stare through a scope and be enchanted by the magic inside. I'd giggle as I wiggled my toes and watched my greenish-yellow bones respond. No one cared about radiation back then, especially excited little boys.

Kenny and I walked hand-in-hand a few steps behind my dad. As we arrived at the Buster Brown store my dad kept walking past. I was about to tug on his coat when he turned around and said, "We're going to a new store today." He stopped and crouched down and looked at me. "When we get there, I'll help you and Kenny try some shoes on."

Why wouldn't the shoe salesman be helping us?

"Then you will take your brother outside and walk around in your new shoes. I'll pay for the shoes and meet you out there. Do not come back in the store."

Why was that so important? I nodded my agreement. It wouldn't help to argue with Dad.

At the new shoe store, no happy chimes jingled when we opened the door. No shiny red rocking horses for us to climb on. Nothing but row after row of racks crammed with shoeboxes. We walked to the children's section.

"What size are you and your brother?"

I shrugged. How was I supposed to know? A man always placed my feet on some sort of measuring contraption. I spotted one, grabbed it, and gave it to my dad.

"You boys sit down here, and take your shoes off."

We both sat on the padded wooden bench and followed the command. My dad measured our feet and brought a stack of boxes. He took the shoes out of all of them and spread them in front of us.

"Try these. Walk around. How do they feel?" We did that several times before he seemed to settle on what shoes we should purchase, and then he whispered to me, "Remember what I said? Take your brother and walk around outside. I'll meet you there in a minute."

I took Kenny's hand and moved toward the door. I glanced back and saw my dad putting all the shoes back into boxes and stuck our old shoes into the boxes of the shoes we were wearing.

I knew what that meant.

We weren't outside long when dad came out, and we quickly headed away. He didn't say a word, but as I looked down I noticed he too was wearing a new pair of shoes.

Being young and accomplished in crime began with the shoe store, but it soon escalated to other endeavors. Many times we'd grocery shop at one of the bigger stores, and my dad would bring a concealed paper bag. He'd fill it up and then order me to carry out of the store.

If caught, he'd simply say he meant for me to carry it to the checkout lane.

Going with my dad to shoplift was a normal boy's day out. He liked taking me. He figured a man with his son wouldn't arouse suspicion. He did get caught a couple times but somehow always eluded arrest.

It was like bonding time. Or that was how Dad saw it anyway. He usually worked nine-to-five, but his hours began at night and finished shortly before dawn. As a pastry chef he often worked alone at high-end clubs or restaurants preparing fresh bread, cakes, and other pastries so they were ready for customers in the mornings.

"Bobo, it's Friday, and you know what that means?"

I sat next to my mother on our plastic-covered couch. The "Life of Riley" blared so loud I barely heard him. I carefully rose so I wouldn't stick to the sofa. I joined him in the kitchen where he stood at the stove with a spatula, wearing only his underpants. The smell of eggs and bacon wasn't as appetizing at night as in the morning. But it was his breakfast, being a night-worker and all.

He glanced over at me and let a smile leak from between his cigar-clenched teeth, "It's Friday, and you know what that means?"

He always asked me with these exact words. Almost like a secret code only he and I knew. He repeated it every few months until I went to high school, when he knew my eagerness to help had stopped.

"I get to work with you!" I had equal parts excitement and dread at the thought.

"Yeah, tell your mother. We'll be leaving after I eat." He grabbed a fork from the counter and began eating straight from the frying pan. He reached over the sink for a bottle of bourbon and laced his coffee. "We'll have fun, like always."

No matter where he worked, the design of our Friday nights together looked much the same. When we arrived he'd put me to work on the pies. I would then help ice some cakes and possibly fill some éclairs. Shortly before midnight I'd be allowed to eat as much ice cream as possible, then I'd spread out a tablecloth or two and curl up reading my comics until sleep knocked me out.

"Bobo. Bobo, wake up. It's time to get busy."

Groggy, with just a few hours sleep, I knew what it meant. I started rubbing the palms of my hands together.

"What are you doing?" My father looked down on me like I was as dumb as a stump.

"Just watch." I took my now warm palms and placed them on my eyelids. "It's something the nuns taught me. I guess it's supposed to help wake your eyes up."

He reached down, lifted me by my arms, and handed me a box.

"When you're done with your crazy eye rub, go in the cooler and start filling this up. Get about six of everything, except the turkeys. They keep a better count on them."

And so it began. We would fill boxes and bags with steaks, hams, butter, and other food items. Whatever he thought wouldn't be missed. We'd keep them in the cooler and freezer, until it was time to leave. He'd give me the keys to the car, and I'd open the trunk. My role then became one of a lookout. When it was safe, he'd carry the stolen goods to the car and we'd head home.

The times I aided my dad with his thefts were the only occasions I felt close to him. Not that it was an excuse. I knew even then I had the choice to not take a path of dishonesty. But it was a chance to please my dad.

To be connected.

Chapter 9
Elvis, and Sam Giancana

"Are not five sparrows sold for two copper coins? And not one of them is forgotten before God. But the very hairs of your head are all numbered. Do not fear therefore; you are of more value than many sparrows."
Luke 12: 6-7

The tri-city area of Moline, Rock Island, and Davenport was great. The best of all my schools, my house was a dream come true, and my bike, though a bit girly, was mine. All mine. But my hope for a normal life was crushed shortly before the end of the school year.

"Bobo, come over here." The nuns in Moline didn't mind calling me by my nickname. My teacher stooped down, and looked closely at my face. She gasped and pulled back. "Follow me."

I trailed behind her flowing black robe as she stormed to the principal's office. What had I done wrong?

Great. Lisa Ann must have ratted me out when I said I was going to kick Tommy's butt. "I'm going to tell Sister Teresa," she'd taunted. "I'm going to tell you said a bad word, and you'll be in trouble."

"Lisa Ann, please don't tell. You heard me wrong, I said 'I'm going to kick you, BUT I won't.'" By the wicked smile that spread from chubby cheek to chubby cheek, I knew she didn't buy it. She sang my crime to the entire playground. Funny how the word was worse than the threat.

"Bobo said a bad word! Bobo said a bad word! And I'm going to tell. He's going to get in trouble. He's going to get in trouble." The girls all flinched like I was something smelly. The boys gave me short nods acknowledging I was cool.

A week passed, and I thought I'd weathered the storm of Lisa Ann, but the death march to the principal's office suggested otherwise. I readied the same defense I used at the playground.

"Wait over there." My teacher pointed to one of the most dreaded things a student could be directed to–like an elementary-school guillotine—the row of chairs outside a principal's office. A short time later a door opened and with one look at the principal's face, I knew this wasn't about saying a semi-bad word.

"My God, look at his face!" Sister Bridget, my teacher, seemed concerned. Sister Teresa, the principal, simply looked frightened. Sister Teresa took a small mirror off her wall and positioned it so I could see my face.

Pimples? I thought only teenagers got them.

Sister Teresa kept her distance. "Did your mother let you out like this?" She sputtered.

"I guess so." I didn't really know if I was "like this" when I left that morning.

"Well, it looks like you have…" Sister Bridget looked at her colleague, as if looking for agreement, "…measles."

"Or chickenpox," Sister Teresa chimed in.

"My mother told me I had measles when I was little, and I couldn't get them again." I was happy to help.

Both nodded at each other and simultaneously said, "Chickenpox."

Sister Bridget took some paper off her desk and wrote on it. "Take this and give it to your mother. We don't want to see you back here until you are completely well."

No school, and I didn't even feel sick. How had I gotten so lucky? What would I do with all my time? I skipped all the way home.

Until I turned the corner to my street.

Police cars lined the street in front of my house. A uniformed officer stationed on the front steps. My heart sank into my stomach. I looked up at my house as one would look at a loved one before they shut the casket.

"Can I help you son?" The police officer stood tall and spoke in a deep voice. Authority.

"I live here, sir." I looked him directly in the eyes, but he avoided my gaze and looked beyond me. His head swiveled as if searching for something—or someone.

"Bobo, what are you doing home?" My mother was still in her pink terry-cloth robe. She looked just like she did the first time she faced the police on *That Day*.

"Here's a note." A man wearing a wrinkled grey suit quickly appeared and snatched the paper.

"Hey, that's mine."

He scanned it, looked at another man in uniform and shouted, "It's a note from his teacher. If you haven't had chickenpox, you'd better stay clear of the kid."

My mother looked down at me, her eyes dark with hopelessness. "Bobo, go to your room and get into bed."

"But, I feel fine. Can't I go out and ride my bike?"

She stared at the men in the living room rifling through some papers. "Huh? Sorry honey. What'd you say?" She clutched the note and fumbled in her pocket. "Bobo, go in my bedroom, and get my purse."

When I returned, she took the bag and started rooting around in it. She took out a package of Camels and a lighter. After she lit her cigarette she dug deeper in her purse and handed me two quarters.

"I can't make you anything to eat right now." She didn't even notice the paper bag I clutched in my sweaty fist, the lunch she prepared for me this morning.

"You take your bike and get yourself something to eat. Come back after our guests have left." *Guests?* I knew police would never be guests in our house.

Part of me wanted to stay. To witness what was happening. But, a bigger part of me wanted to get away as fast as possible. Without a word, I carefully went out the front, climbed on my bike and started pedaling. Before long I was in downtown Moline.

I passed by a hardware store, a shoe store, and a dozen tractor yards. Just as I decided to make my way back, I saw the marquee on the Roxy Theatre. "Love me Tender, Starring Elvis Presley." Elvis' first movie was right there in front of me, and I had two shiny quarters in my pocket. It was a temptation I couldn't resist.

I parked my bike and paid my admission. With enough money for a soda, popcorn, and even some candy I entered the nearly empty theatre. I was so excited to be seeing Elvis, I'd almost forgotten about the police.

Midway through the film I wondered why Elvis would do a movie where all he did was act. I wanted to see him sing. When he did, it was the slow title song. He didn't even move his hips. I felt cheated. By the time Elvis was dying on screen, I was ready to leave. Then, a beam of light blinded me.

"See, look at his face." I could barely make out two men. "Kid, why aren't you in school?"

"The sister sent me home. I have chickenpox."

"Well, you can't stay here, you're sick. We'll refund your money, but you've got to go."

I happily pocketed the quarter they gave me to even cover the popcorn and drink. What a cool day it had turned out to be.

Then I remembered. How had I managed to forget what was happening at home? As I pedaled I knew our good life in Moline had ended. I didn't know what happened, but I knew it wasn't good.

I'd go home but try to stay out of sight. Maybe I could learn something important if I stayed quiet. There was a police car parked in front and two men were sitting in it. If they had captured my father, I didn't think they'd be sitting there. I headed around the block and drove down our alleyway. It wasn't quite dark, but shadowy enough to sneak into my backyard unseen.

Our backdoor was too far on the side of the house and could be seen by the police. If I could find a way up to one of the windows, I knew I could get inside. I looked up at my bedroom window and instantly saw the solution. The apple tree!

I climbed and shimmied to my window. It easily slid open, and I fell in headfirst. The house was dead silent. I tiptoed to Kenny's room. Empty. The phone rang.

Was it my mother? Maybe it was a trap.

I peered down the stairs, and listened until the ringing stopped. Afraid the police would see me if I went down, I sat at the top of the stairs and waited. Every noise—the howl of the wind, a branch tapping against a window, the imagined loud beating of my heart—seemed exaggerated.

If only I believed in prayer. Ever since my Christmas prayer went unanswered I'd stopped praying.

When darkness covered the house I tiptoed down the stairs. The streetlights flashed ghostlike shadows into the house that eerily displayed open drawers and tossed papers.

What were they looking for?

Careful to not be seen, I crept into the living room. The curtains were drawn and it was dark as dirt. I stepped on something stiff and crunchy. I bent and lifted a plastic sheet that crinkled with my touch. My eyes slightly adjusted to the dark and noticed the couch looked deformed. I inched closer and ran my palms over the cushions. Cotton stuffing sprang into my hands.

They had sliced open the couch searching for something. The plastic sheet must have been its cover.

What had happened here?

Ring! Ring! Ring!

The phone startled me. It was only inches from my grasp. I reached for it, its vibration startled my fingers and I snapped my hand back. The ringing stopped.

I looked around for a note, but if there was one it was too dark to find it. I sat on the cushion less sofa. Maybe I should go outside and ask where everyone was. No, they're the enemy. I'll just sit and wait.

Ring! Ring! Ring!!! Not again, the phone wouldn't shut up.

I walked up to the receiver. What choice did I have? "Hello." I could barely whisper the word.

"Bobo, is that you?"

It was a woman's voice, but not my mother's. "Yes."

"You okay?"

"Yes, who is this?"

"It's your Aunt Martha."

I had no Aunt Martha. What were they trying to pull?

"You know the one who makes the peanut brittle."

Ah. Aunt Mary was using a phony name.

"Are you alone?"

"Yes, the police are outside. They don't know I'm here."

"Good job. This call is probably bugged, so pay close attention. Do you still remember my phone number?" Hers was the emergency number mother made me memorize.

"Yes."

"Give the first three numbers."

"2-3-9."

"Good, sneak out of there and find a pay phone. Call the operator and say you want to make a collect call to Chicago. Give her my phone number, and when we talk I'll tell you what to do."

"Okay, but what—"

"No time now. Hurry, and be careful."

Just then a bright light streaked through a window. It slowly moved to another. They'd heard the call. They knew I was in there! I dropped to my knees and crawled. When I reached the dark window, I inched up to peek out. The beam came from a searchlight on the police car.

Oh no, one of the car doors opened.

There was no time to be afraid. I bolted up the stairs and made my way to the tree branch. In the dark, my escape looked much more daring than my entrance had felt. I took hold of the branch with both hands and jumped. As I dangled, I listened for noises. I thought I heard something from in front of the house, but it seemed clear back there.

I swung my legs back and forth. Soon I was hanging like a monkey in a tree, both legs and hands now attached to the branch. I inched my way to the trunk and quickly made my way down. Lights were flashing inside the house. I headed for my bike, but it didn't have a light on it, and I might get noticed. I cut through some yards and made my way on feet to a closed gas station. I entered the phone booth on the side of the pumps, reached up and dialed "O."

"Operator."

It was the first time I ever talked with a telephone operator. I needed to calm down. "I need to make a collect call."

"Person-to-person?"

"No, a collect call."

"Would you to call a particular person?"

"Yes, my Aunt Mary."

"Do you know her number?"

"Uh, it's uh..." I forgot! How could I forget that fast?

"Do you have her number? If not, is she listed?"

"Listed?"

"Yes, I'll need her name and address. If she's listed I can look up her number."

I didn't know her address, or even her last name. I took a deep breath and thought hard. Thankfully the number soon escaped from where it was hiding in my brain, and I repeated it to the operator.

"And whom may I say the call is from?"

"From me."

"And your name?"

"Bobo"

"How do you spell that?"

At least she didn't laugh at me. There was some talking in the background.

"Bobo, is that you? You okay?"

"Aunt Mary, what's going on?"

"Uh, your family had to leave Moline and ... well ... let's just talk after you get here."

"But, you live in Chicago."

"There's someone on the way to pick you up. He'll call me once he gets to Moline. Where's a good place to pick you up?"

"How about my school?"

"I don't think so, they may be watching it."

"How about downtown? The Kresge is open late." The dime store was only a block from the theatre I went to earlier that day. It was one of my favorite places because of their chocolate phosphates.

"Great. When you get there, find another pay phone and call me."

"Okay, but Aunt Mary I'm not feeling too well." My eyes burned, my head hurt, and I was itching like crazy.

"What's wrong?"

"I think I have chickenpox."

"Oh dear, better not tell your driver. Make sure and sit in the back seat."

I hung up and headed downtown. Without my bike it was a long walk, so I waited for a city bus. The driver gave me back twenty cents from my quarter, and I chose a seat in the back. I almost fell asleep, but the bumpy ride kept me awake.

There was a pay phone next to its front doors and I called my aunt. "Kresge's is right by the Roxy Movie Theatre, near the bridge."

"Okay, you stay there. What's the number on the front of the phone?"

I looked up, but couldn't read it. After all, I'd had to stand on my toes to dial.

"It's too high, I can't see the number."

"I need it in case something happens."

Two teenage girls came out of the store. "Can you help me? I'm too short to see the number on this phone, and my aunt needs it."

The taller one acted like she didn't hear me, but the pretty blonde said, "Sure."

I repeated what she read to my aunt. "Thank you."

The girl smiled. "Aren't you a little young to have that many pimples?"

"Those aren't pimples." I reached up and scratched my forehead. "I've got chickenpox."

"I-c-k!" They said it loud, long and in sync, then hurried away.

"When will this guy come? How will I know him?"

"Is there a somewhere you could sit?"

"Yes, there's a bench at the bus stop. It's to the left of the store."

"Stay there. Don't get into any car unless the man knows my name and he calls you Bobo. He should be there in less than an hour."

Should I go in and get a phosphate? Hard to pass up, but I wasn't feeling too good. I walked to the bench and sank into the seat. I would just wait it out. The downtown was well lit, especially the theatre marquee. I pretended I was invisible, but knew I wasn't, so each time a police car drove by I pretended to cough so they wouldn't recognize me.

A fugitive. I wondered if my dad always felt like this. It was sort of like a rollercoaster. Frightening, but thrilling at the same time. The same kind of feeling tingled when we'd stolen the shoes. I walked out of the store ready to be caught, but excited at the same time.

A long black car, like presidents ride in, drove up and stopped in front of the bus stop. I couldn't see in the window, but it soon rolled down and a man's head leaned out. The streetlights reflected off his shiny black hair. A huge crooked nose engulfed his face and made his eyes look tiny.

"You Bobo?"

I softly whispered, "Yes sir."

"Can't hear you, boy. Are you Bobo, and are you waiting to be taken to your Aunt Mary's place?"

I leaped to my feet, headed to the car and loudly proclaimed, "Yes sir, I'm ready to go." Remembering my aunt's warning, my hand reached for the back door.

"So you want to sit in back do you?" He chuckled. "Okay, I'll chauffer you."

Wow, this back seat is bigger than our entire car! Two sets of seats faced each other. I sat on the one facing forward. It was as large as, and softer than our sofa. Before the police ripped it up.

Our furniture. Our home. What would become of it?

A window that separated the front and back seats slid open. "If you want something to eat open the cabinet right below me. Just make sure you stay out of the booze." He laughed and closed the window.

I turned a handle on the wood frame in front of me. A door came down flat and revealed some ice in a bucket, bottles filled with different colored liquids and a bowl filled with potato chips. I grabbed a coke bottle, found an opener, and flipped the top off. It was warm, but the bubbles felt good on my sore throat. I curled back into the big comfortable seat. Too tired, and too sick to worry about all that happened. Sleep came hard and fast.

I dreamed I was floating, and as my eyes partially opened I found I was. The man had me under his massive right arm like a sack of potatoes, and was carrying me up a flight of stairs. If I stretched my hands and legs out I'd be flying like Superman.

He knocked on a door.

"Who's there?" It was my aunt's voice.

"It's me." The door opened. "Where you want him?"

"Is he awake?"

The man shrugged.

I squeezed my eyes shut. Although conscious, I didn't want to be, nor did I want them to know. I wanted this to all be a dream, and to wake up back in my house in Moline.

"Put him on the couch." He gently laid me down, and I played dead. I peeked and saw my aunt go to her purse and reach inside.

"How much do I owe you?"

"Nothing, the kid's dad talked with my boss and made an arrangement. It's all taken care of. Besides, when the boss found out the kid's name was Bobo he wanted to help. After all, his nickname is Momo."

Momo? That was even funnier than my name.

My aunt moved with the man to the door. "Thank you so much for taking good care of him, and please thank Mr. Giancana for his help." After she locked the door my aunt came into the living room and sat next to me. She turned a lamp on and smiled at me. "You're awake aren't you?"

I still pretended to be asleep. Too much to face.

"You hungry? How you feeling?"

I gave no answer.

"I think I better get you to a doctor tomorrow. For now, let's get you a bath and to bed."

Just as she started to lift me, I opened my eyes. I didn't need to be carried, and especially bathed by a woman.

"Hello, sleepy head. I'm going to go draw you a bath, if you want something to eat there's food in the fridge."

I looked at her, but said nothing. I wanted to talk, to ask questions and get answers, but I was too tired. I followed her and before long was sleeping in her bed. I don't know where she slept, but I welcomed the darkness and soon was unconscious.

The morning light crept into the room, landed on my face, and stirred me awake. It was my face that my aunt first remarked about.

"Bobo, you got more bumps than a stampede of camels." She placed a thermometer in my mouth. "A hundred and one, any higher and we go to straight to the doctor. I'm taking a week off work to take care of you." She propped me up with some pillows and brought in a tray with some orange juice and pancakes.

I downed the juice, but pushed the food away.

"I'll know you're okay when the bumps go away, the temperature recedes, and you feel like eating."

Three days later I ambled into the kitchen. She must have heard my stomach begging for food because she had a huge stack of hotcakes and syrup waiting for me.

"Are you ready to eat?" Her lips matched the red of the curled ribbons in her hair. Her smile was as genuine as any I've seen. "Maybe we could go to a movie today."

"Aunt Mary, what's happening? Where is my mom?"

Her grin faintly lessened. "I'm not exactly sure. All I know is your mom and dad called me the other day and asked me to take care of you for a little while. Your dad had you picked up, and here you are."

Aunt Mary didn't have the answers I needed, so I stopped asking questions. No sense making her sad or worried. But I stayed by her side the next three days. We saw a Jimmy Stewart movie, went shopping so I could have some clothes, and ate lots of sweets. She was so nice, I almost forgot about my lost family. Almost.

On Friday there was a knock. She peered through a small hole in her door, looked at me, and silently mouthed, "Be quiet." She pointed to her bedroom and brought her lips down to my ear. "Hide!"

Already under her bed I heard, "Who is it?"

The apartment was small and the answer was easy to hear. "Police."

There was some shuffling, and I could tell there were two men with my aunt. The one with a high-pitched voice did most the talking, but I couldn't understand most of it.

Then the bedroom door opened. "Bobo, you can come out now."

It was my aunt's voice, but there was a set of men's shoes moving toward me. They stopped and stared as I peered out from under the bed.

"It's okay, come on out."

I shimmied out the opposite side of the man's shoes and stared at a skinny policeman.

"Good hiding place, son. Let's go in the kitchen to talk."

How could Aunt Mary have betrayed me like that?

She nodded and winked.

I looked around but couldn't find the other policeman. The skinny one seemed to read my mind.

"Looking for my partner? He's right outside the door."

"Bobo, it's okay if I call you Bobo, isn't it?"

I nodded a yes.

"I've got a few questions for you." He smiled and seemed nice, but I knew the tricky ones always acted friendly. "I told your aunt that two days ago we began a stakeout on her place, in case your dad showed up. When they saw her with a young boy, they figured it was you, so there's no reason to deny you were here. She agreed you'd both answer my questions, and we'd let you stay here. At least until everything gets sorted out."

He took his hat off, and carrot-colored hair sprang out. "Where's your dad?"

"I don't know."

"Your mom?"

"Don't know." My head hung low, and I barely croaked out the words.

My aunt jumped to my rescue. "Officer, you're frightening the boy. Neither one of us know anything."

The questions went on for a while, but they were easy to answer—I really didn't know anything. My aunt was strong in her denials and only hesitated once. "So, how'd the boy get here?"

No answer.

"Explain to me how an eight-year-old boy can get all the way to Chicago to stay with an aunt who doesn't drive?"

"There was a knock and there he was."

He smiled and looked over at me. "Well, son how did you get here?"

I had become quite good at telling lies, but not to policemen. I paused long enough for him to ask again. "How'd you get to your aunt's from Moline?"

"Bus."

"You took a Greyhound?"

Huh? "No, a bus."

"How'd you get from the bus station to your aunt's?"

"A taxi."

"So where did you get all the money for this?" His face looked like he wasn't buying anything I was selling, but his eyes signaled he was starting to. I felt it best to jump in and add more before he asked the obvious.

"I snuck back in my house when I saw everyone was gone. I knew where some emergency money was hidden with a note telling me what to do. I just did what my mom wrote."

Bingo! I could tell he bought it.

"Do you still have that note?"

"He gave it to me when he arrived. I probably threw it out."

Ooh, good one.

The skinny officer stood, closed the notepad and said, "I'm going now. There may be some detectives and FBI agents coming by Monday. Will you be home?"

"In the evening," my aunt replied.

Aunt Mary watched through the door's peephole until they were gone. She walked over to the living room window, slightly drew the drapes back, and stared at the street below. Without looking at me she said, "You did good. I don't like the idea they been watching us, and I hate lying."

"There they are. Come here, look." My aunt pointed at a blue car. The redheaded policeman leaned down to speak to the two men sitting in it.

"Yep, there they are, and it doesn't look like they're going away anytime soon." She grabbed her purse, took me by the hand. "It looks like time for plan B."

Chapter 10
Plan B

*"The lives that have been the greatest blessing to you
are the lives of those people who themselves were
unaware of having been a blessing."*
Oswald Chambers

"What's plan B?" I hadn't even realized there was an A.

"Just stay close." She held my hand as we walked down the three flights. We turned away from the front door and descended toward the Super's apartment. My aunt knocked and an old man wearing a blue Chicago Cubs shirt opened the door. They talked in a language I didn't understand. He looked at me, nodded approval, and we entered his flat. We followed him to his kitchen and out a door that led to the far side of the building.

"*Grazie, ciao.*" My aunt waved to the man and took my hand as we headed to the alley. We walked a few blocks and stopped at a small diner that looked like a trailer. Sliding into a booth my aunt ordered me a chocolate sundae.

I was beginning to like plan B.

"You stay here. I'm going to make a call." She used a pay phone near the toilets. I kept one eye on her as I ate my ice cream. I was licking the spoon when she returned.

"Did you talk with my mom?"

"I talked with both your mom and dad. They asked me to say hello and to tell you that they loved you."

I was sure they never mentioned the love part, but it was nice she wanted me to feel good. "Are they coming back for me?"

"They had to go out of state and don't feel it's smart to return yet."

"So will I go to them?"

"Your dad doesn't think that's too wise. The police will be coming back looking for you at my place. If you're not there, or I don't have a good explanation where you went, I could be arrested. Also, although we were pretty tricky sneaking out, the police might have had someone stationed outside the Super's door. They could be watching us right now."

I craned my neck to look out the large window next to me. "I don't see any police."

"If they are good, they won't be seen. You don't want your dad captured do you?"

"No."

"Well, right now it's too risky for you to go to them."

"Will I stay with you?" As long as I didn't have to go back to my Aunt Agnes' place.

"I have to work, and with summer break you'll have no one to be with you all day.

"I can watch out for myself."

Her red lips creased to a huge smile as she reached over and patted me on the head. "I'm sure you can, but we don't even know if the police will let me keep you."

"If I can't be with my parents, or you, where will I go? I really want stay with you." My bottom lip quivered like Kenny's. I bit down on it.

"Bobo, I would love to have you stay with me. But, who knows how long they'll be watching me. We knew there was a chance the police would show up, so we had an alternate plan. You would have to stay somewhere else this summer, and we would probably have to tell the police where. The only place that made sense was your grandparent's farm in Tennessee."

"Does this mean I'll never stay with my Mom and Dad again?"

"Why do you ask that?"

"Maybe they don't want me anymore. If they did, they'd find a way to get me." I was losing the battle against my tears.

My aunt slid next to me on the plastic bench. Her chubby arm drew me to her and squeezed gently. "Bobo, your parents may not show it, but they love you very much."

"Then why don't I feel like they do?" I'd never said this out loud. It hurt my heart at night in bed when I thought it, but to say it made it seem so real.

"They are going through some terrible things. Give it time. They very much want you back with them. Besides, you'll love it on the farm. All summer different cousins come and stay some. Before summer ends you'll be back with your family."

She took both my arms, moved me slightly away from her, and looked me in the eyes. "So, how about it?"

The idea of a farm did sound cool. I'd have cousins to play with, and I'd never seen my grandparents. Plus, my half-brother was there. My mother had Butch when she was young. When her husband died in the war, she let her parents raise him. I'd get to be with Butch. Ten years older, he was always nice to me.

"Good, we'll have to do some shopping. You'll need some more clothes and some shoes to play in. I've got an old suitcase you can use."

"When do I go? How do I get there?"

"The plan is you'll leave Sunday. We'll take a bus to the train station and you'll take a train."

The excitement at the thought of my first train ride collided with uneasiness. "You won't be coming with me? I'm going alone?"

"No, I can't go. I've got to be at the office early Monday, and after taking these days off work I barely have enough money for the clothes and your ticket. Bobo, if I didn't think you'd be just fine, I wouldn't let you go."

Aunt Mary had never lied to me.

We headed to Sears, and our arms were soon busy carrying three shopping bags full of clothes, shoes, and even some comic books—and nothing was stolen!

"Are we going back through the alley and the Super's apartment?"

"Nope, we'll go in the front door. Let's surprise them." When we arrived at her stoop, Aunt Mary put her bags down next to me.

"Wait here." She confidently crossed the street and headed straight to the car with the two men in it. The driver rolled his window down and my aunt said something to them, and then returned.

"Whatcha say?"

She lifted the bags and headed up. "I asked if they wanted some coffee, or some sweet rolls."

I grinned. "Didn't they ask how we got out unseen?"

She chuckled. "No, they must have figured they'd blown it. They looked like little boys caught with their fingers in the cookie jar."

Aunt Mary let me into the apartment. "Go get the brown suitcase out of my closet, and I'll help you pack."

I found the old case, but it was full of something and very heavy. I used both my hands to drag it into the living room.

"Oh, I'm sorry. I forgot I was keeping some papers and family albums in it. Let me take it." With a grunt she heaved it on her couch. She grabbed a paper sack and handed it to me. "Here, take this bag of rolls down to the policemen. Tell them I'll bring coffee after it brews."

"But they're the police." Why would she want to be nice to the enemy?

"Yes. They just got a job to do, and so do we." She lifted pictures out of the suitcase. "Here's one of your daddy when he was little."

I held the old photograph close to my face. Somehow I never thought he had been young.

As Aunt Mary tucked me into bed that night, she leaned close. "I want to ask you something. I know you're a Catholic now, and I was for a long time. But, have you ever read the Bible?"

"No, but I did read the Catechism."

"Well, the Catechism and all Christian teaching come from the Bible. Let me read some of it to you." She took a red leather book out of her drawer and began to read about Jesus's last days on earth. I knew the story, but it seemed more real coming from the Bible.

"Bobo, I'm packing a Bible for you. I hope you read it. Scripture says if you believe in Jesus as your Savior, accept Him as Lord and welcome Him into your heart, you will be saved. That's what happened to me. I visited my sister in St. Louis last year and went to hear a young preacher named Billy Graham. It changed my life." She took me by the hand and kissed me on the forehead.

"Would you like to be saved? Would you pray to let Jesus come into your heart?"

What she said was appealing, I loved my aunt and she was so sweet to me. But, I didn't get it. How can Jesus be in my heart? I was having a hard enough time accepting He was in a wafer at communion time. I told her yes, and her tears exposed her happiness—but it was a lie. It was the lie I have hated most.

"Wake up, wake up you sleepy head. Get up, get out of bed." The song challenged my eyes to open, but they fought the urge. "Cheer up, cheer up the sun is red. Live, love, laugh, and be happy." Was I back in Michigan and Mom was starting another day singing? But, no, my mother had a good voice, and this one sounded like a goat.

I felt a hand nudging me, and my eyes opened to Aunt Mary's smile. She always had a huge one, but this one seemed limitless. I remembered last night, and was ashamed of my dishonesty.

"This is our last day together. I've made you French toast, with whipped cream, and we'll do anything you want today."

"Anything I want?"

"Yes, you choose."

My mind raced with ideas. Are the Cubs playing at home today? I'd love to see the new Hitchcock movie. Then it hit me. "What about Lincoln Park Zoo?"

"If that's what you'd like, that's what we'll do. You'd better get up. We have a long bus ride ahead of us."

After breakfast Aunt Mary, carrying her purse and a small picnic basket, took me by the hand and led me down the stairs. As we walked down the stoop it was impossible to miss the two plain-clothed policemen in the car across the street.

"I've got an idea." My aunt tugged me, and we headed to the car. The men inside weren't the same ones I brought the sweet rolls to.

"Morning boys. Just thought I'd tell you we're on our way to Lincoln Park Zoo."

The men looked surprised and a bit unsure what to say.

"We will wait for the bus on Ashland, and take it all the way to North Avenue. Then we'll wait for another bus and take it to the park. I know it'll be slow and boring, but I thought I'd tell you."

Hmm, she made it sound horrible. Did I even want to take such a long and dreary voyage?

"There is another option."

The police glanced at each other.

What was Aunt Mary up to?

"Instead of following behind a slow bus, you could drive us. It would be easier on you both. I'm just thinking of you guys, I know this job must be boring."

The driver shrugged. "Lady, I'm not sure we could do that. There may be rules." His partner nudged him and whispered something to him. "Give us a moment. We'll need to get permission."

"Make sure and tell them this was a great way to keep us in your sites all day. After all, Lincoln Park is a big place. You wouldn't want to lose us in the crowds."

She was good. She could sell a ketchup Popsicle to a lady wearing white gloves.

The driver rolled the window up as the other picked up the microphone. We waited on the sidewalk. In a few moments the officer in the passenger seat popped out of the car, opened the back seat, and leaned in. He exited with his hands full of paper cups, newspapers and bags. He looked at us and smiled. "Gotta clean the place up for our guests."

He deposited the garbage in a big oil drum nearby. When he returned, his grin widened, and he stepped aside of the door, made a half-bow and swept his arm in the air. "We would be pleased if you entered our humble vehicle."

My aunt giggled and said, "Thank you, my dear sir."

Wow, I'm going to sit in a police car. It only took a couple miles to realize police cars weren't that big a deal. There were lots of voices coming from the radio, but no different than taxis. Maybe if they put the siren on.

"Officers, will you be able to drive straight up to the zoo gates?"

"Lady–"

"Call me Mary."

"Okay, Mary. I'm Bill and the driver is Mick. We can do better than that. We'll drive you straight into the zoo. There's a special gate for us."

A police escort? How cool. Was I being disloyal to my father? "I don't want them hanging around us at the zoo."

She smiled. "I'll talk to them. I'm sure they'll stay back and out of sight."

We pulled up to a huge gate. A guard left a little hut and walked over to the driver. They signed something on a clipboard, and the guard pushed opened the gate.

Elephants on my right and the Reptile House on my left, I could barely contain my excitement. Directly ahead clowns carried strings of floating balloons and elated kids, with tired looking adults, everywhere. Most of the children carried popcorn, peanuts, ice cream, soda, or cotton candy. The place was fantastic! How could I be so stupid that I forgot it completely?

"So what do you want to see first?"

We walked past some grazing zebras. I looked back and didn't see the policemen anywhere. "Did Mom ever tell you about the giraffes?"

"You mean the ones you road on Zoo Parade?"

"Yes! Do you think we could find where they're making the show?"

She smiled down, took my hand and said, "Let's look." She stopped someone wearing blue coveralls. He pointed down to the left, so off we went.

We passed some peacocks, a bunch of ostriches, and six African Buffaloes. Then, I saw a structure with a big picture of Marlin Perkins holding a chimp. "Over here." I pulled my aunt toward the building.

"Hold on, Bobo, you'll tear my arm out of the socket."

Please be filming today. Please be filming today.

There was a sign on each of the double doors. Closed. No audience today, filming on location.

"Sorry Bobo, it looks like we're out of luck. Where do you want to go now?"

I wanted to pout, but the smells, noises and energy around me soon rekindled my spirit. "Everywhere, I want to see it all, especially the giraffes."

We spent the entire day examining every inch of the zoo. Although the sign said not to feed them, my aunt purchased some marshmallows and we tossed them at the very eager bears.

We had lunch at a picnic table under a huge oak tree. The bags of peanuts, ice cream bar, and the pink cotton candy had taken their toll, and I was barely able to get down half of my chicken sandwich.

We wandered on until I finally caught sight of a giraffe head above the tree line. I ran past the grove of trees until they opened to a clearing where a giraffe family nibbled from the highest branches. They were so tall! Not just tall, but towering. How was it possible I rode on one of those beautiful beasts when I was even smaller than I was? The young giraffes even soared over me.

I tried to remember the picture my mother showed me. I sat on a giraffe and Mr. Perkin's stood next to me holding a microphone. Were any of the animals I looked at the one in the picture?

"Bobo, how're you holding up? Your little legs must be getting tired."

We'd walked a lot. That was for sure.

"The Bird House is up ahead a bit."

Birds? I've seen plenty of birds. Just when I was ready to ask to go home, I saw a big white truck with the NBC logo on it.

"Look." Reinvigorated, I ran toward the Bird House. Everyone was heading out. They must be done with their filming. Smothered by the small crowd gathered there, I couldn't see a thing.

Suddenly, two arms lifted me up. Bill, one of the policemen, had me in his hands.

I gazed over the crowd and saw him. "Mr. Perkins! Mr. Perkins!" I frantically waved and yelled out his name–nothing. "Mr. Perkins, it's me, Bobo. Remember? I rode the giraffes!" My voice was as loud as I could make it, but again nothing.

The officer reached in his pocket, took a badge out and shouted. "Make way, police."

Everyone stepped aside and we walked right up to Marlin Perkins.

Looking confused, the TV zookeeper asked, "How can I help you officer?"

"This young man," he placed me back on the ground, "would like to meet you."

My aunt, now by my side, put her arm around me.

"Do you want an autograph young man?" Mr. Perkins reached into his pocket and brought out a pen.

"No sir, I'm Bobo. Bobo Hall."

He still didn't know. "I used to ride giraffes on your television show."

A weak light of awareness seemed to appear in his eyes. "The little boy with the cowboy outfit?"

"Yes!" He remembered!

"Well, you've grown into a fine young man." His glance at my aunt seemed to confuse him. He probably remembered my thin and pretty mother, and Aunt Mary was, well, not quite that.

"My mother's not here. This is my Aunt Mary."

He shook her hand and said, "I've got an idea. I bet a lot of the viewers who saw him on those giraffes as a little boy would love to see him ride out one more time. Talk with my director over there," he pointed to a tiny bald man, "let's see if we can get a date. Does he still have a cowboy outfit? If not, we can get him one."

Ride a giraffe again? Yes! Yes! Yes!

"I'm sorry, but he's leaving town tomorrow. I don't know if he'll return." Aunt Mary looked pained.

There had to be a way. I had to get on that giraffe.

"Too bad, take care son. Make sure to keep watching the show." He patted me on the head, climbed into the truck, and rode away.

No! Turn around. Tell me we can do it now. Please.

My aunt's smile was dead and her eyes misted when she bent down to me. "I'm so sorry."

Nearby a large balloon escaped from a little boy's hand and floated away. His little fingers reached out, but it was gone forever. Like that boy, I knew there was nothing I could do. No begging or tears could change the inevitable. It wasn't my aunt's fault. I didn't want her to be unhappy.

"It's okay." My smile was a lie, but not my desire to see hers again. "At least he remembered me. Can we have an ice cream cone before we go?"

Her grin spread across her face. "Bobo, sometimes you amaze me. You seem to be able to handle anything. More ice cream may ruin your dinner, but you earned it."

The policeman said, "Let me go get it. What flavor?"

I stayed silent on our drive back. It was hard to because Bill and Mary talked nonstop.

When we arrived back at my aunt's place, she handed him a piece of paper. "Give this to your boss. Tomorrow, my nephew's taking a train to his grandparents' farm in Tennessee. All the pertinent information is on the paper."

By the time we reached the apartment I was sleep walking. It wasn't late, but the day had taken its toll. I was in bed before the sun left the sky. I lay there resolved to dream only good dreams. But my mind took over and created a mélange of zoo animals and policemen determined to destroy me as I hid on a train. None of the police were nice, and there were no giraffes.

Chapter 11
Southbound

"Stop judging by mere appearances, and make a right judgment." John 7:24

The streets were nearly deserted as the taxi carried us toward the station. My tummy fluttered. I'd never ridden a train before, and meeting my grandparents would be great, but I'd miss my aunt. If only—was it wrong to wish she were my mother? I pushed the thought out of my head.

"There it is." My aunt pointed ahead at the towering old building with a big clock.

Seven-fifteen. We had to hurry. We entered a marble cavern of activity. Garbled announcements sent people with suitcases scurrying to their tracks. My aunt purchased my ticket, and we walked over to a colossal window overlooking Lake Michigan.

"Look up." My aunt pointed to the dome.

The early morning sun bounced bright orange light off the water below, through the window, and skyward. The sunbeams, shadows, and chandeliers seemed to be playing tag. I let my eyes trace the lines several times.

"That's God sending you a message."

"Me? God? What kind of message?" Surely she knew that God didn't bother with me.

"That your future is bright. Only God could put on such a light show. I have faith it was for you."

"How do you know that's the message?"

"I'm not sure, but it's my hope. If you believe in Him, all things are possible. I know times have been tough for you the last couple years, and are not exactly looking too hopeful. But, if you belong to Jesus, He will never abandon you."

She pointed up. "Look at the glow reflecting from the sun. It's like the dazzling brilliance of Jesus. And the steady shimmering from the crystal lighting reminds me of the Father's glory. The shadow that moves between the lights is like the Holy Spirit. It exists, but you can't grip it."

My neck craned watching the spectacle, then the sun changed positions, and it disappeared. I looked at my aunt and she seemed so happy, so at peace, I knew she believed what she said—I wish I did. Was her faith enough for me, too?

"It's time to go." She looked sad. I watched her face as she readied my things. Would she cry?

We walked outside and sat on a bench close to the station. As people and baggage filled the long platform, my aunt reached in her purse, "Take this." She folded two ten-dollar bills and squeezed them into my hand.

I'd never held that much money in one time in my life.

"That's for you. There'll be some food on the train, buy what you want. Whatever's left, get a soda, ice cream, or something fun while you're with your grandparents."

I nodded and carefully pocketed the bills. "Thank you."

"You're welcome, Bobo." She wiped at a tear.

We heard it before we saw it—the chocolate brown and orange train approached.

Aunt Mary stooped down and held me tightly. "Now, pay attention." She pushed me back so she could look into my eyes. I knew she was serious. "You'll be just fine on the train. It'll take you straight to Memphis. You get off there and walk towards the terminal, but don't leave the platform. Go to the bench on the platform closest to the terminal doors. Your Uncle James will be waiting for you."

"If for any reason he's not there, you call me collect. There's a paper in your bag that has James' number and your grandparents' in case you can't reach me."

I nodded. "I know how to make collect calls."

"I know you do, sweetheart." She'd stopped crying, but the tears had done their damage. Two streaks of black trickled down from her painted eyes to her now smiling lips.

I reached in my back pocket, pulled out my handkerchief, and rubbed the smudges from her cheeks. Her tears returned, but so did her laughter.

"Bobo, I'm going to miss you. If I ever have a child, I hope he's just like you."

I would miss Aunt Mary, too. Maybe she'd decide to keep me. I watched the train approach. She'd better decide in a hurry.

The heavy train pulled in and tons of people disembarked, while others searched for an opening to push their way on.

"We'll just wait here until all the arriving passengers have come off. I snagged you a ticket in the fourth coach. It's the observation car. You'll sit upstairs and have a great view. If you have any questions, ask the conductor. Here's a sack with some cookies and a carton of orange juice."

When it was time, she walked with me to my seat and opened my suitcase. "Here are some comic books for the ride." She closed the bag and placed it above my head. As other passengers jostled around us, I sat on a big leather seat next to the window. She knelt on the seat next to me and bent to kiss both my cheeks.

"I love you Bobo. Don't forget that. And most of all don't forget that God does too." She made her way down the narrow aisle and off the train. I watched until I couldn't see her anymore, then I placed the bag and comic books in the little pouch in front of me and stared out the window. I listened for the famous "All aboard," but it never came.

With a lethargic grunt the big train began to move. We passed homes and cars at a speed I could've matched on my bike. Suddenly, "Sixty-Third Street" was shouted and we groaned to a stop. For the next hour the snail-paced train made stop after stop. At that rate we'd never arrive.

A brown suited conductor punched my ticket and had one question, "You traveling alone?"

"Yes, I'm going to my grandparents' farm." Would he get mad? Was it wrong to be alone?

"Have any questions? Is there anything you need?"

I thought for a moment, and then asked, "Can I go to the engine car?"

"No, I'm sorry. For safety reasons I'm not even allowed there. If you need me, ask any of the conductors. I'll stop by at times to see how you're doing."

"Can I go into the other cars and look around?"

"Sure, just be careful. The doors between the cars are sometimes tough to open. You may need some help. We have two dining cars. They're more like coffee shops than restaurants, but some pretty good food. At twelve-thirty we stop in Carbondale. There are lots of vendors there. They have better toilets than the train, but make sure you're back on before we leave. It's a very short stop."

After he left I stared out the huge window expecting exciting views, but mostly it was dull and ugly. It seemed riding a train wasn't as exciting as I imagined, at least not yet.

The overhead speakers crackled on. "Carbondale, extended stop. Fifteen minutes." I jumped up eager for a change in scenery.

I joined a trainload of passengers passing by vendors selling food, toys, yarn, and books. I flowed with the crowd towards the station house. My first goal was the toilets. I tried the one on the train, but when I slid open the door, the odor was so bad I gagged and did an about-face.

Assuming many would be rushing to fresher restrooms, I weaved through the traffic as fast as I could into the small house. An arrow pointed toward the Men's room. Two doors?

Whites.

Coloreds.

Why separate toilets for colored and white folks? I'd have to ask the steward when I got back on the train.

Once the train began to chug again I was ready to start my exploration. The conductor passed through and I asked, "Where's the dining car?"

"There are two. Don't use the one up front. The one you'll want is two cars down from us, to the right."

Sliding the door open took both hands and all my leg strength. The space between the cars was loud, slightly scary, and wiggled in every direction. I almost had to jump to the next car. I struggled to get that door open, and the instant I did, a cloud of smoke engulfed me. My eyes burned, and that familiar scratching in my throat reminded me of my mother. If I'd been riding with her, we'd have probably sat in that car.

I pushed into the next cabin where fifteen tables were surrounded by four bolted-down chairs, and a sign over a counter that read *Tavern Lounge Car*. A man in a red uniform answered requests for food and drink. Most folks sat at their tables reading a book or a newspaper. It looked like the many bars my parents had taken me to—dreary.

"Sir...sir." I eyed the hamburgers on some of the diners' plates and my stomach begged for them.

"Sir?" I waved my hands, but he paid no attention. " Sir!" Being little in a big person's world is tough. I looked around for others to help, but the few that noticed quickly disregarded me. I was an insect, worthy of a swat, but not much more.

Giving up, I headed to the front of the train. The conductor had said not go to that one, but my tummy was in charge now. Maybe I'd have more luck at the other lounge. The moment I entered the third car something was different, but I wasn't sure what. When I reached the next car, it was obvious.

I was the only white person.

Eyes followed me as I made my way to the first car. One little girl said, "What's he doing here? I'll bet he gets in trouble."

As I crept toward the final car the noise grew louder. I pushed open the heavy door and entered a new world—

one filled with laughter, music, and dancing. The room was packed, and dark. Not so much the lighting, but the color of everyone's skin. Two couples swaying in tune with the beat froze when they saw me enter. Someone turned the music down. I still had my hand on the door.

"Boy, does your momma know you're up here?" She was very big, wore a pink flowered dress, and had everyone's attention. Including mine.

"No ma'am."

The smaller, skinny lady sitting at the counter next to her laughed. "She'll tan your hide if she finds out."

"She's not here."

The big lady stepped up to look me over. "Whose you with?"

"No one, I'm alone. I'm coming from Chicago to see my grandparents."

"Watcha' doings up here?" She dragged her words a bit. She sounded like Ma Kettle from the movies.

"I'm hungry, and no one would serve me at the other dining car."

"This boy is hungry." She announced it so all could hear. "Let's make space for him at the bar." She walked to the middle of the counter and patted on a metal stool. "You'se comin' in or leaving? Makes up your mind boy."

I cautiously walked towards them. A very tall man wearing a white straw hat lifted me and placed me on the red plastic seat.

"I's Esther and my friend be Florida."

Florida smiled and flashed two gold teeth.

I gawked at them, and she noticed. She spread her lips wide and tapped on them with a fingernail. "My husband got them for me three years ago for Christmas. What'cha think?"

"They're beautiful."

Florida clapped and shouted, "This boy gots taste."

"To the white boy—" a man rose a glass high, "what's your name?"

"Bobo."

"To Bobo." Other glasses were raised, and without ridiculing my name they toasted me into their midst. With my novelty status officially reduced, the music returned, and the party resumed.

"Is it someone's birthday?" I asked Esther, but Florida jumped in.

"It's always someone's birthday, why you askin'?"

"The music. It seems like a party. The other dining car was nothing like this."

It was Esther's turn to reply. "White folks got it all wrong. They reason life is serious times that sometimes get happy. We think it's good times that sometimes get bad. Those in the back of the train lose a day of joy by hating the trip."

She made a lot of sense.

"You a smart boy to come join us." Florida patted me on the head, and handed me a plastic menu. "Whatcha' want to eat?"

I looked at the card. I had never chosen off a menu before. One entrée made me laugh.

"What's this catfish?"

"Y-u-m-m-y, I loves me some catfish. They fry it pretty good here, but not's as good as I do."

Esther nodded in agreement with Florida's words.

A fish that's a cat didn't sound all that good to me. "How about a hamburger?"

"When the man comes, order one and some chips."

I hadn't noticed no one waited on them. But now that she mentioned it, I craned my neck to look behind the bar. No one to be seen. When the red-uniformed man appeared, he was white. The one serving in the other dining car wasn't. The ladies ordered my food and a coke, and almost everyone else placed an order, mostly drinks.

When the man left Florida said, "It'll take a while. He only comes in every fifteen minutes. If they's behind, orders come cold."

I took a few sips from the small Coke bottle and asked, "Why doesn't he stay here?"

They looked at each other. Florida said, "Esther, this is your area. You want to fill the boy in?"

"I don't know. Why bother him with our world?"

"He's gots ta learn sometimes."

I was curious and swiveled towards Esther. "I'm not too young. After all, I'm traveling alone to Memphis."

"That's something no colored momma would ever allow." Florida's words were compassionate, yet angry.

"Florida, it's not our place."

"Bobo, it is Bobo isn't it?"

"Yes."

"You been in the white man's diner in the back right?"

"Uh, huh."

"What color was the attendant?"

"Just like you." Why did that matter?

"The railroad has no problem having a colored man wait tables and take orders for white folks, but they would never trust one to wait on us in the colored diner. The white man working back here doesn't want to spend too much time with us, so he only comes in every fifteen minutes to deliver and take orders."

"This is a colored dining car? I saw a colored and a white toilet back at the train station. Is that a rule for the railroad?"

"Son, it ain't just the railroad, its life. You heading south. You'll see water faucets, restaurants, even schools that are labeled that way."

Schools? It seemed silly, even mean. "Is that why the front of the train has no whites?"

"Yes. Oh, they'll deny it of course. We all buy our tickets at the same counters, but the clerks always gives us seats in the front of the train."

Florida grunted and sputtered, "They sits us in the front of the trains, but we has to be in the back of buses."

It made no sense to me. Some people use a bad name to describe colored people back in Chicago, but the same could be said about anyone. We'd all been called a bad name. That didn't mean we needed a separate toilet.

"You ever been around folks like us, Bobo?" A man leaned over Florida's shoulder.

I shook my head. Except for the Maxwell Street neighborhood, I'd never been this close to any. They seemed no different to me, just darker. I noticed the bar area quieted and many tuned into our conversation.

"Why is it like this?"

Esther looked at Florida, and she shook her head. "Y'all have to ask the white folks that."

Florida looked like she wanted to add something, but Esther slapped her hand. "Let the boy be. That's enough. He a good boy, let's pray he stay that way."

Chapter 12
Summer on the Farm

*"I am reminded of your sincere faith, which first lived in
your grandmother Lois and in your mother Eunice and,
I am persuaded, now lives in you also." 2 Timothy 1:5*

The conductor helped me exit the train. At the end of the
platform a tall dark-haired man stood as I approached.

"You Bobo?" The man had a kind enough face.

"Yes sir."

"Great, let's get a move on." He grabbed my bag, and
we headed out the terminal. My uncle's grey truck
lumbered through Memphis, and then plodded down an
old highway until darkness took over. The windows were
down and the old vehicle screeched like a washing
machine, talking was impossible. Seemed that was
probably the way my uncle preferred it, anyway.

What would the farm be like? Would it be like Tara
in *Gone with the Wind,* or like the one in *Grapes of
Wrath*? The dry pink earth and lack of green hinted at
the latter.

We arrived at a small house desperate for a coat of
paint. My uncle parked on a parched front yard begging
for grass and moisture.

A tiny lady exploded out the screen door and hurried
to my door. Before my uncle could turn the engine off,
she had me in her wispy arms and tossed me up and
down like a beach ball. She gently set me down and gave
me an enormous hug.

Was she a midget? She wasn't much bigger than me.
How'd she manage to pick me up like that?

"Gotta go, Ma. I'll stop by next Sunday for dinner." My uncle winked at me. "Bye, son. You be good, now. You hear?"

She tugged me toward the house.

A porch light revealed the shadow of a tall, thin figure standing on the other side of the screen.

"Bobo, you come on in. We saved you some supper." My grandma lifted my suitcase and took my hand.

"So this is Billie's boy. They tell me you don't like carrying my name?" The tall man smiled down at me.

"James, don't be teasing the boy. He just got here and he doesn't know what a joker you are."

Carrying his name? "No sir. That's not it at all." I didn't want to start off on the wrong foot with my grandfather. "My parents must have given me my Bobo name. I'm Jake...uh...Jim ...ah, James Hall."

Grandpa laughed. "We'll call you Bobo if that's what you want."

"Let's get you unpacked and some food in you." My grandmother led me into a tiny bedroom and gestured to the bed. "You can put your things there and deal with them after you've had your supper."

In just a few steps, I'd seen the entire house. How could a whole family fit in there? "Did all of your children sleep in that tiny room?"

She wore a pretty blue dress and looked a little like a doll, a doll with wrinkles. "No, honey, we've had a couple big homes before. One burned down and our last one we sold. It's down the road some. This one's about all we need now. Room for us and a visitor now and then."

"Does Butch sleep on the other bed in my room?"

"No, your big brother lives in Memphis mostly. He's staying at a cousin's house and works at a plant. He also sings at some honkytonk on weekends."

I tried to hide my disappointment he wasn't there. It wasn't my grandparent's fault. "Is he a good singer?"

"Was pretty good in church, but now sings that awful rocky rolling be-bop stuff."

"Rock and roll?"

"I suppose. It's too loud, and if you ask me, it's from the devil. But, I suppose that's because I'm getting old. Have only heard it a couple times, which was twice too often."

A gigantic pine table anchored the room. She held a chair out, inviting me to sit at a smaller table to the side, crowded with food. "Sunday's, when everyone comes over, we eat at the big table. But, we'll eat here most times." My tummy rumbled at the aromas from the food on the table and the huge black stove.

"I hope you like pasta. We have that every Sunday. Today we have ham, corn, beans, mashed potatoes, fresh bread, and my homemade apple cobbler."

That much food? Just for supper?

When I finished eating, I headed for my room. That's when I realized something was missing. "Grandma, I need to use the toilet."

She entered the tiny bedroom and saw me garbed in my new blue pajamas. "James, Bobo needs to go to the potty. That's your territory."

Grandpa yelled, "Bobo, come out here to the kitchen."

He stood at the sink pouring water from a big jug into two glasses. The straps of his overalls slumped by his sides. "I guess you never been on a farm before, so I need to introduce you to what it's going to be like." He walked over to the long table, placed one glass at the head and the other in front of the seat next to it. He took the head seat and nodded towards the other one. I took that as a cue to sit. I sure didn't need that water though.

"I suppose we need to get all things need discussing discussed." Grandpa took a long drink from his glass.

Grandma entered and headed to the sink to finish cleaning the dishes.

"I'll tell you our house rules, what we expect and other *cibo squisito*."

"Cibo sqiii...?" What?

"In English James. Bobo, he means some tidbits you

might want to know." My aunt dried a plate, but her attention was obviously on our conversation.

"First the rules…" He sat straight and looked serious, and then a big set of white teeth shined a beautiful smile. "There are none. Just treat everyone like you'd want to be treated, and have fun. We are happy to have you, and we want you to enjoy your stay."

What a nice thing to say.

"And what we expect from you…" He tried to look stern, but his face betrayed him. "… Is exactly nothing."

"That's right." My grandma joined in, "You don't have to do a thing. No chores or duties. Only join in when you feel like it. This is your vacation."

That didn't seem quite right. I didn't mind helping. And was it really only a vacation? If so, when was it over?

"But this is a farm, and you will need to know a few things." My grandfather was back in control. "You see your grandma doing the dishes?" I nodded.

"Well do you notice something different?"

I pointed. "The water she's getting comes from right outside the window."

Grandpa pushed up from the table and waved for me to follow. He opened the screen door and flipped a light on. He pointed to the left, and I saw a big wooden barrel with a ladder attached to it. There seemed to be a sort of door flat on its top. "How's the water get in it?"

"In rainy season, God slides it right in. Mostly, it's me filling it up from there." We pump the water from the barrel to give it some force. He took a flashlight hanging on the doorframe and flashed it on a well. "Come on, let me show you."

At the well, he took a long pipe and lowered it for quite a while. He then rapidly reversed his motion and drew it up. He pulled a string and water poured out the bottom of the pipe into a bucket next to us. He grabbed a big spoon, dipped it into the water, and lifted it to my lips. *Wow!* It was cold and tasted better than any water I'd ever had.

He toted the bucket into the kitchen and my grandma emptied it into a jug. "In case you ain't figured it out yet, no running water means no indoor plumbing."

I wasn't exactly sure what he meant by plumbing, but I had a nasty suspicion.

"Let me show you where you go when you have to go." He laughed at his own joke and used the flashlight to guide me to a small shed a good distance from the house.

"Now I didn't want to say this with your grandma in hearing range, but if all you gotta do is tinkle, you don't have to come all the way out here. If you're outta sight most anyplace will do, but never on one of your grandma's flowers or bushes. If you do, she'll blame me."

Was he joking?

When he opened the door, I entered a world I vowed to never return to. The smell, the flies, just the idea of what shared the air I was breathing. Didn't they know there was a better way to do it?

I did everything I could to try and keep my vow of not using the outhouse the entire summer but, like Grandpa said, "If you gotta go, you gotta go." A few stomachaches sent me running back there. I'd hold my breath as long as I could and then breathe using my shirtsleeve as a filter.

Butch's fingerprints were everywhere. Grandma gave me a small list and sent me to the country store down the road. It looked out of place. An old building in what looked like the middle of nowhere. Two very old men who looked like contestants in a fat man's contest occupied the two rocking chairs on the crooked front porch. Two younger men dangled their legs off the porch. I soon became the focus of newcomer questions.

"Who're you?"

"What's your name?"

"What brung you here?"

After I answered their questions, the men looked at each other, nodded, and almost in unison sighed, "He's Butch's lil brother."

"Yep. Got Butch's good looks."

"Hopefully not his mischief."

Mischief? I'd have to find someone willing to tell me stories.

One of the men on a rocker looked at one of the younger ones. "He's from up north. Go get him what we get for all Yankees their first time in the South."

Obedient, he shot up and opened the top of a metal box, reached in and lifted out a bottle. His hand was soaked, and little slivers of ice fell on the old wood floor. He delivered it to the man on the rocker, who motioned me over.

"Young man, welcome to God's country. This is where He hangs out, and I got the proof right here in this bottle." He took an opener from his shirt pocket, popped the cap off and offered it to me.

The bottle was slippery and ice cold. I twisted it around and saw the label. *Dr. Pepper.* Was it medicine? Was it a drink made out of pepper? I couldn't drink either of those things. Were they trying to pull a fast one on me? "Uh, thank you sir, but—"

They all started howling.

"He done what they all do," one snorted.

The man who passed me the bottle waved a hand in the air and the laughing died down. He smiled. "I'll never understand why they gave it its name, I heard it once was some sort of snake oil medicine, but go on and drink up."

I raised the bottle to my lips and let a few drops fall into my mouth. It was sweet and not at all peppery. I took a longer swig. Amazing. "Wow, thank you!"

"Good, ain't it? If we had this during the War of Northern Aggression, the South would have won, and you'd be whistling Dixie today."

This started them on a discussion about why the South really won, but it was over my head. I took another drink. Maybe the man was right, this was God's country. Sipping that sugary nectar sure felt like I was in heaven.

I knew I hadn't lived long enough to use terms like "in all my life," but I'd never had a day like the first one on the farm. I rode a tractor, threw muddy food scraps at pigs, plucked eggs out of nests, and even picked some cotton. But, nothing beat the chickens.

"Bobo." Grandma's voice carried into the barn where I played. "The day's moving on, so I got to get supper ready. You want to help?"

"What can I do?"

"I thought we'd have fried chicken. So, we need us a chicken. Would you like to catch one?"

Not only did it sound like fun, I figured it wouldn't be a problem. I was fast, and the chickens wandered all over the place, some no more than a foot away. "Okay, which one you want?"

She laughed. "Whichever one you can catch." She sat on the back steps like she was waiting for a show to begin—and it did.

I darted right and left, but those suckers moved fast. I dove at a brown one, but only caught dirt. They scattered a few feet from my reach, and began to peck the ground like I was nothing more than a minor nuisance. I saw a wooden box, grabbed it, and tried throwing it at the taunting beasts—not even close. My grandma's cackle soon was louder than the squawks from those cruel feathered devils.

"Bobo, thank you for a good laugh." She used the sleeve of her dress to wipe away some tears. "They are tricky, but they can be had."

She grabbed a bucket filled with corn kernels. "Here chickie, here chickie, chickie." She was surrounded by those tiny terrors.

She pushed the bucket over to me. "You try it."

I threw the corn and they came as close as my toes. The bucket dropped and I dove. My hand touched a foot, but I was again too late.

My grandma bent down to scoop the corn back into the bucket. "I've had a little more experience. Watch."

Before I could blink, she darted with a speed no mere mortal should have. Her left hand held the bucket and her right the neck of a very agitated bird. Then her right arm raised and twirled the feathered body around like a lasso. This was a major problem for the chicken because the body turned, but the neck didn't. She quickly moved to a log, grabbed an axe, and *Whack!* the head was gone. She threw the headless animal away from her and it ran in circles until it dropped. She didn't spill one kernel of corn.

"Want to help pluck him?"

I really didn't, but at that point I was in awe of my super-grandma. I'd do anything she asked. Even though the smell of that animal's innards cooking in the pot was worse than a dead skunk.

"Take it outside and begin a-pluck'n."

I pulled on feathers, and watched the other chickens prance happily about. I guessed they were just glad it wasn't them.

Nothing on earth tasted more delicious than fresh fried chicken, especially with mash potatoes, gravy, butter beans, and baked bread. I helped with the dishes then we headed to the front porch to sit a spell. Or that's what they called it.

"Grandma, you don't have a TV." It was more a statement than a question.

She wore a long white and blue dress, different from the denim day dress. Both she and grandpa sat on a porch swing together.

"No radio either. At least not one plugged up."

"Don't you get bored?" No Saturday morning cartoons? No Ozzie and Harriet? What did they do with their time?

She looked at Grandpa, smiled, and took his hand. "Never get bored with good company."

He reached around and squeezed her shoulders.

"Am I going to be here the entire summer? When will my mom and dad come get me?"

My grandma smiled over to me as I swayed on a big rocker, "Not sure, but the plan is you stay here and sometime before school starts back you'll be with your parents. Best not worry about things you can't change. It'll be a good summer. You'll see."

Maybe. But I was starting to have my doubts. "If you got no TV, do you play games? What do you do after you come off the porch?"

My grandma raised her tiny body and took her husband by the hand. "Let's go inside, and I'll show you."

My grandfather sat on a big green tufted chair with a floor lamp leaning over it. The little table next to him had papers on it, and the floor below it was stacked with papers and books. My grandma came into the room with a wooden tray carrying three glasses of tea. I sat on the couch, but she scooted me off.

"Unless we got company, this is my territory at night. You might like the rocker over by the window."

The chair had a cushion and I rocked back and forth. My grandma brought in some yarn and big needles and laid them on the couch. "We go to bed pretty early most nights, but we try and finish each day here together. We talk some, open letters, and read the Word. Maybe TV is more exciting, but it ain't better."

She moved her needles and yarn around and Grandpa opened the first of the letters. "This one's from Sue."

Letter after letter, and there were many with such a large family, but we read and discussed them all. It wasn't as exciting as television, but for some reason, it felt good.

Dark eased its way into the room, and Grandpa turned more lights on. He lifted a huge old leather book off the floor. "Bobo, this here is our family Bible." As he turned the pages, pictures fell to the floor. It seemed there were as many pictures as pages in the book. "Your grandma tells me you had a Bible packed inside your suitcase."

"My Aunt Mary packed it in with my clothes." If Aunt Mary and Grandma and Grandpa believed in the Bible—maybe I should hear what it had to say.

"Never met her, but she's surely a good person to give you such a special present." Grandpa adjusted his reading glasses.

Grandma continued her work as he read aloud from the book. The only sounds were the occasional car ambling down the road, and the chirping of male crickets begging for a mate. Finally, Grandpa said, "So saith the Lord," and closed the book. He kissed my head and left for the outhouse.

That first night, Grandma asked if I needed to go with him. I shook my head. No way.

"Okay, then. Time for bed."

After I got my pajamas on my grandma sat by the side of the bed and smiled." So what did you think of your first day here?"

"It was cool."

"What about having no TV?"

"I kind of wished you did. Does Grandpa read the Bible every night?" It sounded like a whine. I didn't really mean it that way.

"Yes, does that bother you?"

"Well, I'm a Catholic, and we don't read the Bible."

"Your grandpa used to be Catholic, and he did. I think lots of them do."

"He isn't Catholic anymore?"

"No, he was when he first arrived here. There were no Catholic churches here, so he had to adapt. He and his first wife went to a Holiness church, but became Christian Scientists. That's the church I belonged to when we first got married."

I nodded and pretended to know what she was talking about. "Is that what you are now?"

"No," she smiled big." About the time I was having my fifth child without so much as an aspirin, I figured it was time to change." She looked at my puzzled face and said, "It's a little complicated. The Christian Scientists don't believe you should ever take medicine."

"Not even when you're sick?" Why would someone do that?

"Oh, it's not important. We go to the Church of Christ now, but sometimes go to First Baptist in Jackson."

"I don't get it, why so many different types of churches?" Which one was God's?

She straightened the sheet near my neck, "Guess what? I don't know. When Jesus started it, there was only one church. And I'm sure that's the way He likes it best."

"But the nuns say it's a mortal sin to go to a church that's not Catholic."

"Bobo, I don't want to say anything bad about your nuns. They mean well, and are probably trying to protect you from confusion. But, if there are grades given for sinning, God's the one who does the grading."

It kind of made sense.

"Want to say your prayers before you go to sleep?"

"Okay. Now I lay me down to sleep, I pray the Lord my soul to keep. If I should die before I wake, I pray the Lord my soul to take. Amen."

"Amen. Tell me, Bobo, have you ever just talked to God outright?"

Talked to God?" You mean like He's here?"

"Yes."

I shook my head no.

"That's what prayer is. You don't need to memorize what you say to me, you simply talk. When you wanted some more mashed potatoes tonight, what did you do?"

"I just asked you to pass the bowl."

"You didn't need a memorized speech?"

"No, I just asked."

"It's the same with God. He's here, He's everywhere you go, and would love for you to talk with Him."

"But, He doesn't talk back." Last I'd checked, if I asked God for the bowl of potatoes, nothing would happen. I'd have to get it myself.

"But He does." She took my hands in hers. "That's what your grandpa was doing tonight. He was giving you God's words. And sometimes, if you pay real close attention, you can hear the Lord whisper in your ear."

She lifted her tiny body up from the bed. "Try talking with Him. Tell Him your thoughts, and bring your worries to Him. He's waiting for you." She turned off the light.

Each night Grandma tried to coax me to pray the way she said. Sometimes I tried, but it just didn't seem right. I could say the *Our Father* and the *Hail Mary*, but I had a hard time praying anything but what I had memorized. Most times I wasn't even sure I believed there was a God. Why would a God allow my life to turn into one of lies and running? If there was a God, and He did allow that, I didn't want to talk with Him. No one wants to talk with someone they're mad at.

There was a steady supply of cousins who joined me on the farm. Some came for a day, others stayed a week. We spent most days meandering through the maze-like gullies on and around the farm. The pink crevasses were deep, and reminded me of war pictures. Often my cousins and I would scrounge up sticks, pretend they were rifles, and jump in our trenches. The Nazis, North Koreans, and Indians didn't have a chance.

No matter how early I woke, I never beat my grandparents. Working a farm was hard work and started before light. But the evenings were soft and gentle. After dinner we'd sit on the porch rockers and shell beans and peas. I absorbed all my grandpa's stories about coming to America, his many children, and his family in Italy. Even reading from the Bible became precious to me because my grandpa read the words, not because God said them. I loved my time with grandparents.

Then one day the FBI arrived.

I noticed a black car parked down the road. Around sundown a green car drove up and took its place. This went on for three days, then I decided to get as close as I could. Using my gully tunnels I secretly scooted near enough to see two men in dark suits watching the house. They were police...they had to be. Were they there to make me leave the farm? I hurried home as fast as I could.

"Grandma. Grandma! There are policemen outside."

She put down her dishrag and looked at me. "Are you sure?"

"Yes, ma'am. They've been there for three days. I didn't know they were policemen until today."

She went out the back door, took a red cloth, and tied it to a string hanging down from a pole sticking out from the roof of the barn. Grandma pulled the string and it fluttered like a flag. She looked at me and said, "Your grandpa will see this. He knows it's a signal to head home."

The sound of the tractor as Grandpa pulled into the yard stirred my grandma to action. She grabbed a small set of binoculars and trotted out the back door. I watched as she leaped on the still moving tractor. She sat directly in front of my grandpa and took over the steering as he aimed the glasses at the car. Within minutes they were in the kitchen.

My grandpa was soaked in sweat and was very dirty. "Bobo, I know we haven't discussed your situation with you. We figured there was no reason to remind you about what you already knew." He went to the jar of water and filled a glass.

"Well, we knew sooner or later the FBI would be here. Word is they contacted the sheriff your first week here to ask him to keep an eye on you, and to let them know if any strangers arrived."

"The sheriff's one of your uncles," Grandma added.

"Yeah, they must have found that out and sent some agents here to watchdog us. No big deal, now. But, it could be a problem if your mom and dad show up. And sending you back to them just got a whole lot trickier."

I shrugged. It figured. Every time I felt happy, or safe, something like this happened. Why should I expect any different?

Chapter 13
Homeward Bound

"In everything set them an example by doing what is good." Titus 2:7

"Bobo, this Sunday we're having a pig pickin'." My grandpa grinned as he announced it at the supper table.

I stopped chewing. "A what?"

"A pig pickin'. The family gets together, and I roast a hog outside on a spit. We have a big party like this each year before August disappears and the busy fall is upon us. I'll let you help me with the pig."

Visions of chasing a muddy pig around the yard flashed through my mind. "How?"

"Well, I won't ask you to do the bloody work, but you can help me with the pit."

I wasn't too sure about the pig pickin' party. But there was no changing Grandpa's mind. And maybe Butch would come. I'd catch that pig myself if it meant I'd get to see my big brother.

Midday Saturday Grandpa took me around the barn to a hole filled with some charred logs. "Jump down there and pass me the old wood." Then he handed me a shovel. "See if you can scoop some of those the ashes out of there."

My shovel scrapped against the rocks and bricks lining the bottom of the pit.

"Go to the wood pile next to the house for some logs, and dump them in the pit. James is coming over to help with the pig late tonight. That's when we'll light 'er up."

What about Butch? When would he arrive? I didn't ask. Maybe deep down I didn't want to know the answer. Ignorance left room for hope.

Later that night my uncle arrived, and he and Grandpa headed out the kitchen door. I started to follow them, but my grandpa stopped me. "You stay here. We're going to take care of the pig now. We'll come get you when we're ready to light the fire and start roasting."

I sat on the back stoop and watched the beams from their flashlights head towards the pigpen. The eight-year-old boy in me desperately wanted to watch them slaughter the pig, but the human in me was glad they hadn't offered.

I heard some grunts and squeals, and then a piercing, dreadful shriek. I cringed. Maybe even let out a yelp because my grandma opened the door and sat down. She put her arm around me.

"You okay?"

I nodded. It didn't bother me they killed a pig, but it felt good my grandma cared. After a while, the beams of light moved toward the well.

"Ma, you want to draw us up some water?"

"Come on Bobo, you can help me." For the next thirty minutes we filled buckets that my uncle carted away, and then my grandpa returned with him.

"Bobo, let's get that fire going."

I trailed him to the pit and noticed he carried a long stick whose tip was covered with a cloth that smelled like gasoline. He flicked a lighter, ignited the stick, and threw it in the hole.

"Bobo, throw some of these little branches on top of the flame." Soon the fire grew to a blaze.

My grandma then appeared with some long sticks and a bag of marshmallows. "Here, put a couple of these on the tips and let them sit near the flames."

I held them there like she said, turning the stick to keep them from catching fire.

"Okay, when they're as brown as you want them, let 'em cool, and then go ahead and eat 'em."

I blew on one of the marshmallows as long as I could stand it, and then pulled it off the stick. The gooey mess stuck to my fingers and coated my chin as I took a bite. The warm, sticky, sweetness tasted perfect with the smoky flavor and crusty coating. I'd been eating them wrong all those years.

"Hey, what about us?" My grandpa whined.

She laughed, "I got you boys some sticks too."

We spent the next hour watching the glare from the pit and enjoying our toasted treats.

"Bobo, it's past your bed time." My grandma's words sounded like a command.

"Aw shucks, let the boy stay up to see us put the pig on." My grandpa pleaded.

"How long is that going to be?"

"Fire should be hot enough in less than an hour. Let's just sit here and enjoy the night."

My grandma squinted at me. "I don't know. You've got to be tired."

"I want to see them put the pig on the fire. I'm not sleepy at all." I was telling the truth, the excitement had revved me up.

Before a final decision passed, my grandpa started singing. "A mighty fortress is our God, a bulwark never failing..." My uncle's tenor joined Grandpa's rich, smooth voice. They all sang hymns unfamiliar to me, with words that bragged on God and thanked Him for all kinds of stuff.

I watched the smoke rise from the pit toward the almost-full moon. Sitting around the pig pit felt more like church than church ever had.

"James, I think it's time."

My uncle followed Grandpa. I could barely make out their reflections as dim lights moved away. They returned hauling something strapped to a long pole.

"Whew, this one's heavy." My uncle grunted as he and my grandpa carefully lowered their burden across the open pit.

"He should be big enough for even our gang." My grandpa seemed to have no problem handling the awkward chain-linked contraption.

I examined the dead hog wrapped with fencing and chicken wire. An X-shaped stick wedged in the ground supported each end of the pole.

My grandma left for a moment and then reappeared with a big pot and a ladle. She poured liquid from the pot all over the pig as my uncle and grandpa turned it over.

"Now you boys fill up the innards pot and leave it outside the kitchen door." In charge now, she pointed a finger at me, "It's time for you to go to bed."

Worn out, I welcomed her suggestion.

Most mornings the marvelous odors of country breakfasts worked like reveille. First my nose yelled to my stomach, "Wow that smells good!" Then my stomach shouted to my body, "Get up, before it's all gone!" That was all it took, and I bounced out of bed.

But something was wrong, horribly wrong. My nose shouted, "Oh no, what is that?" Then, my stomach churned and moaned, "Got to get out of here before I puke." I rose with one hand supporting my belly and the other tightly clutching my nostrils.

Something must have died because nothing alive could smell *that* bad.

I stumbled to the kitchen where acrid smoke from outside forced itself in through the screen door. Did a smoking pig smell this bad? I opened the door.

"Sorry about the smell Bobo." She stirred the frothy liquid in the pot with a wooden stick. In her toga-like white sheet, Grandma looked like a witch stirring her brew.

"Come here, this'll help." She spun the lid off a jar marked *Camphor* and smeared its contents above my upper lip. The gel seemed to neutralize the smell some, but it wasn't enough to eliminate it. It was more like minty death after the camphor.

"This here is souse meat. It may smell bad, but no good pig pickin' would be worth anything without it."

"What do you do with it?" I figured anything that stunk that bad had to be used as fertilizer for the garden or was medicine for a horse.

"You eat it. I think you'll like it." As much as I loved her cooking, my vow to not eat whatever floated in that pot was stronger than the one to avoid the outhouse.

By noon my grandparents had both bathed and said it was my turn. I had mixed feelings about taking baths on the farm. I liked feeling clean, but I was too old for my grandma to bathe me. When I first insisted I could do it myself my grandpa asked, "How?" I looked at the tin tub he carried into the kitchen and then the pots of water warming on the stove.

"I can pour the water and then get in."

"But, it will take more water to be reheated. Your grandma is an artist in getting it at just the right temperature. Then, you need to be rinsed off with clean water, not the nasty stuff left in the tub."

I could see their point, but how embarrassing!

I'm sure Grandma was especially glad to bathe the smell of her cauldron's smoke off of both of us. After she dried me, she kissed me and said, "Let's talk."

Over the past couple of years, that phrase had become a signal for my brain to yell, "Pay attention," and my heart to cry, "Not again."

She walked me to my bedroom. My suitcase laid open on the bed. Packed.

"Grandpa has talked with your parents, and it's time for you to go be with them."

I was supposed to be happy. Would going back to them mean more danger, more lost friends, more fear? Guilt fought with my worries and won.

"Great." The word snuck out past the lump in my throat and without an exclamation mark.

"They'll be a big crowd here later and someone will sneak you off. You'll take the train home from Memphis."

"Where's home?" Surely I wasn't going back to the house in Moline. Or to Maxwell Street. Or to Aunt Mary's.

"I'm not sure. It's probably best we don't know."

Yeah. Probably best. Music, food, and tons of people filled the remainder of the day. My grandma asked me to not get dirty again, but slews of cousins anxious to join me in my gullies persuaded me to break my promise. I'd almost forgotten it was my last day here when I heard Grandma's voice.

"Bobo, Bobo!" She may be tiny, but her voice was huge.

I followed it to her in the kitchen. Women and babies held court in the house, and the men and older kids stayed outside.

"It's time to go. I'm going to get your grandpa now. Wait here."

I didn't want to cry, but I did.

She returned carrying a washcloth, and Grandpa clutched a paper sack.

Grandma cleaned the dirt off me, as he gave instructions. "You'll leave with James, but he's only taking you to your cousin Festus' place. Festus will drive you to the station."

Not Butch. I'd be leaving without ever seeing my big brother. Had he known I was there? Why hadn't he bothered to visit?

"Here's the train information and some money. The sack has some ham sandwiches in it. You'll be going to St. Louis this time, and your Aunt Dorothy Jean will pick you up at the station." He sat next to me on the bed, and took me in his arms and wept. "We love you boy."

My grandma had joined us and together they sandwiched me with hugs and kisses. I'd expect it from her, but this kind of open love and emotion from a man was strange to me. But I liked it.

"We know you're going through some happenings no little one should have to. We'll continue praying for you and trust in the Lord." With that my grandpa used a sleeve to wipe his eyes dry and held out his hand. He wanted me to shake it, just like an adult. So I did.

"It's been great having you, and an honor to call you grandson." He then left the room.

My grandma wasn't done hugging, but said nothing more until right before I left. She held my hand as Uncle

James instructed me to hide on the floor of his truck. It was parked around back, out of sight. My luggage already tossed in the back, and covered with some sheetrock. She lifted me, kissed me, and said, "Don't forget us, and remember to read the Bible every day."

My grandparents were gracious, lovely, and wonderful–unforgettable. I could keep that part of the promise, for sure. And I'd come back if I could. Anytime. I'd never love the outhouse, but I'd always love being with them. As for the Bible, I knew I'd never read it again.

Not far into our drive we arrived at a house that seemed so old and fragile. I half expected it to implode at any moment. Standing next to a banged up grey truck was a huge young man as big as a bull.

Uncle Festus.

"Imsa prefessnls chitnplucker."

I had to ask him, "What?" three times.

"I am a professional chicken plucker. I'll try ans slows down. I do three things reals fast, plucks a chickn, eats a meal, and I speeks faster'n I can spits." With that he grabbed a cup from his side and spit some brown fluid in it.

I wasn't sure why he made so many words plural, but once I figured out his language, I really liked him. He was funny, told lots of stories and treated me like a friend. He talked a lot about Butch and I figured they were around the same age. It was his first time driving into Memphis and he had to stop for directions many times. When we arrived at the train station he looked nervous.

"A police car." He said it slowly with a special accent on the *po*. "I s'pose to heads back if I sees police."

What to do? If I helped fuel Festus' fear I could be back with my grandparents as fast as it took to drive there. But, it was time to go back to my fugitive life. "They probably meant if the police seem to be looking for us." I watched the police car for any sign of activity. "Let's park, git the ticket, and keep'er eyes open to see if I'm bein' followed."

Festus was a hoot in the station. He tried to act like a guardian but performed more like a younger brother. His eyes lit up like a firecracker when we walked in. "Wow!" Then, he tried to look serious. "I'm heres to pertecs ya, wees needs ta be looking for tha polices."

I spent most of my time reassuring him. When I waved goodbye I worried more about Festus getting out of the city than my own situation.

The train was not the same, nor as nice as the Spirit of New Orleans. I didn't seem as welcomed in the dining car in front, and had nothing to read or play with. As night entered the compartment I nodded off and didn't wake up until the conductor tapped my shoulder. "St. Louis is the next stop. Do you need help with your bag?"

I shook my head and struggled down the aisle with my things. I'd met my Aunt Dorothy Jean when she left off her two sons at the farm for a couple weeks so it wasn't hard to find her on the platform. The next two days at her house, I played with my cousins and waited. And waited. For what?

On the third day my aunt said, "Pack up, it's time to go." No explanation. Nothing.

I carried my bag and followed her to a bus stop. We headed downtown.

Before our stop, I saw them. My mother stood with her arms folded, staring at the bus. My dad sat between Cindy and Kenny on a bench near the bus stop sign. A flood of emotions attacked. My family. Homesickness and longing flooded my senses.

As I climbed down from the bus, Dad and Kenny waved and Cindy yelled out "Bobo."

My mother ran toward us, but instead of grabbing me, she took her little sister in her arms. My mother cried and kissed my aunt while I battled tears. *Was I not missed? What about me?*

Cindy ran to me with her arms held wide, and I hugged her tight. Like I wished my mother would have hugged me. "I missed you Bobo. I got a new dolly. Want to see it?"

My mother glanced down and gave me hug and a kiss on the cheek. She then took her sister by the hand, and they walked halfway down the block as the rest of us followed. I let Cindy drag me over to the bench where she introduced me to her doll.

"You been okay?" My dad glanced up and down the street. He looked worried.

"Yeah, fine."

Kenny said nothing, just stared at me.

"Hi, Kenny."

"I guess this means I don't get my own bed anymore?" His sulking question gave me a hint that our current home was not all that big.

Whack! My dad slapped him across the face.

I flinched. Dad didn't need to hit him. Looked like nothing had changed. Same tempers flaring. Same somber attitudes. Same shame.

"Your brother's been gone, you should be happy he's back with us."

Kenny looked at Dad with a face that could melt steel. He didn't cry, but his eyes turned as red as the slap mark on his cheek. Did Dad see what was behind that glare? He'd better watch out. Kenny was going to be trouble.

My mother ran to Kenny and took him in her arms. She covered him like a mama hen, and then glared at my dad with eyes so dark and soulless that my anger toward them all turned to pity.

Maybe my welcome wasn't what I expected, but I somehow knew my summer had been better than theirs.

Kenny, Cindy, and I curled up in the back of an old blue Pontiac to sleep. When I woke, I stared at a dirty old apartment on the wrong side of the border separating the Italians from the Puerto Ricans—in Chicago.

Chapter 14
Mafia or Priesthood?

_"But if serving the Lord seems undesirable to you, then
choose for yourselves this day whom you will serve..."_
Joshua 24:14a

Until seventh grade we moved so often it seemed
normal. Most of our apartments were in Chicago's
Southside Little Italy. The summer after my stay with my
grandparents we again lived near Maxwell Street, and I
spent much of my time wandering there.

That's when I was introduced to the Sons of Italy.

Walking home three big boys blocked my path on the
sidewalk. I tried to walk around them, but the skinny one
reached down and grabbed the front of my shirt. "Where
you going boy?"

"Home." Why did they care? They were too young
to be police.

"Where do you live?"

I told them and the curly haired one said, "He's from
our area. You Italian?"

"Yes."

"Then you're old enough to know the rules."

Before I responded the biggest boy said, "Kid, two
laws you need to learn. You live in the Sons of Italy area.
You better be careful when you wander away. And, until
you're old enough to join, you'll need protection."

Protection from what? I had a bad feeling about this.
"We'll take care of you, for a price. What's your name?"

What name do I give them? Was this some kind of
trick to get to my dad? How much was this protection?

"I'm Bobo."

"Bobo? Did you say Bobo?" His eyes grew wide and a sinister grin spread across his face.

"Yes." Maybe I should have said no.

The skinny one, still gripping my shirt, tauntingly repeated "He's Bobo. Little Bobo. Little Bobo."

"Yes, my name is Bobo, so what? Let go of me." I defiantly pushed the hand away. I stepped back and took what I hoped looked like a fighter's stance. Crazy, what I was doing. Even I knew that. But it was all I knew to do.

The boys took in my fighter stance from head to toe and then howled hysterically. The bigger one nudged his friend. "Check it out. Bobo wants to fight."

My dad had always said I should stand up for myself. To give it all I had. The problem was I didn't have much to come after them with. Then again, Mickey Rooney always fought people bigger than him. But he wasn't just nine years old.

There seemed to be a moment of decision as the boys looked at each other, and then back at my determined clenched-fist pose. The biggest one stepped up and said, "I like this kid." He put his arm around me and the boys started walking with me.

"Your name really Bobo?'

"Well, it's Jim. Everyone but the nuns call me Bobo."

"Where you go to school?"

"St. Mark's."

The biggest boy pointed at the other two, "That's where they go. I live on the west side. We're all in the eighth grade next year. I'm Nick, he's Tony, and pointing at the skinny one, he's my cousin Jacky."

"I have no money." I said.

"Don't worry kid. We won't charge you a dime." His chin rose in a prideful pose. "We're Calabreses."

After a short stay in Oak Park, we moved back into the city and became members of St. Angelo's and my new school. The first time we visited the church a Ferris wheel, and other rides, sat in the playground for a weekend carnival.

Maybe I could meet the father and get involved.

I approached a nun cleaning the windows on the church's ornate front door. "Sister, is Father around?"

"He's with someone. Can I help you?"

"I just moved here, and I wanted to see if he needed an altar boy."

"Oh, he handles that. He's in his office with Mr. DeStefano. Wait for him in the church. He'll be hearing confessions soon, so catch him before he enters the booth."

Candles at the feet of various saint's statues cast the only light. I sat in a back pew and waited. I jumped at a noise as the side door opened. A sliver of light shone on a small man wearing a black cassock. The Father. Before I could rise, he turned in the doorway and angrily pointed a finger at someone standing outside.

"I don't care what your deal is with Holy Trinity Church, our percentage stays the same."

"Father, I'm just saying expenses are up, and I have to make some money here. The cost of renting these rides alone is killing me. Cotton candy machines break all the time, and the carnival workers are always skimming money."

"Sam, that's your problem. Increase your prices, purchase better equipment, threaten the carnies, I don't care. Our cut stays as it has been since I've been here. Now, I've got to go hear confessions. You want yours heard?"

The man sighed. "Father, you haven't got the time to hear all my sins."

"I'll make the time."

"Nah, I'm waiting for my deathbed confession."

"Sam, don't make light of the sacraments. Besides, in your line of work that bed stays pretty close by. So, we keep the same percentage on the take for the festival, raise prices if you want, but each night one of my sisters will help with the count."

The man snickered, "Ah, don't you trust me, Father?"

"Not as much as I trust the sister." He closed the door and headed my way.

Should I have heard that conversation? I decided to slink down. Sam DeStefano, known as a ruthless hit man for the Outfit, ran many church festivals. The priest who took him on, and won, planted a seed in my heart.

I'd be a priest.

Parish priests were power brokers—and protected. After all, who'd harm a man of God? In my search for acceptance and security—and power—the idea of priesthood seemed perfect. Plus if God existed, if He was real, it'd be smart to be on His team.

In an attempt to stay ahead of the law, our family moved every few months. The summer before seventh grade we moved ninety miles west of Chicago to Rockford, a small industrial city. Dad landed a job with a big bakery. It seemed like the perfect place to blend in. After a short stay in a rented home we purchased a trailer.

"It's a doublewide!" I hadn't seen Mom smile so big in years. "You can walk to school, and there's a path down to the Rock River." Owning something, even a trailer, seemed to give her hope.

Sports crammed my seventh grade year, and eighth I battled puberty. For two years I experienced–normalcy. But, it wasn't enough. With sports and good grades I could earn the love and respect I craved. But the joy of great grades and sports accomplishments crashed into the reality that my parents didn't care.

With no one like Aunt Mary or my grandparents around, chasing girls and winning their affections became an addiction. Anything for a kiss, and then I'd discard them. I went steady with so many girls at the same time I couldn't keep up.

A good friend planned to attend a seminary high school. As much as I wanted to join him, my family couldn't afford a boarding school.

My friend's mother filled out a scholarship application for me. I felt sorry for her, wasting time like that. Good things just didn't happen to me. Especially something that big.

Late in eighth grade, the principal asked me to meet after school. I often did errands or chores for teachers. But two other women and the parish priest were with her.

"Sister, you needed me?" Was it a private meeting?

"Jim, we're so glad you could come. Let me introduce you to the two chairladies of the Legion of Mary." The principal grinned.

I looked from face to face. Everyone smiled. After the introductions, the priest read from a sheet of paper.

"This is to notify you that James A. Hall has been accepted with a full scholarship to St. Mary Minor Preparatory Seminary." The father handed the page to me.

I looked at the paper, but the words all swam together. *Waived. Allowance. Four years.* "What does this mean?"

"This means your tuition, room, and board, and schoolbook costs are all covered. Congratulations."

Wow, it happened? They were letting me go to boarding school? For free? Nothing like that ever happened for me. Ever.

The sister came over and gave me a hug. "You're the first boy to enter the seminary in our forty-eight year history. All the women in the Legion of Mary have been praying for years for someone from our congregation to become a priest." Wow. It was a big deal even to them. They were proud of me. That felt...good.

One of the ladies handed me an envelope. "This is from us ladies, we are so happy for your decision."

From everyone's look, it seemed clear I was supposed to open it.

Five twenty-dollar bills. One hundred dollars!

"We hope this will help with some of your extra costs."

I had never held so much money. I stared at the bills in my hands.

"We will continue to pray for you and your calling."

"Son, you're the one making the valedictorian speech at our graduation ceremony a week from Saturday, right?"

"Yes, Father." Should I change what I'd planned to say?

"After you're done, remain on stage. I want to announce this great news to everyone."

My head swam. I rushed home with the good news. My dad was in his bedroom getting ready to go to work, and my mother was in the kitchen drinking coffee.

"I got the scholarship to the seminary high-school I told you about! They're sending me to seminary! For free!" I shouted as I entered the room.

My mother's jaw dropped as she put her coffee down. She walked over and took me in her arms. Now taller than her, her tears dampened my shoulder. She was crying?

"Al, come here. Our boy's going to be a priest."

My dad peeked out his door. "Good. Is it that school you were telling me about?"

She looked at me, concern etching her face. "Does it pay for everything? I'm not sure what we can afford."

"Yes, everything's covered. I even got some money from the ladies of the church." That brought my dad out the door wearing a playful smile.

"Money?" He moved next to me. "How much?"

I held out the envelope.

He opened it, pocketed it, and turned away. "This seminary thing might just be a good thing."

"Al, how much is in there?" She let me go and moved toward my dad.

"Uh, looked like fifty."

"It's one hundred." What was he trying to pull?

He shot me a nasty look.

My mother held her hand out and gave a stern glare.

He pulled out two twenties and gave them to her. She kept her hand out and tapped her foot.

He pocketed the envelope and shook his head. "Gotta give some to the boy. He earned it."

"I can't wait to tell my friends. Just imagine. I could be the mother of a priest." She practically skipped out of the trailer.

My dad walked up with his right hand out. "Here, you did good. This is for you."

A five-dollar bill.

***

Graduation day.

People filed into the church until it was packed to overflowing. Families crowded into pews. Parents and grandparents dabbed a their eyes as their children passed from one stage of life to the next. High school.

I took my turn at the podium and spoke of transition. "It's time to leave the mistakes and sins of our younger years in the past and go after the future God has in mind for us." It was as good a time as any to subtly acknowledge I'd been kind of a dog to the girls. That way, maybe, they'd just overlook my immaturity rather than hold it against me in their prayers.

After I finished, the priest took the lectern. He covered the microphone with one hand and gestured to me with the other. "Jim. Please remain here a moment." He let go of the mic and spoke into it. "Would Jim's parents please come up here with us?"

Oh great. I leaned over and whispered, "Uh...They're not here."

His eyes widened in confusion. "Your parents couldn't make it to your junior high graduation?"

I looked out at all the grandparents and parents of my classmates. I shook my head. "Uh, something came up at the last minute. They really wanted to make it."

His face softened in what might have been pity. But he erased it before I could be sure. Father put an arm around my shoulder. "Members of St. Peter and Paul's, family and friends of the graduates, esteemed guests, I'd like to make a special announcement. Jim Hall..." He went on to praise my accomplishments during my short time there, ending with, "...and I'm so glad to announce that he has received a scholarship to go to a seminary. Please give a hand to what may be the first priest ever to come from our parish school."

Thunderous applause filled the church. A standing ovation. I'm sure my parents had their reasons, but I'd have loved for them to see that crowd clapping for me. I'd learned not to care at times like that—or at least bury the hurt where my mind couldn't find it. I bathed in the glory and pride swelled my chest.

I stepped down from the platform, and my fellow classmates gathered around me. Some hands slapped my back. Parents pulled me in for a hug.

Ramona Bobble pushed her way through the crowd. Her face looked like a cherry ready to burst from the heat. She muscled directly in front of me, and jabbed a finger at my chest. "Jim Hall, you're a liar, and you will rot in hell!"

Seemed it wasn't all that big a secret after all.

Chapter 15
St. Mary's Minor Seminary

"If it were not for hopes, the heart would break."
–Thomas Fuller

My family jammed into the tiny 1952 Plymouth to take me to the seminary. Crystal Lake was only fifty miles away, but the difference seemed like a million. The town looked unspoiled, like a Norman Rockwell cover for *Saturday Evening Post*. A world away from home.

I peered out the open window at manicured lawns, beautiful homes, and boats on the lake. I cringed when I saw the finely dressed teens, all looking like they stepped out of a TV show. Shame crawled into my heart as I thought of my cheap, old clothes packed in the trunk, and my parents—how would they act? Being away from home didn't concern me, but maybe I wasn't good enough to be at that school.

We drove to the far end of the lake. My new home sat on a hill surrounded by huge oak and walnut trees. A large sign greeted our entrance. *St. Mary's Minor Preparatory Seminary.*

My eyes stayed glued on the old building as we walked up the hill. The driveway circled under a canopy attached to a Victorian stone mansion. The tower above the third floor lent a sense of foreboding—like someone was watching. Attached, to the right of the main building, stood a slightly newer, long stone-and-brick structure with huge awnings hanging from the first floor windows. Another tower soared above everything on the far end.

Under the main canopy, carpet ran all the way up the stone stairs. Carpet outside? A young man wearing a black cassock, belted with a knotted white rope, welcomed us at massive walnut doors.

My mother stood ramrod straight and acted like she knew what she was doing. "Hello, Father. We're here to check my son in."

"I'm not a priest. I'm Tim, a senior here. All students wear what I do. The priests have an extra cape with a hood and a long rosary attached to a belt."

As much as the parquet floors, the carved woodwork, and the marvelous grand staircase impressed me, all my attention was focused on my new school uniform.

I sure won't be able to pick up girls wearing that.

He ushered us to a reception area. My parents filled out a stack of paperwork.

"Hi, I'm Roger. I'll show you around." Red hair and a smattering of freckles across his face and arms gave Roger a friendly appearance. "If you have any questions, feel free to ask."

I couldn't ask my one burning question. Not with everyone there.

"A wealthy merchant built this many years ago. Notice the detail of the woodwork. It's all custom-made from the black walnut trees that grew on the property. The magnificent stairway in front of you leads to the priests' quarters. They are off limits to us, but to our left is our chapel. It's never off limits." He laughed at his joke, but I didn't really find it that funny.

"We begin each day with mass and have community rosary before dinner. There are also four small altar rooms spread around the first floor, so each of the priests can say his mass each day."

I may not believe that much in God, but this small, impressive chapel sure seemed like a place He'd want to be.

We walked to an annex. "To the right are classrooms and the dining hall is to our left. The dining area was part of the original mansion, but most everything else was added on later. We'll now head downstairs."

My parents followed, silently taking it all in.

The basement held an eclectic mix of a Rec and TV room, two science labs, a sports equipment room, and a huge laundry room. At the far end, we entered a space crowded with an assortment of weights and benches.

We climbed three floors up. "The top two floors are identical. The upperclassmen stay on this one, and the freshmen have the one below." Every few feet the green walls were interrupted with a door. I counted at least twenty-five of them.

"To the left are double rooms. Two students share a room, with a toilet between them. To the right are smaller single rooms." I peeked and noticed no toilet, just a bed, sink, desk, chair and bookcase.

"Showers are communal at the end the corridor." It was like a cross between a college dorm and an army barracks, spotless. But it wasn't bad, really. Better than sharing with Kenny.

I stepped into a double room.

Roger's hand shot forward. He grabbed my sleeve and tugged. "Jim, classmates aren't allowed to enter anyone else's bedroom for any reason."

I stepped back into the hall and glanced at Dad. He shook his head and gave me a look of disgust for getting it so wrong.

Moving down the hall, Roger continued. "And all doors have to stay open except for a short period at night. You know, when you get ready for bed."

As we traveled down the stairs he stopped at a window overlooking the grounds and pointed. "Notice the road down the hill. It encircles most of the property. It's a public road we often use for taking walks and, you know, having time alone with God."

Did they make Roger say that kind of thing, or did he really mean it? It was so weird to hear a boy my own age talk like that. Maybe God was more likely to show up on this majestic property than the trailer park I left. He'd certainly never been to that wretched place.

We stopped at the first door on the second floor. Our guide knocked and a tall priest with a long protruding chin opened it. "Folks, this is Father Phillips. He's our prefect."

Dad cleared his throat. "I'm not sure my boy knows what that is."

"A prefect is someone in charge of all the students. Like a principal."

I knew exactly what it was. Dad had no idea.

"Father Phillips, this is Jim Hall and his family."

His long thin body turned toward us. He shook my dad's hand, then mine, and nodded at Mom.

"I'm glad to meet you all. Jim, I'm sure you'll be a great addition here. Mr. and Mrs. Hall, I will do my best to see your son well educated, and hopefully prepared for God's calling." Ichabod Crane closed his door and we resumed the tour.

"Let me see." Roger looked down at a sheet of paper and began walking. "You'll stay in room 208. Usually freshmen don't stay in single rooms, but it looks like you got lucky."

Another favor. I tried to hide my grin.

He turned to my parents. "Mr. and Mrs. Hall, you'll need to stop at the reception desk on the first floor to complete the last of the paperwork. All families must leave the property no later than four thirty."

My mother nodded. "We'll just go get your things and bring them up."

Leaving me wasn't going to be a problem for them.

"Jim, rosary is at five. We'll have the freshmen orientation in the dining room immediately after dinner. Good day." The door shut, and I was alone.

Oh, boy. I'd wanted to pull Roger aside and ask the nagging question, but maybe he wasn't the best choice anyway. I looked around my room. The blond, wooden desk against a window overlooked the back garage area. The sink, next to the small bed, was adjacent to the door.

Freedom!

My parents returned with my belongings and then left before the box of books stopped bouncing on the mattress where they'd dropped it like a hot potato.

During chapel I sat with the other freshmen, filling all the pews on the far side. We took out our rosaries as the upperclassmen led the Apostles Creed. After we recited the Our Father, the race was on.

As fast as humanly possible, the far side chanted, "Hail Mary, full of grace the Lord is with thee..." The upperclassmen looked at us to complete the prayer.

"Holy Mary, mother of God, pray for us sinners..." Judging by the exasperated looks from the older students, we were much too slow.

Again, a rapid "Hail Mary ... fruit of thy womb Jesus." It was like a blur.

Before long we caught on and reduced the Hail Mary down to fewer than seven seconds. Each day, we repeated this mantra and finished the rosary at a speed that would have made Chuck Yeager proud. I wasn't exactly sure why the breakneck pace, but whatever. Maybe God liked it fast.

That's not what Grandma said about praying. But she never went to seminary. I'd have to send her a note and let her know she had it all wrong.

The dining room was actually a cavernous ballroom, but only the huge chandeliers reflected its past grandeur. In an ominous row across the front of the room, priests sat in throne-like seats with the Rector in the middle.

Upperclassmen held their fingers to the lips as we filed between the tables that held slices of bread, butter, and some sweating metal jugs. Each student stood behind their chair waiting silently as a priest read scripture and said a prayer.

"...Amen."

"Amen," we responded and took our seats.

"So, wonder what we get to eat." A chubby boy at the end of the table rubbed his hands together.

The kid next to me elbowed my side and gestured at the bread. "Would you pass that over?" Students chatted throughout the room.

"Silence!" The rector's deep voice almost shook the crystal lights above our heads. His snow-white head towered at least a foot above us all. "As much as you all want to get acquainted, discipline is now part of your life. You stand until all the priests are seated, and you may speak after I ring my bell."

He pressed his robes against the back of his legs and the sat back in his seat, eyeing us the whole time. He picked up his bell and held it up, waiting. Watching. We passed some test because he finally rang the bell.

"Hi, I'm from Boston."

"I'm from Detroit."

"We drove in from Indianapolis."

What would they say if they knew all the places I'd lived? Would they kick me out of school if Dad got busted? I hoped I'd never have to find out. But his luck would run out sometime, wouldn't it?

White-robed nuns bustled through the doors with trays of fried chicken and mashed potatoes. I bit into a crispy leg. Not bad, but nothing compared to the scald grandma could get on a chicken. I bit into the buttered bread and chewed. And chewed. Next time I'd dunk it in my gravy. I swallowed the stale lump and reached for my red juice. I guzzled down several big swigs, and then looked for a place to spit it. How could they have messed up fruit punch?

An elbow jabbed my side. "What's up with this?" The pimply boy next to me grimaced and looked into his cup. "It's bug juice." And so it would be forever known.

That first night the freshmen hung out at the tables waiting for orientation.

The rector stood and cleared his throat. He clasped his hands behind his back, squared his shoulders, and lifted his chin. "I'm Father Constantine. I am in charge of this institution. Tonight you will be given instructions on how you are to conduct yourselves here. First, and foremost, you will adhere to our honor code. It's been copied from the code I introduced while Chaplain, and a colonel, at the U.S. Air Force Academy."

Ah, that explained his stance.

"When you return to your rooms tonight, a copy will be on your desks. Father Phillips will deliver the rest of the orientation."

"Boys, there'll be a copy of the schedule and rules in your rooms. I'll go through them tonight, but ask no questions here. If you're unsure of anything, ask an upperclassman." His softness contrasted with the rector. His back hunched in such a way that his entire carriage resembled a question mark. He spoke with a slight lisp. And why did he constantly play with his rather large nose. Maybe I should go get him a Kleenex. I winced as pinky finger flicked out from the tip of his nose again.

"Monday through Thursday the alarm will wake you at six-fifteen. Six forty-five is mass and breakfast follows. School hours are eight until two. You'll have silent study at your desk between three-thirty and five. Then to chapel for rosary. You're free after dinner until seven-thirty, when you must again be at your desk. At nine you will go to the chapel for Vespers."

Vespers? I looked at the boy beside me and raised my shoulder.

"The priests chant in Latin in the chapel...we listen," he whispered.

Father Phillip stopped his speech and lifted a crystal decanter to fill his tiny tulip-shaped glass a fourth time. His words weren't yet slurred like Dad's, but his red eyes confessed the dark liquid wasn't bug juice.

"There is total silence from seven-thirty until the conversation bell rings at breakfast. If you break that rule, or any other, you'll be given a demerit. If you earn demerits, you lose privileges. You're allowed up to eight demerits per month. Get any more than that and you'll be expelled."

A demerit sounded bad. I didn't mind breaking rules, but hated the idea of getting caught.

"Lights out at nine-thirty. Now, everyone head to the laundry room. You'll receive your robes and cords."

We silently marched downstairs to the basement. No one seemed to know if we could speak. At the rear of the room three racks with robes hung like black sheets. White cords streamed from a nearby circular stand.

The freshmen stared at the robes, then at each other. *Were we supposed to wait?* Where had everyone gone? Finally, a short freckled boy gathered the courage to speak. "I guess we pick them out ourselves." He reached out for the nearest robe. A few other freshmen cautiously grabbed at the robes.

"Do we get more than one?"

"How can you tell the sizes?"

"How do you belt these cords around you?"

"Yeah, and are they called ropes or cords?"

"Why are there three knots in each?"

I blurted, "I think they symbolize the rosary." There were a lot of nods from the other boys.

"No, son, each represents a vow we Franciscan's take when we become priests." I looked through the crowd to see who spoke. Although the voice was soft and sounded young, the "we Franciscans" clearly indicated a priest was in our midst.

"They are poverty, chastity, and obedience."

Everyone moved back and I saw the source of the words. A short rosy-cheeked young-looking man stepped through our crowd. Wearing only slacks and a tee shirt, he didn't look like a priest. His baby face and doughy body made him blend well within the group of freshmen.

"Gentlemen, I'm Father Anselm, the vice-rector here at St. Mary's Minor, as well as your choir director. I'll also be your Ancient History and Latin teacher." He reached up at a hanging robe, partially wrapped it around his left arm, and jumped a few feet forward. His heals clicked loudly when he landed.

He posed like a matador and swished the robe as his imaginary bull charged by. "Ole!" His feet stomped with each pass. "Ole! Ole!"

He then reached into his pocket and pulled out a book—a catechism. With the caped arm held out he lifted the book above his head, and then swiftly brought it down like a sword. "*Mortem obire*—meet your death!"

He fell to one knee, covered the imagined victim with the robe, and held the book high.

We held our breath. Would lightning come from heaven at such an irreverent display? Nothing happened. We broke into applause.

He bowed and again lifted the book. "The words of Christ and the teachings of the church will eventually defeat our foe. The robe has no power, but it shouts you are different than the world. And it's the world the evil one wants. The cord reminds us of our vows, and the belt of truth St. Paul wrote of in his letter to the Ephesians. You'll see truth is what our Christian faith is all about. We are guided by it, protected by it, and able to conquer the devil's plans with it."

I wanted to believe him. Kind of. But if I did, I'd have to believe in a devil. If Satan was real, there was a real hell. And if there was a hell, then there was a God. And how could God make hell? So, it just reasoned none of it was true. Nothing more than a myth. Besides, I wasn't good enough to be a priest like Father Anselm—yet—there had to be more. Perhaps I would find it there.

He lifted the robe and put it on. It engulfed his body and its hem sprayed the floor. "These come in different sizes. There are three racks. The smallest sizes begin on the first one and gradually increase to the giant version I'm now wearing." He lifted the cord and quickly gave us instructions on how to tie it around our waists.

"You each get one robe and cord. Wash the robe each week with your laundry. If your cord gets dirty, clean it in your sinks." He disrobed and placed the garment in a laundry basket. "Wear your robes to school, chapel, meals, and other formal affairs. At other times you're free to dress casually. Are there any other questions?"

I had a big unspoken question and based on the blushed cheeks all around me, most everyone wanted to know the same thing.

Father Anselm chuckled. "Gentlemen, these aren't dresses. You wear slacks and a shirt—a tee shirt is fine—under your robes. "

Phew!

***

"If you fall below C average, you're on probation for the next quarter. Fail to rise above a D means expulsion." Father Phillip's algebra class explained. "You may have forced study times, but no one can force you to study. Discipline is the key. If you don't discipline yourself, we'll do it for you."

They couldn't possibly be any tougher than the nuns.

That first morning passed quickly. After lunch I went to one of the labs for Biology and took a seat in front. Father Gregory handed the first row several stapled pages titled, *Course Outline.* I kept one, turned, and handed the remaining papers to the boy seated behind me. Everyone knew that's what you do in a classroom—pass back the papers. But, I was in a new world.

"What are you doing?" Father Gregory towered over my desk.

Is he talking to me? I glanced to my right and my left. "Uh, Father, I'm passing the papers back."

"Did I tell you that you could pass them back?"

I shrunk at his sarcasm and the steely weight behind his glare. "No Father, but—"

"But? Did I just hear a but?"

Laughter filled the lab.

"What do you think you are doing?" Each word came slow and loud. "You will not smile. You will not giggle. And you most certainly won't laugh in my classroom."

He grabbed a long rubber tipped pointer from the desk and twirled it around like a weapon.

"If by any chance, I decide to share some amusing antidote sometime in the future, you may laugh. But, consider that a ray of sunshine in your humdrum lives."

No one laughed.

Father Gregory walked to my desk. Our eyes met and I thought I saw a slight smile on his face. He walked down my aisle. I felt it wise not to look back.

"All of you who laughed raise your hands."

One hand in the front slowly edged up. The long rosary attached to his belt tapped me on the arm as he rushed by me to the front of the room.

The sound of the pointer crashing down on the desk almost jolted me out of my chair.

His back to us as his words boomed. "I did not see all the hands of the guilty."

The father slowly turned around, and said in a low whisper, "The reprobates who mocked this student," his pointer aimed at me, "must confess by a show of hands." He passed the stick in front of us as he surveyed the room.

"Don't start your first day with me by getting caught in a lie." He leaned forward, and scanned the room. "Be careful, I see everything in my classroom. Now, all who showed pleasure in another's dilemma raise your hand."

The sinister sound of his demand almost made me raise my hand. But then I'd be lying about lying about laughing. What would Father do about that? Afraid to look back, I wasn't sure how many hands went up, but my fellow first row classmates lifted theirs. I glanced to my right, and a small dark haired boy trembled and turned pale.

"Now hold those arms straight out with the palms facing up." Father Gregory walked to the far aisle.

The rod came down swiftly across an outstretched hand. Afraid to move, I listened to the hard slap of wood against flesh, and the involuntary grunts of pain, repeating for the next several minutes.

Done meting out punishments, Father settled into his chair. "Now, you may pass the papers back." Quietly and quickly we obeyed.

But Father Gregory wasn't the worst. By far. I smuggled a flashlight to study English under the covers after lights out for fear of Father Benedict.

I stared at Father Benedict as he gave out our homework assignment. Tall, he kind of looked like Cary Grant. But looks could be deceiving. "Your assignment for tomorrow is to read chapter three and answer the questions at the back of the chapter. Also diagram every sentence on page twenty-three."

What? Didn't he know we had assignments from other classes too? It'd take forever to finish. If we didn't complete the work, not only would we receive an F, but we'd also earn five lashes. Thank heaven for the upperclassmen that taught us cupping our hands took some of the sting from the switch.

Some of the boys were homesick and wanted to leave before the end of the first week. Not me, I loved my new home. Security, without fear, gave me comfort. But I wanted more. I joined the choir, volunteered to act in the Christmas play, and launched a campaign for popularity by joining the football team. A presidential election year, John F. Kennedy could have picked up some pointers from me. I introduced myself to every classmate and teacher. I became the consummate yes-man.

"I love liver." Al Musial sat next to me waiting for the platter of fried onions and innards to reach him.

"I love liver too." I guessed being a seminarian wasn't going to cure me of my oldest habit–lying. But Al Musial? That kid was cool. His Irish good looks and charm...and all that athleticism...plus his uncle was Stan "the man" Musial of the St. Louis Cardinals. If Al liked liver, I liked liver. Even if I had to choke it down.

Father Anselm made every class, even Latin, fun. He became the rector my sophomore year, and his last, at St. Mary's.

After Father Anselm left, I spoke with Father Joseph, the Latin class replacement. "I'm going to hate Father Anselm not being here."

"I bet. It also puts quite a burden on the school." Father Joseph rested his folded hands atop his rather large stomach.

"How so?"

"Father Anselm taught two courses, led the drama department, directed the choir, and in his free time ran this entire place as rector. He traveled many weekends and most of the summer doing fundraising."

"Wow! I never knew that."

"He also wrote three books during his four years here."

He was an author? "Why didn't he say anything about writing a book?" Maybe they were murder mysteries or something fun like that.

"Father Anselm is considered one of the greatest ancient historians in the Church. He served the Vatican before his transfer here."

Oh. Probably nothing interesting in his books, then. "If he was so important, why would he be sent to this tiny school?" They had nothing more for him to do than mess with a bunch of kids?

"Teaching and influencing our future priests and Catholic leaders is extremely important. This school may be small, but one of you may be a future pope. The Franciscan Order also firmly believes we sometimes need to be placed in less impactful roles to help keep us humble. You remember Francis the Polish friar who was our landscaper your freshmen year?"

Right, the guy spoke no English. He'd ride up and down the lawns on a tractor with a smile a mile wide. "Yes sir. He was a sweet old man." He was in charge of our many yard duty days. He'd point at the dandelions, hand me a spoon, and I'd be on my knees. One by one, I'd spoon them out while the friar followed behind with a rake singing hymns in Polish.

"His brother was Maximilian Kolbe. You may have read about the World War II hero who sacrificed his life for a Jewish prisoner at Auschwitz."

I nodded even though the memory was fuzzy. Was that a lie?

"Well, Maximilian may very likely be declared a saint someday. Investigations are going on now. Francis is believed to have been a great influence on his brother's faith. He's also considered one of the holiest and most godly men in our order."

"So they sent him here to keep him humble?" It sounded like he didn't need it.

"No he requested the position. Father Francis often said he felt nearest to the Lord when he worked with His plants."

Odd. "Where was he transferred to?"

"The last I heard, the Pope requested him at the Vatican as prayer partner and spiritual advisor. The Church will soon have its second Vatican Ecumenical Council." Huge news among Catholics. The twenty-first time the Catholic theologians and leaders gathered to address questions of biblical law since the fourth century.

"Brother Francis was chosen to be an important part of these proceedings. Although he requested a simpler life, he acceded to the wishes of Holy Father."

Chapter 16
Initiation

"Education without values, as useful as it is, seems rather to make man a more clever devil." C.S. Lewis

Every boarding school has dozens of traditions, and St. Mary's was no exception. The one with the most fanfare—Freshmen Initiation Day. The third Monday after the new school year began each sophomore was assigned as the owner and keeper of a designated freshman. Some took their task to heart.

"Get up you slave."

What? My eyes fought to adjust to the dark. I glanced at the big clock outside my room. Five in the morning! A flashlight beam blinded me.

"I'm your master today, and your day starts now." The voice sounded familiar, but who was it?

I could hear other voices and the shuffling of feet in the corridor. "In fifteen minutes you must report upstairs at room 317."

I showered and trudged up the stairs after my fellow slaves. What if we mutinied? What could they do to us? I'm sure we all thought it, but no one voiced the idea of a coup.

The third floor hallway already bustled with activity. Mops, brooms, and buckets moved from one room to the next. When I arrived at my destination, I recognized my master-of-the-day, Hasko. Oh no, not Hasko!

I didn't know his first name, or even if he had one. Everyone called him by his last, and never with a smile. He earned a reputation as both a bully and a little off his rocker.

"I personally chose you because I just don't like you."

What had I ever done to him?

"You're so smug. Think you're a great football player, don't you?"

My ego almost said yes, but silence seemed wiser.

"I'm going to have fun with you today. First, clean my room. And it better be spotless."

After many failures the room passed Hasko's inspection. "Okay Hall, go down to the end of the corridor and select your uniform. Come back here right before breakfast."

I'd heard that the sophomore's always furnished the garb for freshmen to wear on Initiation Day. I settled into a line of fellow slaves and waited.

As the sun peeked through the widows, three seniors dropped some boxes on the floor. "Help yourselves. This is your apparel today. You will wear a t-shirt and swim suit under them."

We reluctantly gathered around the brown cardboard containers. One said "Pink," another "White," and two "Red." I recoiled at the words, "Nightgowns!"

"No way. I mean no way."

"I'm not wearing this."

"They must be crazy." The grousing grew strong, but we knew our fate was sealed.

"We have to."

"What choice do we have?"

Really, though, what had they expected from the sophomores?

"Mike, you'll look great in this red one."

"I want the white lacy one."

An overweight boy tried on a small pink one. "I hope these come in different sizes. This makes me look fat."

"That's because you are fat." When I said it, laughter erupted. He looked hurt, so I put an arm around him. "Just kidding."

Thirty minutes later I stood in front of Hasko's room.

"Stand out there where I can see you."

I stepped back. I looked down at the pink gown that flowed down to the edge of my sneakers.

"You look so pretty," he mocked.

What a jerk.

I joined the other gowned students as we followed the sophomores to chapel and then the dining room. Breakfast was delayed so we could serve our masters.

"You two stand on the table and sing, *Mary had a Little Lamb.*"

I joined the smaller boy in a rendition that brought the house down. Even the priests enjoyed it.

I think that's what made Hasko lose it. He couldn't stand that we weren't agonizing over the hazing. We were winning, and it was killing him.

The hazing went on throughout the day, including a humiliating parade. But I kept my eyes on the celebration that was to come when the day ended.

That night we were allowed to wear casual clothes and attend the party. We stuffed ourselves on popcorn and punch—good stuff, not bug juice. Until the main attraction.

Curtains opened to three seniors sitting at a long desk dressed like judges wearing white wigs. What was that about?

Different sophomore prosecutors read a series of accusations attempting to find a freshman guilty, and thus not worthy to be there.

"He eats his boogers."

"He brushes his teeth with deodorant."

Each freshman made a defense. Most were "I didn't do it," or "Not me."

When it was my turn, Hasko shouted out his accusations. "Your Honor, the charges against James Hall are most serious."

I expected the typical absurd accusations, I was wrong.

"He thinks he's better than everyone else."

I tried to fake a smile.

"He doesn't even want to be a priest."

I looked down at my shoes. How had he figured all that out?

"He's faking it when he pretends he likes people."

There was a hush in the room.

A judge struck the table with a gavel. "I think what you mean Prosecutor Hasko is Mr. Hall is a Baptist sent here to spy on us."

The room erupted in laughter.

"What do you say to that charge Mr. Hall? Are you secretly a Baptist?"

"What's a Baptist?"

Claps mixed with laughter, and my heart stopped racing. I glanced to the side and saw one of the priests talking to Hasko.

As much as the initiation experience seemed horrible, I loved it–I belonged. Finally. The son of an escaped convict and cold mother who relied on dishonesty to get by, but I was accepted by the priests, the students, and maybe even God. I was a new person.

***

An early December snowstorm dumped five inches of beautiful white powder over everything. I cranked open my window and grabbed a handful. Perfect! I quickly made a snowball and crept over to Rick Romano's room. He always lingered in bed at least ten minutes after the alarm. As I suspected, his blanket covered his head.

"Rick, Rick."

Two hands reached out and slowly pulled the covers down. "Wha' d' ya want?" He yawned.

I tossed from the doorway, obeying the rules.

"What the—" He shot up and scraped the wet stuff off his face. "Snow?"

"No idiot, heavy spit. Look out the window."

He leaped up and squinted against the sun glaring off the snow. "Snow ball fight after school."

At mass, every boy glanced out the windows several times. I'm sure the number one prayer asked that the snow would stay. Midway through my algebra class, the heavens opened and it started snowing again.

By the time we gathered in the yard at least seven inches accumulated. Some built snow forts. I scooped up snow and molded it into ammunition. Soon a white missile sailed across the yard and smacked into the front of our fort.

The war had begun.

Snow flew everywhere. Coats and hats bore evidence of direct hits. Eventually we all grew tired and headed inside, but the other side was relentless. They would not stop.

Then I saw him.

Hasko ducked behind a tree and poked his head up every few seconds to heave a wet bomb at me as hard as he could.

Okay, I could handle him. We exchanged misses, and then one of his throws hit my chest. *Ouch!* That hurt more than it should have. I bent to see what had hit me— a rock. He'd packed his snowball around it.

My anger surged, and I charged him. I knocked him flat and pinned him.

"You're crazy! You don't put rocks in snowballs!" I'd had it with him. He was mean. And dangerous. And just...mean! I saw a huge stone lying nearby. *Grab it. Take it, and smash his brains in.*

Then he spoke. "I'm sorry. I didn't really want to be mean to you."

I felt my breath whoosh from my lungs like I'd been sucker punched. "So why have you treated me so badly?"

"No one likes me here. This is my second year and I have no friends."

"What's that got to do with me?"

"Your first week here you sat next to me in the rec room. We watched TV together, and you were nice to me. I thought we could be friends."

I scoured my memories but couldn't find it.

"But once you turned into a big football star you ignored me. That hurt, so I wanted to hurt you back." He shrugged.

I slowly rose, lifting my knees off his arms. I held out my hand. "How was I supposed to know? You're a sophomore, and they don't hang out with freshmen."

He grabbed my hand and hoisted to his feet.

Having him on my side couldn't hurt. "Okay, I'll be your friend."

He took off a glove and held it out to shake my hand. He used the same hand to wipe his tears.

How odd that he'd be crying. Seemed a bit excessive. Hopefully, for his sake, no one was watching. I turned slowly to see the members of my snowball-fight team had gathered to watch. I walked toward them.

"Great job."

"What a jerk." Someone clapped me on the back.

"Man you nailed him."

"Crybaby, Hasko. Crybaby, Hasko."

Oh, man, they didn't have to go that far. Should I stand up for him? Hasko sure didn't deserve it, but he was a human being. And he said he was sorry.

"You're the best, Jim Hall."

That did it. Hasko was on his own.

A few weeks later, when we returned from Christmas break, Father Philips called me into his office. "Jim, you have received a letter." He handed me an already opened envelope. "Read it, and I'll then explain the situation, but you will not be allowed to keep it."

It was only one page long. It said he'd missed me, and was sorry he couldn't return to school. It finished with, "I don't know why I did it. It really wasn't me. Someday, when I get better, I still plan to be a priest. Maybe we can serve in the same church." He signed it, "John Hasko."

"I don't understand." I held the paper toward Father Philips.

The priest took the letter from my hand. "John did something very bad, and I will need to send this letter to the police."

He took a deep breath. "Over the Christmas holidays John helped his mother at their dairy store."

"Yes. That's what I'd heard." I sort of remembered he lived somewhere north of Rockford.

"No one knows why, but two days after Christmas he took a knife and killed his mother and one of the girls working there. He placed their bodies in a milk cooler, cleaned up, and went home."

My hands froze and sweat broke out on my upper lip. Killed? As in dead?

"According to the police the only request he's made was to write you. Why do you think he did that?"

Murder. A murderer wrote me a letter. "I have no idea."

So his name was John? John Hasko. A killer.

If I'd known his name, if I'd honestly befriended him—if I had defended him that day in the snow—would it have made a difference?

Chapter 17
A Blue, Blue, Blue Christmas

"Look to my right and see; no one is concerned for me.
I have no refuge; no one cares for my life."
Psalms 142:4

Dear Mom,
   Things are fine here. I work in the kitchen and have good grades. I'm doing really well at football. I got a letter from the women of our church. Tell them thank you for the twenty dollars they sent. See you soon.
   Love,
   Jim

Dear Bobo,
   I'm glad all is well. Since the ladies sent the money, I won't send an allowance this month. Everyone is doing just fine here. Keep up the good work. I'll see you in a few weeks.
   Love,
   Mom

   The letters were always pretty much the same. And each month we had visitation Sunday, but what most boys especially loved were our month-ends when we went home for a weekend. I looked forward to my first visit back to Rockford. I wanted to visit my friends, and be fawned over by the nuns and ladies at my church.
   On Wednesday, two days before I planned to hitch a ride home with a fellow student from Rockford, Father Philip stopped by my room. He closed the door, and sat on the bed. "Jim, I talked with your mom.

There's been some trouble, and you won't be able to go home this weekend."

My heart sank. "What kind of trouble?" It had to be my father.

He fidgeted with the beads on the rosary he wore, and avoided eye contact. "Apparently your dad was arrested. That's all your mother knew. She said she would call me again tomorrow." He stood and placed his hand on my head. "I'll pray for you and your family."

What now? My mother never worked, they had little savings. How would this affect my stay at St. Mary's? Should I be worried about Dad? Why though? It was all his fault. Would I be sent to an orphanage? I didn't want Kenny and Cindy sent to one either, but I had myself to worry about. I needed to talk with someone who would know.

I walked down to Father Philips door and knocked. "Father Philip, I'd like permission to speak with Father Anselm." I was in his choir, and he seemed to like me. The priest nodded and lifted the phone.

"Father, Jim Hall would like some time with you...yes, it's quite urgent. I'll send him down." He pointed a finger at me and then at the door. "Go ahead."

I hurried to Father Anselm's corridor and was immediately ushered into the Vice-Rector's office.

"Father Anselm, have you heard what happened?"

"Yes, my son." His desk seemed too large for him. He motioned at a leather chair in the corner. "Sit down. What would you like to share?" He grabbed a smaller leather chair and pushed it across from me. "I will divulge with the other fathers only what you give me permission to."

I told him everything, even about my thefts. The only things I omitted were my doubts about God—and the ones about wanting to be a priest.

His habitually smiling face looked serious, not sad, but attentive. "Have you confessed stealing that food with your dad?"

"Yes, Father."

"I imagine you wonder what will happen if your dad is...um...detained."

I nodded, and my eyes misted.

"St. Theresa of Avila says to let nothing trouble you, all things pass, but God never changes. He alone suffices. But, I'd say right now it's normal to have some concerns. Let's wait until your mother gives us more information before we let that concern grow to a worry." He leaned close and stared into my eyes like he searched for something.

"I have a concern as well..." He placed a hand on my shoulder. "...And it's you. I promise I'll do what I can to help. Is it okay for me to share all you've said with the other priests?"

I nodded and returned to my room.

After football practice Father Anselm summoned me. "Come sit down."

Father Philip sat in the chair I occupied the previous night, I sat in the other one.

Father Anselm stayed behind the desk looking at a piece of paper. "I asked Father Philip to join us. It seems the situation has changed some, and considering the story you told me last night, you probably won't be shocked." He placed a tiny set of Ben Franklin glasses on, "Father Philip, please interrupt anytime you feel it necessary."

"Jim, your mother called, and we were both able to talk with her. She said your father was arrested for stealing some items at a department store, and she was able to bail him out."

I felt the tension release a little.

"At first she didn't want to say much except you couldn't come home tomorrow. When I told her you had shared everything with me, she told us of their plans." He walked over and opened his door. "Anyone want something to drink? I'm going to have a Coke."

Father Philip asked for coffee.

"I'll take a Coke." I'd rather he'd get on with it.

Father Anselm stuck his head out and gave his order to his receptionist, and then returned to his notes. "Your parents knew once his fingerprints hit the system they'd be after him, so they packed up what they could and left."

They left. As in...left? Mom had really loved that trailer. Now what?

"She said she couldn't say where they were going, and it was best we didn't know. Right before her call, a neighbor informed her the Feds were all over the trailer park."

Father Philip answered the knock on the door and carried a small tray over to the desk. He handed me a can, took his cup, and read a note his secretary had given him. "Excuse me." He picked up the phone. "Tell them it'll be a few more minutes." He cleared his throat. "Sorry about that, where was I?"

"My parents are on the run again, and you don't know where." I fought back tears. How could this have happened? Then again, how could it not?

"Jim, I told your mother to not worry. We'll take care of you. You shared about staying with your aunt, and then your grandparents. This will be much the same. Your mother did say that it might take quite a while before it is safe for you to be in contact with them. We recommended no contact that could be traced until then." He took a big gulp of cola.

Could they get into trouble for helping me? Was it even right, what they were doing?

"Jim, we're all sorry you have to go through this. Do you have any questions?"

"What does this mean?" Take care of me? And why would the priests support my parents staying on the run? Why didn't they want them to confess?

"Well, you'll live here. You'll obviously not get visitors, and you'll spend your month-ends here. A few boys can't make it home every month, so there's company."

This was sounding pretty good. At least they weren't tossing me out. I took my first drink from the cold can. My hands trembled as it gripped the cold aluminum.

"There are two federal agents waiting outside. They contacted us shortly after your mother's call. They want to talk with you."

I gasped. What would I say? I shook my head. "I...I can't talk to them. I don't know what to say."

"Jim, don't lie to them. But, you don't have to offer anything." He gave me a big smile as he went to the door. "You're very bright. Did you know you have the highest IQ of all the new students? I'm sure you'll do fine."

I had no idea about my IQ or whether he told me the truth. Father Anselm was probably trying to make me feel good by bragging on me.

He swung wide the door and stood back as two thin men entered and shook hands with each of us. They looked like federal cartoon characters right out of the funny papers. Blue suits, white shirts, and a red tie. When they sat on the couch they even crossed their legs at the same time. Father Philips and I flanked each side of the couch, and Father Anselm completed the circle as he sat behind his desk.

"Gentlemen, before a boy is accepted here, his parents sign a legal document that effectively makes us his guardian when in our care, which is now. Since he is underage, we will be present for all interrogations." Father Anselm not only sounded older, he seemed bigger.

Thank God for him.

"We're not here to interrogate, just ask a few simple questions."

What was the difference?

"I will also need to ask you and the other father a few questions."

Father Anselm smiled, "Well, why don't we start with us then?"

That was nice of him, giving me a chance to relax and get my thoughts together.

"Have you talked with the boy's parents?" The same agent spoke while the other wrote on a pad of lined, yellow paper.

"Do you mean recently?" Father Anselm was in control.

"Yes, since the...ah, incident?"

"If you mean after his family moved out of their home, then yes."

"Did they tell you, or anyone else here, where they were going or anything that could help us find them?" He seemed to stare down Father Anselm, but the priest didn't blink.

"No they did not say where they were going. As far as helping you, we don't consider that our job. Our role is to protect and comfort young Jim."

The agent's glare shifted to me.

"Jim, have you talked with your parents in the past few days?"

Before I could answer Father Anselm said, "Students do not use the phones here, except for emergencies."

"Wouldn't you classify this as an emergency?" His tone hinted of sarcasm.

"Mr. Hall did not use the phones, all calls are logged."

"Can I see your log for the last few days?"

"No."

The agent seemed surprised. "If you have nothing to hide, why can't I see if he called anyone or received any calls?"

"There are other students here that may have been given permission to use the phone. I will not have them drawn into this."

"So you're saying maybe another student took the call for him?"

Father Anselm sat up straight and flashed a small smile. "See, you already are imagining a conspiracy. His mother called here twice and spoke with Father Philip and me. She knew better than to give out any relevant information."

"Is that true Father Philip?"

The priest nodded, and the other agent wrote something on his pad.

"Jim, I know this is tough on you, but it really would be better for you and for them if they just gave themselves up."

Like he cared about me, or what was best for them. I stared at the agent and stayed as expressionless as I could. Never mind the twitching of my lip and the burning behind my eyes.

"You don't want your mother facing charges do you?"

Father Anselm held up a hand. "Do you really want to add more worry to the boy?"

"Father, would you please let the boy talk?" The agent sounded annoyed.

The priest shuffled some paper on his desk, and then lifted his face. His eyes squinted, like someone aiming a rifle. "Let me make this perfectly clear. We do not know where his parents are. This boy is in our protective custody. If you think you could get a judge to challenge that, be my guest." The priest's face hardened. "I will allow you one more question."

The agent leaned forward, ready to fight. Then, he took a deep breath and sat back. "I understand, just one more question, Jim. Do you have any idea where they might go? Who's helped you in the past?"

"That was two questions. This interview is over."

"It was one question with two parts. At least let him answer the first part." He turned to me. "Do you have any idea where they might go?"

Chicago? Either of my aunt's places? Maybe my grandparent's farm? Before I could give any of those answers, Father Anselm rocketed off his chair and strode to the door.

"Gentlemen, like I said, this interview is over." He opened the door. "We need to get back to our duties here, so have a nice day." He stood with his hand outstretched.

The two agents looked at each other, and slowly stood. "You said I could ask one more question."

"That I did, and you did. But, I never promised an answer. Good day, gentlemen." The lead agent nodded to his companion who looked like he had just been run over by a bus.

After they left Father Anselm smiled. "How'd I do?" He had that little boy look again. "Was I tough enough?"

Father Philip chuckled and said, "You handled that better than I could have. I think your phonebook idea was great."

"Thanks Father, it did make me feel more powerful."

Phonebook idea?

Father Anselm reached behind his desk and lifted two Chicago Yellow Pages volumes off his chair. No wonder he'd seemed so much bigger.

The only freshmen not to go home that October month-end were two boys from California. It wasn't too bad. Thanksgiving was tougher. All the students were gone, and the familiar feeling of isolation poured over me as I ate turkey with the priests. But if I'd thought Thanksgiving was hard, Christmas was the worst.

I sat at my desk and tried to read my book. Under the circumstances, David Copperfield was probably a bad choice. The window at my desk gave me a perfect view into the parking lot. Streams of cars emptied the school of my classmates. One by one they left, excited for the holiday. Darkness fell, and I was alone.

Usually the hallway lights came on at dusk, but Father Philip wasn't there to turn them on. He had joined all but two of the priests, as they all headed home for the holidays. I inched my way down to flip the switch, but light made it seem more deserted. All the rooms, except mine, were dark. The glow from my chamber seemed hollow and lonely.

The end of the hallway, the entranceway to the priest's quarters, was black, like something sinister lay in wait on the other side. Father Philip said I couldn't go into any bedrooms, but the entire building lay open to me. I could go into the priest's side, but I'd visit via the front stairs. I had no intention of getting close to the dark end of my hallway, especially since I'd have to walk past the tower to get to the priests' quarters.

The story of the ghost of Dole Mansion spread through the freshmen body soon after we arrived. Supposedly, the Dole's had a crazy child they kept locked in the tower. One night she committed suicide, and the tale says her ghost remains in the room. Many locals say some nights an eerie glow shines from the tower's window, and they can see a faint shadowy figure hanging from a rope. I didn't know if I even believed in ghosts, but I sure didn't want to find out. I stayed clear of the tower.

Dinnertime arrived, but the dining room was dark. This was different than my Thanksgiving stay. I headed towards the lifeless chapel. Seemed like even God Himself went home for Christmas. I slowly walked up the ornate staircase towards the forbidden zone. When I reached the top I viewed a beautiful old fireplace and a number of rooms.

"Is anybody here?" A shadowy figure moved to my right. Father Andrew. Great! He would be nice to me. He had a pile of clothes in his arms, as he went in and out of some of the rooms. I watched until he emerged from the last room, his hands bare.

"Hello, young man."

I jumped at the sound of another voice.

Oh no! Father Benedict.

"Jim, I was just going to go get you. Is this your first time up here?" He stood outside a doorway, smiling.

I did a double take. That couldn't be Father Benedict. Not if he was smiling. "Yes, Father. I've never been on the priest's side."

"Well, not much to see. Our rooms are slightly larger than yours, but nothing fancy. Come, take a look." The polished hardwood floors reflected the blue molded plastic ceiling above my head. The ornate trim and windowsill decorated what was once a grand room, but the modest furniture made it feel plain.

"Your room's nice Father."

"Not all that nice, but it serves its purpose. Looks like you're stuck with Father Andrew and me for the next couple weeks. The TV room downstairs is yours, and you can have three free candy bars and sodas each day. Just help yourself." He lifted a white sweater and measured it against his chest.

"Looks like this will fit me, cashmere sure feels nice." He passed it over for me to touch.

"Is it a Christmas present from your family?"

"No, they couldn't afford this. I expect I'll get my annual cheese and sausage basket any day now. This actually was one of Father Andrew's Christmas presents."

"Didn't it fit him?"

"It probably does, we're about the same size. Father Andrew received a box of these and some other gifts from his family in Boston. He divided them up and passed them out to all the priests."

"I saw him going into some of the rooms. Didn't he like his gifts?"

"It's not about liking. We Franciscans take a vow of poverty. We don't make a big deal about it, but whenever we get anything, we try to share it with our brothers. When the other priests return from their holidays at home, they'll do the same."

The idea of giving away a gift was foreign to me, but it greatly impressed me. "Do you do that with money? What if someone gave you a million dollars?"

He smiled again. "That's a question we are asked before taking our final vows. My answer was that I'd take it, and then contact my superior to see how the church could best use it. I figured we should never turn down donations."

"Sounds right to me." Though I'd keep some for myself for sure. Maybe only share half of it.

"You'd think so, but my answer was wrong." He took the sweater and carefully folded it on his bed. "I had to learn an individual is never to accept donations. If someone wanted to give a lot of money to the order, or a specific mission, they needed to be directed to a superior. If someone wanted to give me a great sum of money, I should decline."

My chin dropped. "You would turn it down? Why not take it, and divide it like the sweaters?"

"There is a story in the Bible that tells of a young man who came to Jesus for advice. Jesus told him to sell all he had and give it to the poor. He didn't take Jesus' advice, so he walked away in sadness."

I nodded. We'd just studied that in class.

"The scripture tells us his problem was he had great possessions. You see, once you have something of value, it's very hard to give it away." He walked over to an old cabinet, opened a drawer, and placed the sweater in it. "Most priests don't take the vow of poverty. St. Francis saw how money and riches corrupted the church. Although he came from a wealthy family, he took the radical step of living a poor and simple life. He started an order of priests and nuns who believed the same...the Franciscans. Someday, you may do the same."

He meant well, I was sure. But money was the only way to have happiness and security. With it, I could take care of myself and not worry about anything. Without it, I'd have to rely on other people forever. That settled it. I'd never be a priest, at least not a Franciscan.

"Enough about the order, let's go eat. I told the sisters to not worry about us tonight, we'd go out." He placed his hand on my shoulder. "Let's get Father Andrew."

It was like I'd stepped into another dimension.

"Father Andrew," he yelled down the hallway, "I'll get the car. We'll meet you out front." I followed him downstairs to one of the garages. I sat next to the priest in the front seat of the blue Chevy Corvair, my teeth chattering.

Father Benedict faced me. "So, where do you want to go eat?"

I shrugged my shoulders, but I was sure the night and my heavy coat masked my answer. "I don't care." Just the thought of getting out was enough for me.

"I bet you'd like the malt shop."

"What boy wouldn't?" Father Andrew asked as he closed his door.

"Then the Crystal Lake Malt Shop it is."

The design and jukebox music made it seem like we stepped into a TV program. Packed with teens, I was almost surprised that Wally Cleaver or one of Ozzie and Harriet's boys weren't part of the crowd.

Father Andrew pointed to some empty stools, "Looks like we'll have to eat at the counter."

Good, sitting at a table meant talking. I had no idea how to carry on a conversation with priests.

"No wait, that booth is opening up."

Oh no. I shuffled to the booth. What could I talk about? They didn't watch television, but maybe they'd be interested in my giraffe stories anyway.

We all ordered cheeseburgers and fries. I added a chocolate malt, and they had Cokes.

"Father Andrew, is there any law that says you can't have chocolate malt and a banana split during the same meal?" Father Benedict rubbed his belly.

"None that I know of."

"Well Jim, you up for dessert?"

Ugh. I couldn't eat another bite. But... "You bet."

"When you're done, we'll go bowling." Wow, what had gotten into Father Benedict?

The two weeks at the seminary were a strange mix of loneliness, boredom, and fun. The priests did all they could to make me happy. Bowling, movies, and many trips to the malt shop filled my nights. On the last night Father Benedict took me alone to an Italian restaurant for pizza. "I hope your time with us wasn't all that bad." He poured himself some red wine from a bottle wrapped in a wicker basket.

"I really appreciate you and Father Andrew taking me to all the neat places, and buying me all the meals. The ice skates you gave me for Christmas are cool." What would the other boys say?

"We were happy to, but I've got a favor to ask."

"What is it?"

"It's obvious I don't act this way in the classroom."

"You mean nice?" Whoops. Maybe that was rude.

He smiled. "Yes, nice. You see, my desire is that you learn the most you can in the shortest span of time. I wish I had the natural gifts of Father Anselm. He is interesting and makes his classes come alive. I don't, so I take the tough approach."

"So you really are nice, but act mean to scare us into learning?"

He laughed. "I'll have to share that assessment with the other priests. Hopefully, I am nice. My discipline may seem rough, but I think my intentions are right."

"So what's the favor?"

"Don't tell any of the other students about the real me. Don't share what we've done. You can say Father Andrew took you places and bought you the skates, but I have a reputation to live down." He held out his hand. "Deal?"

I shook his hand. "Deal."

My parents stayed out of contact until late May. Month-ends and visitation days came and went. I wanted to miss them, but I didn't. It was easier being abandoned than being chased.

Chapter 18
Hunger

*"He has made everything beautiful in its time. He has
also set eternity in the human heart; yet no one can
fathom what God has done from beginning to end."*
Ecclesiastes 3:11

"Tonight President Kennedy has a very important
announcement. We will all gather in the rec room after
dinner to watch it," Father Norbert told us during lunch.

Strange. We'd never been ordered to watch TV,
especially if it interfered with studies. That night I joined
the others and watched the hope and pride of all good
Catholics, President Kennedy, as he laid out the proof
Soviets had missiles in Cuba. Armed with nuclear
bombs, those bombs were aimed at United States cities.
Terms like "acts of aggression," and "world nuclear
missile war" left no doubt of the seriousness. The
moment the President said his farewells to the nation,
Father Norbert turned the television off.

"I think it would be a good time to go to the chapel
and pray." He somberly stood by the door and ushered
the boys from the rec room.

There was no horsing around that night. In fact,
some boys cried. What was the big problem anyway? We
were the USA. Nothing bad would happen to us. Our
military would take care of any threat and we'd be fine.

But then why did the priests look so solemn? Some of
them were even wiping at tears. As they filed into the
chapel they were ashen with worry, maybe even shock.

We were going to war.

In bed that night I remembered the President's words, "Capable of striking most major cities in the Western Hemisphere." I looked out my window. Would I see the cloud and flash of light when one hit Chicago? I bet no one could sleep.

The next day Father Anselm made the announcement. "Sorry I couldn't be with you last night during the President's speech. There have been a number of calls from your parents. We told them exactly what I'm going to tell you. You are as safe, if not safer here as anywhere else. This is entirely in God's hands. This is a time of trust." He smiled and placed his tiny reading glasses on the bridge of his nose.

"Will the following students please come to my office right after we are dismissed? He read eight or nine names off. They all were freshmen.

"Father Benedict will now address you."

Like a drill sergeant he rose to attention and barked out orders. "After breakfast you will go immediately to your rooms, take the blankets off your beds and proceed back here to the dining room in orderly fashion. You will be given further instructions then."

Should we salute?

As we headed to our rooms I noticed a number of cars pulling into the drive. It didn't take long for us to learn they'd come to pick up the boys on Father Anselm's list. I guess their parents were too worried to be apart from their sons during such a scary time. I didn't have to look twice to know that my parents weren't among those families.

Father Benedict stood near the entrance to the kitchen. "Jim Hall, please follow me. The rest of you stay here." Uh oh. What did I do?

"Jim, you are the kitchen supervisor, so your role will be crucial. If there's an alarm, you immediately come here. Each student will arrive with his blankets and lay them on the counter. You will point to which food items they will carry in their blankets. The canned goods go first and then the dry food, no perishables. Everyone will take his filled blankets to the basement until an all clear is sounded. When all the food is gone, you head down. Understand?"

I nodded. But that meant I'd be last to get to safety. How did I get signed up for that job?

We walked back out. "Mr. Hall will be inside..." He pointed a finger at the door instructing me to go back in the kitchen. I faintly heard him yell out instructions, and then they started marching in. One by one they entered, and I directed the action. After I helped fill three blankets, Father Benedict opened the door and leaned in.

"I didn't mean for them to actually load their blankets today, this is only a drill." He saw my concern. "But, it's probably good to see how much can get in them. You reshelf them while I bring the others downstairs."

I restocked the cans. Seemed kind of unfair to be the last to the basement. Should I complain? Or was it just my duty? I'd never been much for duty.

During these tense days I also rehearsed for the play, Julius Caesar. Each night, after our evening prayers the cast headed downstairs and Father Anselm worked with us. We usually finished around eleven, and quietly made our way to our rooms. Four nights into the missile scare Father Anselm let us rehearse without him, and the teenage giggles struck. Everything was funny, and no matter how hard we tried, we couldn't stop laughing.

"I've got an idea, but it's pure evil." The life of a seminarian offered few chances for wickedness.

"Oh?"

"What? What?"

"Why don't we wake up Boynton and Sellers?" They were two juniors who loved giving us a hard time.

"What's so bad about that?"

"We tell them to take their blankets, fill them with food, and head to the basement."

There was a long pause. Rick, usually the class clown, was the first to chime in. "Let's do it."

"Okay, I'm in." The others agreed.

It was a simple plan. With our flashlights we'd station ourselves along the corridor outside their rooms, down the stairway to the kitchen and down to the basement.

"They both have roommates. What'll we tell them?" Rick's question introduced a wrinkle I didn't expect.

"It won't look real if we don't include them in the plan." I answered.

We all moved to our posts. Mine, in the kitchen. I leaned against the wall by the racks of dry goods. I closed my eyes and envisioned how we'd planned the trick to go down. After about sixty seconds, I expected one of our targets to arrive.

I heard the slap of bare feet running down the hall.

There he came.

But instead of either Boynton or Sellers, a bleary-eyed senior stumbled in, his face white as a ghost.

A sophomore ran into the kitchen, his blanket clutched in his fist.

Suddenly dozens of students jammed into the doorway creating a bottleneck. One boy's blanket fell and cans flew everywhere. Students shrieked and grabbed food as fast as they could.

"Do we take the soap boxes?"

"I'll get the cereal." The crowd all looked to me for direction. Someone flipped the lights on.

I had to get out of there. I slunk away into the shadows and felt my way back to my room, no sense turning on my flashlight. I stopped by Rick's door. "What happened? It looks like the entire floor was down there."

"It kind of got out of control. I woke Boynton and his roommate up and they started down the hallway as planned. But, they made so much noise others asked what was up. Before I knew it the hallway was full of blankets and classmates. What was I to do?"

Why hadn't we imagined that would happen? Stupid! "Okay, if questioned, we say we overheard someone say to get up because there may have been a bombing. We don't know who...we simply did what we were taught to do."

I scuttled to my room and pretended to be asleep when someone flicked the light on. Through squinted eyes I saw a long crooked finger motioning me out of bed.

Oh, dear. Caught.

Father Philip didn't say a word as I followed him to Father Anselm's office. He opened the door, and I cringed when I saw my accomplices.

Father Anselm wore a blue velvet-like robe, and his usual smile was nowhere to be seen. "Ah, the last of the culprits arrives. I understand you were the ringleader, so the last shall indeed be the first—in punishment that is."

I glared at my fellow plotters. Some friends.

I received the most demerits of all of us, and we all were given extra chores to perform. But the priests did show us some compassion. They never let the rest of the students know we were responsible for half scaring them to death. No telling what the seniors would have done to us. Memories of initiation day still made me shiver in disgust.

As with the nuns in earlier grades, my excellent marks and good behavior bought me favor with the priests. Until Geometry. I'd always been good at math—but this transcended my natural ability and even went beyond the limits of my superhuman cramming abilities. Plus, the weekend before the first big Geometry exam was also the weekend of a big game. If I couldn't cram, I could do the next best thing—cheat.

I wrote all the formulas on a paper and smuggled it into the classroom. I flipped open the top of my desk and placed the cheat sheet right on top. Once the exam began, I pried open the desk ever so slightly and peeked inside to find my help. Wow. How easy. I was sure I'd aced that test. Only problem, Tim Piasceki sat across from me.

Tim was a day student and one of my best friends, though a bit different. He didn't enjoy sports, or most anything fun, really. He was more solemn and religious than anyone I knew...except the priests. He even prayed in the chapel on his free time. He was an obvious choice as one of our class' two members on the Honor Committee. When I was selected as the other member, I thought of it as just another feather in my cap. I never thought it meant much of anything. Tim, however, took his role seriously.

He approached me right after the Geometry class. His eyebrows furrowed and cast dark shadows on his eyes. "Jim, why were you opening your desk during the test? Were you cheating?" He actually looked sad, and a bit hurt.

"Yes." Why did I say that? I always deny everything. "Uh, I was just refreshing my memory." Tim seemed to take my sin personally. Like I'd done something to him.

"Do you want me to report this, or do you?"

Right. The Honor Code. We had pledged to report infractions even if we were the guilty party.

"I'll do it." Where were those words coming from? If it were anyone else I would have had a million excuses. But Tim—something about him called me to a higher level. Maybe it was his sincerity. And his trust. "I'm sorry."

"Jim, you might want to bring that up with the Lord. He's all about forgiveness."

There was a trial, and I plead guilty. I lost my position on the committee, and received a zero on the test. After the hearing Tim said, "I wish I hadn't seen you. But, God must have wanted you to get caught. Maybe you were at a crossroad, and He wanted you to see there are consequences to dishonesty."

Maybe, but at the moment all I felt was embarrassed and hurt. A totally honest, godly person makes the dishonest ashamed.

"Are we still friends?" He held his hand out and I shook it.

"Friends." And I meant it.

My parent's disappearance continued through the remainder of my freshman year. In late May Father Anselm told me they had called, and I would join them after school closed for summer break. As a choir member, I stayed a few days after break to sing at the senior's graduation service. After the service Father Benedict approached me.

"Are you packed?"

"Yes."

"Bring your bag and come the back way to the garage."

I toted my lone suitcase. The garage and the car's trunk were both open. The seminary owned four cars and one truck. All the cars were baby blue Chevy Corvair's with motors in the rear, and trunks in the front.

"Jim, we're worried about being followed, so it might be best if you hid in the trunk until we get to the train station."

It almost sounded like a question. "That's okay, I understand."

"Here's your ticket and an envelope with instructions on what to do when you reach Chicago. When we get to the station I won't immediately let you out. I'll wait until right before the train leaves, then you hop out and run."

I never knew I was claustrophobic until I crawled into that trunk and the father slammed the door shut. The bouncing, the tight space, the stale air, and most of all, the darkness, seemed to close in on me and grow smaller and smaller. I was surely going to be crushed to death or suffocate if that door didn't open soon.

The car stopped. I heard some noise, then daylight. "Go, hurry!" The priest grabbed my arms and lifted me out. I grabbed my suitcase and fled to the train as it slowly churned forward.

I believe I broke every speed record to reach the chugging train. I threw my bag up a staircase, and reached for the rail. A hand grabbed my arm, and with a powerful yank lifted me to safety.

"Kid, you got a train to catch?" The old man laughed hard at his joke. "Why in the world did you do that?" I eyed his plaid shirt and grey hair. He couldn't have been the conductor.

"I'm on my way to see my parents."

"Can't hear you, kid. Between the noise and my old ears, my hearing ain't what it used to be." He lifted my bag and opened the door to the left. I followed him and watched him place it in an overhead tray. I sat across from him, face-to-face.

"So, what were you saying out there?"

"I was late, but I didn't want to miss my train. I'm on my way home."

"What you been doing in Crystal Lake?"

"I go to the seminary there. It's a boarding school."

"Seminary? You look a bit young to be a priest."

"I'll be fourteen in August." I'd concentrate on my age, not the idea of becoming a priest.

"Well, they sure make priests young these days." He gave me a sweet smile, reached into a small duffel and took out a chocolate bar. He broke it and gave me half. "So what's your name?"

Wait a second. Was he trying to win me over to get information about my parents? But his disheveled appearance sure didn't look like a policeman. The lines on his face said he'd lived many years, and most of them were full of smiles. "I'm Jim, but most people call me Bobo." Why'd I tell him that? I hated that nickname.

"Well Bobo, I'm Charles, but most everyone calls me Chuck. I'm on my way to see my daughter. She has a son about your age. Is this your first time on a train?"

"No sir, but the first time on this one."

He rifled through his bag as I read my instructions.

"When you arrive go to Bus #19B Roosevelt Rd. Get off at Ashland. Take the southbound Ashland Rd bus. Get off at 47th street and call this number." A phone number was scribbled in a different color, and beside that was a hand-written note.

We all wish you well, and may everything work out for you and your family. We can't wait to see you next school year. Father Anselm and the staff.

I pocketed the note and sighed.

"What's wrong?"

"Nothing." I shrugged.

"Son, I've been on earth too many years to not recognize a lonely spirit. You want to talk about it?" My feelings were twisted, I wanted to be with my family, but again I didn't. How do you share something like that?

"No, I'm fine."

"Son, you are only as fine as you allow yourself to be. And I don't believe you've done much allowing." He lifted out a book and held it up for me to see. "This is something I try to read from every day."

I caught a glimpse of the title. *Man to Man*.

Chuck leafed through some pages. "I can't seem to find what I'm looking for, but I remember a few things that might help you."

Help me with what? He didn't know a thing about me.

"Son, the writer says that just as fish were made for water, man was made for God. In Ecclesiastes God says He placed in us all a desire for the eternal. That He gave us all something the author calls God hunger. But, the more you try to get away from Him, the more your life is empty. You'll never be at peace. Does that make any sense to you?"

I nodded. I guessed I understood the theory, but what did it have to do with me?

He sat back and smiled. "I'm not sure why I wanted to share this. I suppose I'm just a pushy old man. I doubt if you'll much remember me, but try and hold on to the one truth that all men are hungry for something, it's how you fill that hunger that makes a difference."

Chuck talked with me all the way to Chicago. Before we departed he asked, "Have you started shaving?"

I shook my head. Though it was getting to be that time. I felt my prickly chin.

"We'll, let me leave you with something practical." He opened his bag and lifted out a razor.

"First make sure your face is wet." He took out his hanky. "Pretend this is a washcloth. Get it as hot as you can stand."

He went on to explain the finer points of giving myself a great shave. But what stuck with me most about Chuck was that idea of the hunger he described. Hungry. No other word could describe the longing, the churning of my spirit.

After the train ride, I hopped the bus and followed the instructions. When I reached my final bus stop, I climbed down and found myself staring at the open door of a corner bar. Spanish music blared onto the street and, from the stares of those who passed by, a white teenager carrying a suitcase wasn't the norm. I could see a graffiti covered phone booth halfway down the block, in front of a store with *Lavanderia* stenciled on its window. But worse, the phone was absent a mouthpiece. A group of older boys moved my direction when a woman carrying a baby approached.

"You lost?" She looked me over top to bottom and smacked her gum.

"Looking for a phone, ma'am." She was almost black, and spoke with a heavy Mexican accent. Her sleeping baby was wrapped in a bright orange blanket. Man, he had to be sweating in his little cocoon.

"I see you get off the bus. I figured you must have picked the wrong stop. My apartment is down the block, you can use my phone."

I looked down the street in the opposite direction. Those older boys had gathered into a tighter group, ready to pounce. It had to be safer to take my chances with the woman. I followed her to an old building that smelled of beans and chili powder. Her place was small, but neat and clean.

"You can use the phone over there." She pointed to a table next to her gray couch.

"Thank you. I'll hurry." I put my fingers in the little holes and dragged the dial around, waiting for it to bounce back into position for the next number. It seemed to take twice as long as it usually did.

Finally, my mother answered. "Where you at?"

Hello to you, too. "I'm at a lady's apartment, near the bus stop."

"Will she let you wait there, until I can come get you?"

"Ma'am, if it's not too much trouble, can I wait here until my mother can come get me?" She laid her baby in a small crib near the kitchen.

"Sure, no problem."

After relaying the address to my mother the lady brought me a glass of coke. "Your family, they lives here?"

"I guess. I've been away at school and never have been here. It's summer break."

"How long you been gone?" She squinted at me.

"About eight months."

"What kind of school keeps a boy from his family for so long? You not been at a reform school, have you?" She shot a nervous glance at her baby.

"No, a seminary."

"Ave Maria." She made a sign of the cross. "You going to be a priest?"

"It's a Franciscan Preparatory Seminary." She could draw her own conclusions.

"I never had a priest in my apartment."

"I'm a long way from being one."

"It's a blessing to be able to help someone called by God." She stood a bit taller.

Oh great. I was probably committing some mortal sin by letting her think she was helping a future priest.

"You probably lives on the other side of Damen Avenue. Mexican on this side, white on other. Be careful when you over here, too much anger. Much danger for you on this side, especially when dark."

A loud buzzer interrupted us, and the lady jumped up and raised a window. She leaned her entire torso outside. "Your son is with me," she called to the sidewalk. "Okay, I'll send him down."

She turned back to me with a soft smile. "What is your name?"

"I'm Jim."

"And I'm Rosa. It was a pleasure to meet you Jim. I can't wait to see you again."

She planned to see me again? When?

"In heaven, Jim, in heaven."

Ah right. Heaven. We'd have to see.

My mother looked older. Not just a few months, but many years. After quick hugs and pecks on the cheeks, we walked away from Damen Ave., and deep into the dangerous side of town.

To describe the living conditions of our apartment as dreadful would be like calling Disneyworld a nice little amusement park. Roaches competed with the rats for food and space. Some of the bugs were so huge, I'm sure they won most of the battles. Then there was the odor. The entire building smelled of a combination of urine, rotten food, and mold. To top it off, the foul air outside was worse. The stench from the carcasses at the nearby Union Stock Yards made my eyes water.

I had to get out of there. Such a selfish thought, but I couldn't help it. I had to go as soon as I could. As far as I could go.

"Bobo, I'm sorry about where we are living. I'll get us a better place soon."

"I understand, Dad. I'm sure you will. It's not so bad." I pasted on a fake smile.

Two out of three of my responses were true. I did understand how, and why, they were there. I believed he would work hard to get a better place, or be arrested trying. But, the apartment was worse than bad. I couldn't imagine how my mother kept her sanity. It was great to see Cindy. She was a pretty, sweet little girl. Kenny seemed to resent my arrival, maybe because he had to give up space on his tiny bed.

I stayed away from that dump as much as possible that summer. Most days I'd take the long bus ride north to Al Musial's house. To me, he lived the perfect life. He had lots of loving relatives, his father was a mailman, and they owned a small neighborhood grocery. As often as I could, I stayed overnight with him. I was ashamed of my apartment, my parents, and my life.

Al had two bikes, and we rode everywhere. We'd stand outside of Wrigley Field during batting practice waiting for homeruns to clear the wall. Returning a ball to a ticket attendant gave us free admission. Daily softball games and weekly trips to Riverview Amusement Park competed with the occasional trip to Lake Michigan's beach.

I wouldn't have made it through that summer without Al's friendship.

In fact, his family store was a source of income for me as many times Al and I were asked to help out. Being across from a high school, and with summer school in session, it stayed pretty busy.

One afternoon as I stocked cans, Al's mother approached me. "Jim, I hate to bring this up but it seems like my cash drawer doesn't balance on some of the days you work." She twisted her hanky between her fingers.

"What do you mean?"

She looked down. "Well, it seems when you work we often come up five or ten dollars short."

I shrugged. "I don't know anything about it."

"Jim, are you sure? I just want to know the truth. Be honest, and it will be fine between us."

I stared straight in her eyes. "I didn't take anything. I've never worked alone. Al always works next to me. Is there anyone else who might have worked by themselves those days?"

She looked down at the ledger. Her lips moving like in prayer. When she raised her head, her eyes looked drawn. "Maybe I just made a mistake."

On the bus home that night strange emotions were at war between my head and my heart. It was like the cartoons with an angel on one shoulder, and the devil on the other.

Angel: "You should feel very guilty. These people were so kind to you, and you stole from them."

Devil: "You did need the money didn't you? The little bit you took couldn't have hurt them. Besides, your family is poor. How else could you afford to go to Riverview Park?"

Angel: "But, you didn't have to go to the amusement park that often. Even worse, you hinted your best friend might have taken the money. Imagine how that would have hurt his mother."

Devil: "She's old. She probably figures it was her mistake. What could you do, confess?"

Then a new battle ensued.

Angel: "While I'm here, you need to be told how selfish you've been this summer. Your family went missing for months, and when you get a chance to be with them, you don't."

Devil: "It wasn't your fault they disappeared."

Angel: "It wasn't your mother's, or your brother and sister's fault either. You could spend more time with them."

Devil: "In that rat-infested stink hole? If they could have, they would have been with you at Al's all summer."

Angel: "It's your family, and that comes first."

Devil: "You are your family now. Either put yourself first, or end up just like them.

Just like most cartoons, the devil smacked my angel on the head with his pitchfork and triumphed. His last argument cinched it for me. I couldn't stand the thought of ending up like my family.

I'd see to it that didn't happen.

Part Two

"I will give you a new heart and put a new spirit within you." Ezekiel 36:26

Chapter 19
Manipulations

*"We are liars if we say we know God and do not keep
His commandments – and His truth is not in us."*
1 John 2:4.

Confession, my chance to beat hell. Or, at least earn a lighter sentence. Daily confession for a potential atheist? When it came to religion, I wasn't taking any chances.

I went for the reduced sentence any way possible. Reciting prayers didn't cost anything, didn't cause physical pain, and didn't require constant good behavior. The longer the prayer, the less time I'd have to spend in purgatory.

Another get-out-of-Hell-for-a-day card appeared when a priest mentioned medals blessed by the Pope. "If you're wearing one when you die, you will only stay in purgatory until the next Saturday after you pass away."

I bought one and added a little caveat to my prayers. "Lord, when I die, may it please be on a Friday night?"

I asked another priest at St. Mary's about my magic medal, but he brushed it off. I think I saw a twinkle in his eyes. "The priest who sold it to you was a bit mistaken, boy. No object can do that. It's more about how good you are."

What? Was the priest mistaken, or having fun with our fear and pocketing some cash in the process? Surely a man of God wouldn't do that.

But I had to go back to being good?

Well, there were no better works than attending Mass and going to confession. Right? I already went to

Mass each morning, I'd just go to confession more. That would do it.

Only one problem. I went to confession, but I lied. Not always, but often. I learned how to pick out the perfect priest. I avoided the ones with the reputations for being tough and sought out the ones who would proverbially pat me on the head and send me on my way.

"Your best bet," a friend told me, "is to go to the churches where the priest might not speak English that well. Go to the Hispanic church, and then confuse the guy."

Ooh. That sounded smart. God couldn't hold it against me if the priest didn't understand me.

"You give him small sins, like disobeying or lying," my friend whispered. "But, you don't want to get grilled on the, you know, personal stuff. So, after you offer up the obvious sins, you close with 'and I'm sorry for any sins against the sixth and ninth commandments.'"

Right. The thought and deed commandments. Every boy's nightmare.

It wasn't the church's fault, really. No one ever taught me an insincere confession would be accepted by God. In fact, I prayed the Act of Contrition daily...knew it very well.

> *O my God, I am heartily sorry for having offended Thee, and I detest all my sins, because I dread the loss of Heaven, and the pains of Hell; but most of all because I love Thee, my God, Who art all good and deserving of all my love. I firmly resolve, with the help of Thy grace, to confess my sins, to do penance, and to amend my life. Amen.*

Oh, I prayed it all right. I just didn't mean it.

But the summer after my sophomore year two federal officers taught me what it meant to be absolved of wrongdoing.

We moved up to a slightly nicer neighborhood and into a much better apartment. Since the Musial family wasn't an option any longer, I joined neighborhood softball games or played stoop ball against the apartment stairs. A Cubs games, though, drew me indoors.

Mom opened the door to a knock.

I leaned back to see. Two men in dark suits. A lump rose in my throat. *Here we go again.* Could I get to Dad in enough time to warn him? How would he escape that windowless room anyway?

"My father's not here." I stood to defend my mother.

"Son, we know he is. Mrs. Hall, would you ask him to come into the kitchen?"

Why didn't they have their guns drawn?

Mom went back, and Dad sheepishly came out wearing dark slacks, a T-shirt, and black socks. No shoes?

He was surrendering.

"Son, we'd like to talk to your parents in private." The agent didn't take his eyes off my father while he spoke.

I backed out of the room, eyes locked on Dad. Would they take him away?

The door softly closed until the lock clicked. I pressed my ear against it. I heard muffled snatches of speech. I pressed in harder. But that made it worse.

The door opened and I caught myself before I fell on my face.

"Sit down and wait." An agent pointed to the sofa, turned the TV up and left, closing the door again.

My whole body began to tremble. What would my mother do this time? Were they going to arrest her as an accomplice? Would I be able to go back to St. Mary's?

Mom opened the door and motioned me in, face damp with tears.

Dad sat at the table staring down at a sheet of paper. "It's over. Bobo, it's all over!" Dad waved it over his head.

"What's over? Where did the cops go?" I ran to the window and looked down to the street. Were they getting handcuffs?

"Look." He handed me the document and pulled Mom into his lap. Her grin as wide as I'd ever seen it.

I scanned the official-looking document. It had my dad's birth name on it and many of his aliases. The top read, "U.S. Marshall Service/FBI Case Record."

They had record of all of that? That wouldn't go well for Dad. Busted. Big time. But why did they look so happy? "I don't get it."

"Read to the bottom."

I saw the words that excited my parents so much, and changed our lives.

Status of Report: Deceased.

Deceased, as in dead? "What? How? I don't get it."

My mother went to the kitchen table and lit a cigarette. She took a long drag, and collapsed into the red plastic chair. "They listed your father as officially dead so we wouldn't have to worry anymore."

This made no sense. "Why?"

"They said they looked at how long we've been running, how we had a son in the seminary, and that the original crime was so long ago. They just both agreed to do something good for someone, and they chose us." She shrugged.

Why would a couple of feds risk their careers for an escaped convict they didn't know? It couldn't be a bribe. My parents were broke.

I studied their faces for clues. They looked free but weary. As though the weight of all they'd endured settled on them, into them.

But it made no sense.

Chapter 20
Going Bad

"There are all sorts of things in this world that offer to give [to] you, but they never quite keep their promise. It may be hard for an egg to turn into a bird: it would be a jolly sight harder for it to learn to fly while remaining an egg. We are like eggs at present. And you cannot go on indefinitely being just an ordinary, decent egg. We must be hatched or go bad."
C.S. Lewis

Madly in love. With Mary Alice.

Or so I thought. Only problem with dating, it cost money. My parents gave me no allowance, so I scoured the newspaper for jobs until someone hired me to sell magazines door-to-door.

I had my pitch down pat. "Good morning, I'm Jim Hall. I want to tell you some exciting news. The Time-Life Corporation is introducing a new way to help us neighborhood kids out. Do you get the paper delivered?"

No matter what the response, I continued with, "I'll be able to deliver your favorite magazines to you, just like the newspaper. What makes it especially exciting is Time-Life wants this to be a huge success, so they're giving you four free magazines. Let me show how this works." They could subscribe to Time and Life Magazine at a special discounted price. I'd give the impression that, like a paper route, money would be collected by the delivery boy. "Cancel at any time. Initial here please."

I received five dollars for each sale. I made twelve sales my first three days. I soon took home more than a hundred dollars a week. My mother kept seventy-five, and I kept the rest. I was rich! It was being dishonest but the reward was worth it. The poorer the people were, the less they needed the magazines. But, they were the easiest to sell. They heard free and nothing after that.

I took Mary Alice to movies, ice cream shops, and bought gifts for her family. Despite the seminary's wisdom on avoiding physical contact with girls, I chose a different path. Kissing soon graduated to the next level, but never enough for her. I refused to go all the way. Not because of any religious convictions, but because of a real fear of being a teenage dad.

Two weeks before the end of summer break, I gave notice at work.

They tried hard to dissuade me. "Why quit when you're doing so well? You're a natural."

"I'm going back to school."

"Kid, you don't need school. We'll up your commission to seven bucks and make you a closer. You'll double your wages. I bet that's more than your old man makes."

That night at dinner I told my mother and father about the offer from work. Mom seemed to favor it. "We can up his rent." Of course that's what she'd think of first.

But my father looked like he could spit nails. "They want a boy your age to just drop out of high school? What kind of people are they?" He slammed his fork down. "You're done there. Today was your last day. I'll stop by there tomorrow to tell them and get your final check."

The extra money had sounded nice, but two weeks without work sounded even better.

Late the following day the phone rang. "Hey Jim." My boss said, "We're sorry, really sorry about asking you to drop out of school. Please tell your dad I made this call, and I'm very sorry."

I'm not sure what he said or did, but it looked like Dad's visit made quite an impression. He'd finally done something to protect me. What a shame it was so little—and so late.

I quit St. Mary's before Christmas my senior year. I wanted at least one semester at a school that girls attended. Walking in the doors of the public school was like symbolically sloughing off all the teachings about Jesus and morality I'd learned. I embarked on a quest for girls. Many girls.

***

After graduation I went to UCLA, and did some acting. Not the best profession for someone plagued with insecurities. But I graduated and then returned to Chicago. That is, *we* returned–after all, I was married.

I wasn't looking to settle down, but sometimes it doesn't take much to change a young man's mind.

"I'm pregnant." Few words struck a college boy with more fear than those two. But like a good Catholic boy, I married her.

We left for our honeymoon, and I soon realized I'd been duped. Pregnancy can only be faked for so long. Mother Nature has her own way of telling the truth.

That's when I stopped going to church.

Shirley was very nice, and I even liked her. She was smart and great company, and even a fantastic cook. But what I admired most was how she manipulated me. It seemed like God gave me a dose of justice—the liar was out-lied. Outsmarted at my own game. I had to give her kudos for that.

But, I didn't love her. I couldn't. I was too much in love with myself.

My accounting degree could easily land me a job in Chicago dealing with numbers, but I wanted something more exciting. Leaf Brands Candy Company hired me to sell their Whoppers Malted Milk Balls and Rainblo Bubble Gum to grocery stores. It was easy work, but boring. Before long I earned a promotion. As the Marketing Coordinator I monitored which display and location sold best in the stores. It was more like accounting than sales, and I soon looked elsewhere.

I saw an ad in the Chicago Tribune. Union Camp was hiring salespeople. I landed the job right away and sold vacant lots at Apple Canyons Lake, a new recreational property. I learned more about sales, and deceit, than I'd even known.

The resort was near Galena, Illinois, two hours from Chicago. Union Camp took a few thousand acres, carved up four hundred for a future lake, designed a golf course and stables, and began selling lots. When I arrived, the lake was full and everything else neared completion. A tall Texan, who managed a twelve-man sales team, quickly introduced me to my job.

"Kid," the only name he ever called me, "land sales is the great wild west of selling. All you need is courage, a big gun, and some ammunition. The gun is learning the lots and your presentation. The ammunition is the secrets your fellow salespeople share with you. But you'll have to supply the bravery."

After door-to-door magazine sales, I could handle the courage side. I was anxious to sell. People drove into the property and became an "up," assigned to the next salesperson in line, determined by the month prior sales. Top salesperson started the day first, and the bottom last. Problem—many people only wanted free gifts promised by the telemarketers.

"You drive up to our beautiful lake, enjoy a short tour of the property, and receive your choice of a set of pots and pans, or a clock radio."

It didn't matter why they arrived or if they happened upon the property lost. They were the next up, and maybe the only chance that day for a sale. I memorized my pitch, walked the lots, and drove people around the property. But no sales the first week.

Each night the salespeople headed to bars to discuss their day. That's where I learned my craft.

Four other salespeople joined me at the tavern's wooden bar when Ken, a gray-haired old geezer, directed his question to the group.

"Do you think he's ready?" He gave a nod toward me.

"A week without a nibble might prompt him to pay attention." Frank, the top salesperson, said. He flashed hundred dollar bills, and people flocked to him.

"Jim, do you want to know why you aren't selling?" Ken was a top salesperson, too, but no one would guess it from his looks.

I shrugged. "It's just bad luck. Everyone I took out was too broke, or they only came for their prize."

Ken lifted a glass of dark liquid and took a swig. "You got to make your own luck. Of course no one drives hours from home wanting to buy vacant land that someday may be a neat place to have as a second home. All they want are the goodies. You simply got to trick them into believing they got to have the lot."

"Trick them, how?" My ears perked up. There was a formula for this?

"You first create a story about yourself to make them trust you. Then, you build the lot up as something better than it is. Then you take it away."

Hmm. That was my method of getting dates. It would work for sales too? "What kind of story? Take it away?"

"Guys, let's work this out." Between drinks, each threw out ideas.

"He's young. We got to use that."

"A college boy."

"He's new."

After they each had about three more drinks they presented me with a role.

It was like I was back acting in Hollywood. "Hi, I'm Jim Hall. I'm an accounting manager here. All the sales people are busy, so I was asked to show you guys around. That is, unless you want to wait until a salesman is available."

They created a basket of lies I could use to help sell the lots. Using their script, and other sneaky sales ideas of my own, I moved up the sales ladder. It was dishonest, but no more so than my childhood identities. My false confessions. The magazine sales. At that point, who cared? Judging by the checks I deposited each week, God sure didn't mind.

Besides all the land sales, that year was especially marked by three events that impacted the rest of my life. I had an affair with Rhonda who worked with me at the lake. I met Dennis, my future business partner. And I conducted my first business transaction with the Chicago mafia.

The affair, like many, started innocently. Flirting, a lunch together, dinner, a few kisses, and then a motel room. She knew I was married, but I told her how my wife tricked me into marriage. I promised that I loved her, eventually I'd leave my wife, and we'd get married. Rhonda was the first of many girls I sold with that script.

Dennis joined the Union Camp sales force a few weeks before me. When most of the lots were sold, many of us were sent to a real estate school in Wisconsin. Wisconsin, leery of out-of-state recreational land salesmen invading their state, made it extremely difficult to get a real estate license. We had to prove residency and pass an exam designed to flunk over ninety-eight percent. Shirley and I moved to Milwaukee for the residency requirement, and I studied hard to pass the test. Only seven of the more than five hundred who took the exam passed. Of them, Dennis and I, the only ones from our sales team.

We needed to be close to the property. Dennis and I rented a lakefront lot in Reedsburg, Wisconsin, about two hours from Milwaukee. We became good friends and top salesmen. We spent the next two years as Wisconsin drinking buddies.

Before the move to Wisconsin, I ran into one of guys from the old neighborhood. He made me an offer I couldn't refuse.

Chapter 21
The Mob and the Indy 500

"When tempted, no one should say, 'God is tempting me.' For God cannot be tempted by evil, nor does he tempt anyone; but each person is tempted when they are dragged away by their own evil desire and enticed. Then, after desire has conceived, it gives birth to sin; and sin, when it is full-grown, gives birth to death."
James 1:13-15

A typical January Chicago day—ugly and uglier. But I'd promised Shirley a deep-dish pizza at Pizzeria Uno, so I drove toward the restaurant hoping the light mist wouldn't turn to sleet. I let her out at the door and searched for a parking space.

I spotted an opening three blocks down on Ohio Street. I pulled ahead to back in when a white Cadillac swerved into the opening headfirst. With its rear sticking out, the driver maneuvered up and back working into my space. Livid, I put my car in park and went to confront the driver.

My gloved knuckles pounded on the driver's wet window. It rolled down.

"What do you want?" He looked to be a few years older, and much tougher than me. I hesitated, but my anger took control.

"Man, this was my spot." The mist morphed to a steady cold rain and my carefully brushed hair flopped like a mop after a swabbing.

"You think I care? Get out of here before you get hurt." Less a threat than a promise. I knew I should let it slide, but my pride was bruised.

"You either move, or you'll be sorry." I hoped my bulky winter coat made me look more dangerous than I was. The door swung open and the muscled form of a man rose above me. I looked up at his sinister grin. I'd smile too if I were as big as him. I took the stance I learned in the Golden Glove boxing matches. There were a couple problems. It'd been years since I fought, and my body was now as soft as a marshmallow. I was doomed, so I tried to out talk him.

"You don't know who you're messing with. My brother's the head of the Sons of Italy."

"Is that so?" He looked down at me like he was trying to figure me out. Maybe this tactic was working, so I plunged ahead.

"Yeah, and I'm friends of Nick Calabrese." I had no idea if he'd heard of him, but the name sounded tougher than my brother's.

"You are, are you? Just how good a friend is he?" As a salesman I learned to listen to the tone of my prospects voice. Something wasn't right. I didn't know what, but I didn't think he was buying.

"Really good, and trust me, you don't want to get on his bad side."

"I'm glad you believe that, because I'm Nick Calabrese. And, I don't take fondly someone using my name without my permission." His smile was replaced with a mad dog sneer.

Uh oh. My boxing stance changed into two hands waving defensively.

"Nick, it's me, Jim Hall. You know, from the old neighborhood."

"Jim Hall? I don't know a Jim Hall."

"Bobo, I'm Bobo!" A car honked at us both to get out of the street. I figured he wouldn't do anything in front of a witness so I slowly retreated to my car.

"It was nice to see you again, Nick. Sorry about all the confusion."

"Ah, I was just razzing you. I figured you were Kenny's brother. By the way, he's no longer head of the Sons of Italy. They kicked him because he got into too many fights. They did the same to me." He smiled and my back regained its spine.

"You heading to Uno's?"

"Yeah, my wife's already there."

"Great, you can introduce her to me. That is, after you find yourself a parking place. Now get out of mine so I can finish parking."

After walking the extra three blocks I found Nick waiting for me near the door. Shirley was at a table for two.

"There's my wife. I'll introduce you."

"No need, I'll introduce myself." Nick not only gave his name, he took my place at the table.

"Go grab yourself a seat and join us. I'm sure they won't mind the three of us sharing a pizza." Nick entertained us with stories from the old neighborhood, paid for the food and drinks, and then slipped me his card and whispered, "Call me tomorrow."

The card burned a hole in my pants all through dinner. What could he want?

The God of my grandparents and Aunt Mary struck at my conscience with a loud, *Run!* The demons of my father softly whispered, "Go for it."

The next morning I called before nine. "Nick, this is Jim...ah, Bobo." No longer a victim of my dad's choices, or foolish adolescent making dumb choices—this was a grownup decision. Besides, it was only a phone call. Nothing but talk.

"You know where the Calumet Forest Preserves are?"

"Yes."

"Can you be there at noon? I've got someone I want you to meet."

Meeting in the woods on a cold winter day seemed strange. Mob movies always used isolated places like that to whack double-crossers because it was hard to bug a forest.

I arrived a little early and drove to the parking lot, and waited. A black Mercedes pulled in close by, but no one got out. A little later Nick's car parked next to mine. He rolled his window down. "Let's go for a stroll."

Yesterday's rain had crystalized. Each step crunched like we walked on shards of glass. Nick stopped by the children's play area and pointed at the swings.

"Let's sit." The seat was so cold I thought my rear would stick to it. I sat next to him. "Get on the other side. I want to see your face."

"Been a long time since I been on one of these." He started swinging. I wasn't sure what he expected, so I stayed still. His black boots dug into the earth and he stopped. "You're too serious. You need to loosen up some. I know what you need, a way to make a score."

Money, hopefully.

"The future is about smart guys like you. All the guys are sending their kids to college. The Outfit will soon be run by suits. All they need us dumb guys for is the dirty work." I wasn't that interested in his predictive powers. My mind stuck on the word score.

"I have a friend who needs someone clean, smart, and trustworthy to help him. When I saw you yesterday I figured it was fate. You're exactly what he needs. I get a percentage, and I'm sure he'll cut you a great deal."

"What do I have to do?" My heart raced so fast I no longer felt the cold.

"Let me introduce you to my friend." He jumped off the swing and headed toward the idling Mercedes. I crawled behind him into its back seat.

"Mr. D, I'd like you to meet Jim Hall."

"Jim, it's good to meet you. Please call me Bill." He didn't turn around or offer his hand.

"Mr. D, I can vouch for Jim. He's bright, college graduate, has no record, and I think he's your guy. I didn't give him any particulars. I figured you would."

The mysterious man explained that he and his family were involved in many interests, including the novelty stands at the Indianapolis 500 and various state fairs. Because of new regulations, he needed someone squeaky clean to run the three weekends at Indy and the week at the Minnesota State Fair.

"You would get a cut of the take. You can figure to make at least ten grand." Ten grand for about fifteen days of work sounded great.

"That's it?"

"Yeah, nothing to it. We got a deal?" A hand shot over the seat and I shook it. "Nicky will be your supervisor. Do what he says, and you'll do great."

Nick took that as a signal to open the door and exit.

The pavement was a mix of wet broken concrete and rocks. The wind blew discarded food wrappers around our legs as Nick gave me further instructions. "This is an important first step. I'll get you some paperwork to fill out. You didn't get yourself in trouble with the law while out at that hippy college did you?"

"Of course not."

"Not even nailed for some stupid sit-in or smoking some of that Mary Jane?"

"I'm clean."

"These organizations will run a criminal check. If you don't get approved Mr. D and his family will be angry with me. And I will be angry with you. *Capiche?*"

I very much understood.

"We'll meet before May and go over your role." He slapped me on the back, waved a goodbye, and headed to his car.

My shoulders hitched up an inch. I was going to work with the mob, and it wasn't even illegal. At least it seemed straight.

Seemed straight. Those words echoed in my head. Hopefully they wouldn't become famous last words.

The first part of April I was helping Shirley pack for our move to Wisconsin when Nick called. "What is this I hear? You're skipping town?" His voice had a chuckle in it, so I kidded back.

"Yeah, I'm trying to get away from guys like you." The dead air made me think my response was a bit too flippant for his taste. "We got to move to Wisconsin so I can get a real estate license."

"We need to get together soon. Meet me tonight at the pizza place." He hung up before I could ask for the time. I could call him back—nah, I'd get to Uno's early enough.

I was into my third drink when he appeared. We grabbed a table and ordered. "Here's how this works. At the Indy there are small wooden concession stands near each exit and entrance. Each one will have two people working it." He lit a cigarette and took a sip of his Chianti.

"Each morning they go to our warehouse and get boxes of souvenirs. They buy them from us on consignment. We give them our price, they mark up the goods as much as they can and keep the difference."

"How do I get the people to man them?"

"No problem at Indy. Lots of Chicago folks we know who'll drive down to make some money. Some of them will make two hundred a day at the trials and twice that at the race. Minnesota is another story, but we'll talk about that after Indy."

I waved at our waitress to order another Bourbon Old Fashion.

"Each night they check in what they have left and get a credit. They also turn in all their cash. We take our share, and hold what they earn until we all settle up in Chicago a week after the race."

"Why don't we let them just keep what they earn right then?"

"Oh, they'll pocket some. But we tell them it's for their protection. Mostly it's to make sure they show up the next day. You'll check them in and out, make sure they don't run out of goodies to sell, and do the necessary accounting."

"What's my cut?"

"Fifteen percent."

"Of the entire take?"

"No, just what we get."

"Do we sell enough to make what your friend said?"

"Just wait and see. Those drunken race car fans throw their money away."

***

When I arrived at Indy, I drove down the street circling the racetrack. It reminded me of Maxwell Street. Pole trials started the next day and people packed in like pickles in a jar everywhere I looked. Yards filled with campers and cars. The street turned into the sidewalk. Careful to not run anyone over, I inched toward the service gate. An orange-and-white striped sawhorse and a policeman guarded the entranceway. I showed him my badge and car permit and he motioned me in.

I waved at Nick as I climbed the stairs up to the warehouse.

A huge bearded man opened the door. "Can I help you?" He seemed friendly enough, but the shotgun strapped to his shoulder told a different story.

"I'm Jim Hall. This is my operation."

"Sorry, Mr. Hall. Mr. Calabrese said you'd be arriving. Back there's your office, but I also set you up a desk in the warehouse. You'll use that one to do your business with the contractors, the guys running the stands. " He flung his gun around, and laid it on his lap as he sat.

Nick opened the door. "Make yourself useful." He threw me a clipboard. Everything's in, go do an inventory and then we can start boxing." The goal was to have each stand's cartons full of novelty items before morning.

I looked at the sheets and opened the boxes all stamped, "Made in China." Cheap, very cheap, black and white checkered flags priced out at a dollar. I knew they couldn't have paid more than a dime. As I opened boxes full of overpriced sombreros, T-shirts, coffee cups, and mugs. I understood how they'd make their money. It may be legal, but the mark-up was criminal. Even worse, the prices would be doubled to the happy fans.

The experience at the Indy 500 was like none I'd had before. At night another armed guard joined us and we'd sleep in cots in the warehouse. The final count the first weekend was thirty-six thousand. My notes showed we were holding fourteen thousand dollars due the contractors. I quickly computed the remaining twenty-two thousand take at fifteen percent. Wow, thirty-three hundred for a few days' work. Next week was supposed to be around the same and double the next. I could make over twelve thousand dollars. But, Nick had a different accounting system.

"Nick, we did great." I handed him my paperwork. Around us were paper sacks of money, cloth bags of coins, and boxes full of miscellaneous junk novelties.

"Come with me, let's talk." We went back to the tiny office. "It's a bit more complicated than your numbers. Some of this stuff came back damaged. We'll need to subtract that from the contractors take. Then there's the matter of using the wrong price list."

"What 'wrong price list?'"

"The one you been using. See where it says the flags were sold to the contractors at a buck? Well, they were supposed to get them at seventy-five cents. He took a folded paper from his pocket and handed it to me. Exactly like my list, but all the prices were twenty to twenty five percent lower.

"I don't understand."

"This is the list I will be using to report back on how much we made. We subtract the damaged goods from the contractors, but don't change their take."

"I see, we charge the contractors what we think we can get, just like they did with the fans. This list is what we report back with. But, why bother? It seems the take is still the same."

Nick looked at me like I was being dense. "Think about it."

The dim light bulb in my brain finally began to glow. "Ah, we report the smaller amount."

"You got it. No harm, no foul."

Ideas ticked through my mind like a bomb ready to explode. A kind of double cross, but I liked the idea of a bigger take.

Nick went out to get us all some burgers and I recalculated the numbers based on breakage and Nick's price list. When he returned, I handed over my findings."

"Bottom line, the contractors make fifteen hundred less, your partners make thirty five hundred less, and there's five thousand left over." I was almost afraid to ask, but knew it needed to be settled.

"What's my share?"

"You get your fifteen percent." I was worried he'd say that. I'd make no more, but be in the middle of trying to trick whoever set this operation up. "I'll tell you what, you get your normal percentage on the official take. I'll give you twenty-five on the overage. Start counting it out."

For my three weeks at Indianapolis I pocketed over five thousand cash, and made another ten thousand at our settlement meeting. I handled the Minneapolis State Fair alone. Nick agreed I could keep fifty percent of our special accounting money. The fair was harder because we used Carnies in the booths, and they had to be manned all day. I met Andy Williams, the Osmond singing group, and net fifteen thousand for my week's work.

Once back in Wisconsin, Dennis and I broke every sales record. But we were wild men. We stayed out every night drinking until the bars closed. We often showed up at work so hung over we couldn't see straight. Parties, drinks, sales, and women were my steady diet that summer.

Late into the year Dennis and I visited a competitor's office armed with proof of our sales success. The owner flew us to his resort in northern Wisconsin. We accepted jobs there. Before long at our new stomping grounds, we had a surprise—our wives.

I'd visited Shirley only twice that summer. Dennis and I moved to a house on the eighteenth tee of a golf course. We'd travel to Minneapolis or Duluth each weekend to get drunk and pick up girls. The first day of November I got the call.

"Hi, what's for dinner?" Shirley asked with a challenge in her tone.

"Say what?"

"Edie and I are packed up, and we're following the moving truck. We should be there by six."

We had two girls in the house, staying for the weekend. "What about your jobs?"

"We quit, see you soon."

Four p.m., and we had to make the girls disappear and check for any evidence. Dennis and I scrambled and accomplished the near impossible. Everything was in order when the wives arrived.

I'm sure both wives knew their marriages were in trouble and made this drastic move in an attempt to save them. For me, a small detour in my self-indulgent life.

By the second winter we were all ready to head back to Chicago.

It was time to make some money, serious money.

Chapter 22
Striking Oil

"For this people's heart has become calloused; they hardly hear with their ears, and they have closed their eyes. Otherwise they might see with their eyes, hear with their ears, understand with their hearts and turn, and I would heal them." Matthew 13:15

J. Paul Getty once said, "The formula for success is rise early, work hard, and then strike oil." I considered Chicago my oil field, so I went searching for my well. Dennis searched for temporary ways we could make money. If we landed a good paying job there, we'd stay. We always had the option to go back and sell land in Wisconsin in the spring.

He saw an ad for a sales job near Loyola University with Universal Office Supplies. When I learned it was for inside telephone sales, I balked.

"I'm a salesman, not a telemarketer."

"But it's cold out there, and the owner says we can make some good money."

Dennis was ready to take the job, so I set the condition. "Let's give it two weeks. If either one of us wants to leave, we both do."

They primarily sold toner for copy machines. They would lowball Xerox and other companies and try to convince the prospect the ink was just as good as the manufacturer's. After reading some research studies, the toner was basically the same, but I made only fourteen dollars commission per sale. It would take an awful lot of sales to make any significant money.

"Dennis, either we go elsewhere, or I've got to change the presentation to increase the sales numbers."

"Are you going to ask the boss?"

"No, I'll play around with it first."

Within a day I created a pitch that changed the telemarketing world, and led to the phrase Toner Bandits.

"Hi. I'm Jack Scott calling from the toner warehouse. What's the number on your copy machine? You know, it's the number in front right by the name."

After getting the number, the heart of the pitch began. "The reason I'm calling is we need some help. We made a shipping mistake and sent a case of toner, you know, for your copier machine, to the wrong location. I figured instead of going through the trouble and cost of shipping it back, I'd give you a call. If you can help me, by taking the case, I can give it to you for the warehouse price. You know, for helping out."

There was no lost shipment and no special discount, but it led to a heavy increase of sales. Then an idea struck. It seemed no one knew what they paid for toner. I increased the price by ten dollars. And then twenty. Finally I tried eighty-nine dollars per can, seventy more than the retail. A few less sales, but the average commission skyrocketed. Within three weeks I averaged eight hundred dollars commission per week, a tremendous wage.

The company had two other locations in California. Within three months I managed sales at the Chicago office, and four months later became national sales manager. At the age of twenty-five I earned more than a grand a week and drove a Cadillac.

Dennis worked in the resell department. Wanting to make as much as me, he designed a pitch as Machiavellian as mine. "Even if we sold them enough toner to last years. I tell them their next order is ready to be shipped. They haven't a clue, so they say 'ship it.'"

Sales exploded. Overrides increased. But I hungered for more. One night at a local tavern I shared something with Dennis. "What do you think they pay for this toner?"

He shrugged his shoulders and took another drink of his bourbon.

"I'm thinking it can't be too much if they used to sell it at nineteen dollars. If we found out the source, we could start our own business."

Dennis' eyes widened.

"Man, you have access to the files. Find out where they get it from."

The next weekend we jumped on a plane to Los Angeles to meet the owner of the manufacturing plant. After a tour of his facility, I asked the question that changed our lives. "We're the primary reason the sales at Universal Office have increased. We're thinking of opening our own company. Would you sell us the toner directly, and at what price?"

The portly manufacturer rubbed his chin. "I don't want to get the owners of Universal mad, so this meeting never happened. But, I got a feeling you guys are going to do great. I want to be part of it. Universal pays one dollar per can. If you start with a minimum order of five thousand, you get the same price."

A dollar! Hmm, six cans to a box. So six dollars per box, and we sell it at eighty-nine. It didn't take a math genius to figure the amazing markup.

Dennis' face looked numb. He said what I was thinking. "You've got a deal."

On the flight back I set out our plan.

"We'll continue working at Universal and secretly start up the business. We'll smuggle sales from your reorder department. I'll ask Ross Fascetta to be a partner. He's now my top sales person. We can funnel half of his new orders over. We'll build up a nest egg before officially leaving."

Dennis waved the flight attendant over for another drink. The enthusiasm for our new scheme reddened his chubby cheeks. "We'll need someone to run the business until we come over. We also need to incorporate."

"I know someone who might be able to help."

***

I figured Nick Calabrese could steer me toward someone who would go along with our unethical and possibly illegal scheme.

He knew the perfect lawyer. "I'll set you up with a meeting with Johnny Ciccone, but we need to talk before you meet with him." I'd met Johnny in my youth, but had only vague memories of him.

That was Nick's way of saying, "not over the phone."

"Where?"

"I guess our pizza place."

That night, over pizza and red wine, Nick explained what he couldn't on the phone. "You're a bright kid, and could go places. I'm not introducing you to just an attorney, but the most important Italian one in the state, maybe the country. You know what I mean?"

He meant this lawyer was connected. I nodded.

Nick stopped talking when our deep-dish pizza arrived. When the waiter left, Nick glanced around the room and then continued. "Johnny's dad is John Ciccone, Sr. Ever hear of him?"

I shook my head.

"That's because he's smart. He doesn't want his name to be known. He's the Don, the head of the Chicago Outfit."

"I thought that was Aiuppa or maybe Tony Accardo."

"Accardo handed the reins over to Giancana before he semi-retired. When Giancana was wacked, Aiuppa took control. Aiuppa is sort of retired now, leaving Ciccone in charge. He's ruthless, and no one crosses him."

"His son is an attorney?"

"It's the future. Lots of the old guys send their kids to law school. Considering how much time they spend in courtrooms, it seems like a wise move." He laughed. "Johnny is more than a suit. Word is he's the underboss. For sure he's the consigliere for the Chicago family. I send you to him, and you do good—he makes money. He then is indebted to me. It's the way it works."

"Okay, what about someone to run our business until we are ready to leave Universal?" Nick's face had a smudge of sauce above his lip that looked like a red mustache. For some reason a vision of my Aunt Mary flashed in my mind, and I wanted to reach over and wipe it.

I wondered if the memory of my aunt was a kind of warning God sent me. If it was, I ignored it.

"I already asked Johnny and he gave me this guy." His mustache grew with another bite of pizza. He reached in his pocket and pulled out a small folded piece of paper. "Mario. Mario Lassorella, do you know him?"

"Never heard of him."

"Johnny recommends him. This means he can be trusted. Bring him in."

I didn't like the idea of be dictated to, but the appeal of having such a powerful attorney and ally overcame my hesitation. I called Mario and he invited us to meet him the next night at a nightclub outside the city.

A large board outside announced the evening's entertainment. "The Amazing Mario! Hypnotist and Comic Extraordinaire."

Was this our Mario?

We were escorted to a table next to the stage. Dennis looked at me like I really blew it. "I thought we were meeting with a potential partner, not going to see a cheap club entertainer. How can we talk while there's a show going on?"

Ladies well past their prime filled the room. The few men looked like they had been forcefully dragged. Cigarette smoke merged with green and red strobe lights. The beams shot on the shiny gold velvet curtain to give the room a Christmassy feel. A little bald man shuffled onstage.

"Ladies and gentlemen, without further ado the Amazing Mario!" The women cheered and the men groaned. The curtains rose and a tall man in a white tuxedo jogged to the middle of the stage. His dark curly hair and prominent nose reflected a likely Italian heritage.

His comic monologue was dull, and thankfully short. He seemed to know why everyone was there–hypnosis.

"I need six volunteers." Women swarmed forward with their hands held high. He chose four and two of the men whose arms were forced up by their dates. Six seats were brought on stage and his act began. With a little hocus-pocus, he soon had his targets in a trance.

"When I reach the count of five you will awaken. You will not remember anything, but whenever you hear the word *hand* you will act like a chicken."

They all awoke and Mario continued, "Thank you all for being good sports." Turning to the audience he said, "Let's give them a hand."

All six of them strutted around like chickens.

Dennis laughed.

The act turned raunchier and even funnier. When the curtain came down Dennis looked at me through slightly drunk eyes. "Well, it looks like your guy didn't show up. At least we had a laugh or two."

"Dennis, I've a sneaking suspicion we weren't stood up." Just then the Amazing Mario walked up and introduced himself.

"I'm Mario Lassorella."

I shook his hand.

"I'm Jim Hall and this is Dennis Fader." Dennis looked at me with dazed confusion.

"I thought it might be cool for you to see my act before we sit and talk."

"Mario, it was very entertaining, but I can't help but wonder why Mr. Ciccone recommended you."

"He knew I was looking for something. I can't make a living doing this. I'm a good manager and very good at sales. What exactly are you planning?"

I gave him the plan and we agreed to hire him at Universal Office as a salesman, so he could learn the ropes. We would keep him on the sales floor a couple weeks, and then move him into the reorder department right after that. That gave us time to find a warehouse and office.

The four partners all met with Johnny Ciccone to draw up the corporation papers in National Toner Warehouse, Inc. I was the President, CEO, and Chairman of the Board.

"Well guys, good luck." Johnny shook each of our hands. "Toner, the powder for copiers? Is there any money in it?" When I told him the markup his eyes lit up.

"That's better than dope."

I nodded and grinned. When had Bobo changed into this person?

I wasn't just hungry for money, I was ravenous. I had to find the amount that would satisfy me. But once the downward slide began, the speed increased, and my soul sank deeper and deeper.

As I left his office, Johnny leaned over and whispered. "Call my secretary and set up a dinner for you and me. Let's get to know each other better."

I met Johnny at a tiny Italian restaurant near downtown. The place was packed, and I waited in a line for the Maître D'.

"Sir, do you have a reservation?"

"I'm not sure, I—"

"We are very busy tonight. No reservation, no table."

"I believe Mr. Ciccone might have made one."

The short mustached man went from practically ignoring me to almost tripping over his feet. "Did you say Mr. Ciccone?" If he'd had a palm frond, he'd have waved it at me.

"Yes, Johnny Ciccone."

"I'm so sorry. No one informed us of his desire to dine with us tonight. How many will be joining you?"

"Just us two.

Seated at a table next to a fireplace, I watched in awe as Johnny came toward me. It was like watching a celebrity. Men rose to shake his hand. Women waved and blew kisses as if the Pope had entered the room.

I sat up a bit straighter because as soon as he sat down, all eyes would be on me. My life would change yet again.

I wasn't sure if his first question was a test, or just some conversation.

"Why are you letting them be full partners with you?" Meaning Ross, Dennis, and his chosen Mario.

"I'm creating a team more than a dictatorship."

He waved his hand dismissively. "They are obviously following you, and you have the clout." It wasn't a question, so I stayed silent. He changed the subject to sports, but I couldn't pull my mind off his original point as we wined and dined, and enjoyed impeccable service.

I walked with him as we exited the restaurant. He grabbed my hand and clasped it. "This could be the start of a great friendship. I want to thank you for bringing Mario in. I don't forget favors. If you have any problems with him, call me. I'll take care of it."

The voice in the back of my mind wondered what that meant. But the voice in the front, the one calling the shots, silenced it.

We found offices in northwest Chicago, paid the rent, ordered phones, and shipped the toner in. Meanwhile, Mario worked out of a little office he had in Melrose Park. We funneled business and everything seemed to be going great the first month. Then something suspicious happened.

One of the customer service people at Universal Office Supply came to me with a complaint from a client whose record wasn't in their files. I figured it was a reorder we billed from our new firm. "I'll handle it." I contacted the company, fully expecting they were confused by the different company name. And I was right.

I explained it was part of an internal change and their billing would now reflect National Toner Warehouse as the distributor. That seemed to do it.

Problem was, I had no record of their order. I let it slide, but a small antenna of concern began to rise.

A few days later I intercepted two more calls also billed by my new company. When I couldn't find these orders I knew something was wrong. The next day there were three more suspiciously missing orders. I called the first to ask if they had paid, and they had. Since I controlled all deposits, I waited for their check, but it didn't come.

After two weeks I called the first company that had complained. "I'm just reviewing our records. Have you paid the invoice?"

"Yes, we took care of it right after your call."

"We never received it. Could you contact your bank to see if the check cleared?"

"We just got our statement. Let me look at it before I call them." A minute later they returned. "I've got the cancelled check in my hands. It was deposited with a Texas bank."

"Which bank was that?" I wrote down the name and called them. They informed me a National Toner Warehouse had an account with them, and a Mario Lassorella was the designated officer. The swindlers were being embezzled.

I went to Ross and Dennis and presented my evidence.

Dennis was livid. "How much?"

"So far, thirty-two hundred."

"Let's go give him a visit."

Ross stayed at Universal Office to cover for us. Dennis and I drove out to confront Mario who was his usual affable self.

"What's up guys? I'm surprised to see you this early in the day."

Dennis approached a set of golf clubs sitting in the corner. "Nice clubs. My favorite is the two-iron." He slid one out of the blue bag.

I followed his lead and took a five-iron out.

Dennis swung his club and shattered Mario's coffee cup. Liquid brown oozed down the desk and dripped onto the tile floor.

"Hey! Why'ya do that?"

I took my weapon and hit Mario on his left arm. It wasn't meant to break anything, just get his attention.

"What the...? I don't understand." Mario clutched his forearm.

I took the list of orders I knew he stole and recited the names of the companies. Mario tried to feign ignorance, but he was better at hypnotizing than acting. "You owe us thirty-two hundred dollars." I took mock baseball swings with the club.

The iron inched closer and closer to his head. He recoiled into a corner and defensively raised his arms for protection. "I'm going to take every order form, and anything else that is ours, out of this office. While I do, Dennis will practice his golf swing. You will sit on the chair in the corner. Don't so much as move. I'd hate to see Dennis mistake your head for a ball."

I emptied the contents of the office into Dennis' Chevy Suburban, and returned to give Mario his severance pay. "I want you to go to your desk and sell your percentage back to the firm for one dollar."

He didn't hesitate in doing as I said. I handed him a check. "Get your personal checkbook out, and make out a slip for a one dollar deposit." He seemed to be looking around for an escape route, but Dennis had the door covered. He opened a drawer and did as told.

"Please hand me your checkbook." He did and I checked his balance. "Good. Are these the only monies you stole?"

"Guys, it wasn't that big a deal. I planned on cutting you in. I—"

Dennis hit the desk so hard the wood splintered. Mario's face looked like he saw a ghost.

"That's it. There's no more."

"Okay, write out a check for what you owe us. Dennis will go to your bank, deposit your dollar, and cash your check. I will wait here." While Dennis was gone, Mario tried to smooth talk his way out of this jam, but he was trying to fool a professional con artist—no chance.

Within three weeks I uncovered another four grand he owed us. I couldn't leave work, but Dennis and Ross called Mario and said they were on the way. A few hours later they returned with quite a story.

"You'll never believe what happened when we pulled up at his place." Dennis looked excited, like he couldn't wait to tell me. Ross looked like he needed a sedative.

"Before we could get out of the car, three squad cars surrounded us. They yanked us out and slammed me to the ground. One cop shoved Ross over a car hood. When they found my gun, I figured we were in some big trouble."

"You took a gun?"

"Yeah, I figured he probably packed his golf clubs away. So, they yelled, something about extortion and jail, and I shouted Mario was robbing us. This slowed them down some and one of them pulled me aside. After I told him how Mario embezzled from us, the policeman changed his attitude. And when I dropped the Johnny Ciccone name on him, the river parted. He told me they were just doing a local guy a favor. They took off faster than we arrived." Dennis looked like he was on top of the world.

"Oh, that's not the end of the story. Don't ever send me out with Dennis again for something like this." Ross was always the cautious one, almost timid.

"He..." Ross pointed his finger at Dennis, "he came into the office like he was Al Capone after Eliot Ness." Ross was breathing so hard I thought he would hyperventilate. "He took the gun and shoved it in Mario's face, made him kneel down and pray."

"It was beautiful." Dennis lit up one of his ever-present cigarettes. "I thought he was going to wet himself. He cried and begged like a little girl."

"I was afraid he'd have a heart attack. Dennis, you were out of control."

"I was perfectly in control. Not only did we get the money, he paid us another three grand to never return again."

I figured Mario earned the fear, and his extra payment made us even. That's what I told Johnny as I gave him Mario's resignation letter. From Johnny's words, I'd say he didn't agree.

"I'm shocked he would do you this way knowing I recommended him. If you feel satisfied, then fine. But, I must apologize for his actions. I now owe you, and I hate debts. As partial payment, your incorporation fees are waived. As far as Mario, he dishonored me and stained my word. I don't take this kind of offense lightly, but that's between us."

Johnny caught me before I left his office. "Let's go to dinner tonight. I want to introduce you to a dear friend and my accountant. I hope he can be both with you."

Tony Rizzo did become our accountant, and my close friend. As for Mario, I soon forgot him. But, someone didn't. A year after I told Johnny of Mario's actions, my partners and much of our staff took a cruise from St. Thomas to the Caribbean Islands. When we returned there were two urgent messages. One was from the F.B.I., and the other from Johnny. I called the feds first.

"We've been trying to contact you and your partners since last Thursday. Where have you been?"

"We were on a Caribbean cruise. I took all my managers."

"Where were you last Thursday?"

I thought for a moment. "Thursday and Friday were sailing days returning home from Caracas, Venezuela."

"Can that be corroborated?"

"I'd say so. Between our partying and the casino, we weren't exactly a quiet, unnoticeable group."

"If that's true, it looks like you all have perfect alibis."

"Why would we need an alibi?"

"Your ex-partner, Mario Lassorella, was found shot to death and stuffed into the trunk of his car. It was passed to our division because it looked like a mob hit. We've learned your business breakup wasn't exactly amicable. But, I guess we'll look elsewhere." The moment I hung up on the feds, I called Johnny.

"Johnny, I got your message. It was marked urgent."

"Just wanted to make sure you guys had fun on your cruise."

"Did you hear about Mario?"

"Mario who?"

"Lassorella."

"The name escapes me."

"You know our ex-partner."

"Was that his name? What about him?"

"He was murdered last Thursday."

"Gee, sorry to hear that. I was in Palm Beach at a convention last week. So I've been out of touch with local news. Maybe I'll send flowers to his gravesite. See you guys soon, bye."

It looked like he had a perfect alibi as well.

Chapter 23
Money, Power, and Women

*"I denied myself nothing my eyes desired; I refused my
heart no pleasure. My heart took delight in all my work,
and this was the reward for all my labor. Yet when I
surveyed all that my hands had done and what I had
toiled to achieve, everything was meaningless, a chasing
after the wind; nothing was gained under the sun."*
Ecclesiastes 2:10-11

Our business averaged fifty thousand dollars per week
within a year. Because the sales were so full of lies our
return rate hovered at thirty percent, but the hefty mark-
up more than made up for it. We doubled our revenue
year two. Our salaries and bonuses were getting larger
and larger. We held board meetings in exotic locations,
and traveled first class. Tony and Johnny acted as board
advisors and confidants. I learned about the Chicago
Outfit from Tony. While I wasn't a member of the mafia,
I took part in the enterprise. Best of both worlds.

Throughout the world one mafia rule remained
universal— all must be of Italian decent. After that, each
organization took on its own shape. While Chicago had
similarities to New York's mob, and the mafia of movies,
it was a unique entity.

When Sam Giancana was murdered, and Johnny's
dad took control, the organization structure morphed
more into a corporation. The CEO was the boss, often
called the Don or Godfather in movies. His executive
V.P's were the underboss and consigliore. Sometimes the
same man.

Under these execs, a franchise-like operation existed, run by the capos, with exclusive territories throughout Chicago and its suburbs. They paid franchise fees and a percentage of all money earned to those above them. Each capo managed a crew of made men, or soldiers. They might have different specialties. Gambling, prostitution, protection, and robberies fell under the usual domain of the soldiers' assignments. A good earner might be awarded a branch, or neighborhood to run. They used the threat of pain, or worse, to control their territories.

Numerous associates included bagmen, tough guys, or other mid- to low-level flunkies. If Italian, they often dreamed of becoming made. If not, it was a way to make money with little skills or brains—often the most frightening of all the members because they had the most to prove.

But, the real goal was big money, and that came from other directions. One of the most valuable assets of the mob was the senior associate. Usually they weren't made. The guy might not even be Italian. They were politicians, labor leaders, bankers, police, or anyone who could give the organization the greatest commodity—power. And power equaled money. The doorways to perceived respectability and the best means to mask illegal revenues. If you didn't have powerful and plentiful senior associates you never could become or stay a boss.

The conversation I overheard as a child in church about carnival money was likely with a senior associate. My dad never had enough money or clout to be that high up, but he obviously associated at times. Why else would Sam Giancana's chauffer drive me to Chicago?

My time with Rizzo, Ciccone, and others rarely put me in much contact with anyone below capo status. Like corporate America, the chief executives rarely mix with the staff. Most social contact with Johnny happened at his Italian restaurant in Melrose Park, west of Chicago. Great food, but always an adventure. Walking in guaranteed your picture would be taken. Dennis and I tried to spot the feds in nearby parked cars. Dennis loved waving and mocking poses for their cameras.

The general public sat upstairs. Reservations were required for downstairs, and only those known and trusted could enter. A tremendous amount of mob business conducted in that cave-like room.

"Tony, what's going on down here? It's like one big meeting room for shady looking people. What's the deal?" Rizzo was sitting at the bar, separated by a bedded doorway.

"This place is clean. It's swept for bugs four times a day. Because we meet in a basement, they can't use any of their sophisticated equipment to listen in from across the street."

Often, Johnny's father occupied a corner table. I watched the orchestrated table-hopping in awe. With Sinatra or Tony Bennett songs serenading them, requests started with a capo. They'd return to their table and wait for an audience with Johnny or his dad.

While we ate, it wasn't unusual for Johnny to get up ten times, to join a discussion at another table. When he returned, no one mentioned his absence. Sitting at the table of someone so powerful gave me a rush. Friendship with Johnny seemed a perfect addition to my snowballing success in business.

Dennis and I began planning an operation in another city. I'm not sure why we chose Atlanta for a second office. Maybe the cold of Chicago, and everyone referred to the southern city as "Hotlanta." We arrived in November 1976. I was twenty-nine, rich, and hungry for more. The city was beautiful, so were the ladies. Most importantly, because so many divorcees headed there for jobs, the women greatly outnumbered the men.

I dated a Falcons Cheerleader, and enjoyed the stares when we walked into a restaurant. But, like money, no matter how much I had, I wanted more. Dennis and I ran wild trying to get our fill.

At a nightclub, I asked. "Why don't we move here?"

"Who would run Chicago?"

"It's running smooth now. Even Ross can't screw it up. We'll keep Chicago as the home office, but we'll get an office open here and have blast doing it."

"What about the wives?"

"What wives?" That was our running joke. We both lived so far removed from our spouses it was like we were single. I never told a girl I was married—I usually didn't stay long enough to cause suspicion. Ladies, booze, and money were all ways to fuel my hunger for more.

That changed in May 1977.

Ross visited Atlanta to see the building for our new operation. The first night we went bar hopping off Peachtree Road. A sign read, "The Casbah Disco and Late Night Club."

"Let's check it out."

Around back and up a long set of steps, we entered to a Thelma Houston song, and an empty club. Odd for that time of night. The bartender explained most of their action happened after two in the morning. We finished our drinks and rose to leave when I spotted two ladies dining in the empty restaurant area.

"Ross, let's go check them out."

Then I saw an angel. The disco lights ricocheted off the mirror balls overhead and reflected back to a beautiful blonde dressed in white.

I had to meet her.

"How's the food?"

She then did something no girl in Chicago would. "It's really good." She lifted her fork. "Here, have a bite."

I let her feed me as I dropped into the seat beside her. I'd heard southern accents before, but none like hers.

"I'm Jim, and this is Ross."

He pulled a chair up to the other girl.

I'm sure she introduced her friend, but all I heard was her name.

"I'm Judy." Her smile, her voice, her everything entranced me.

Ross went home with the other girl, and I drove Judy to her apartment. I learned she was recently divorced from a husband who left her for another man. She covered the hurt well.

Then she hit me with, "I have three little girls. We come as a package." She so overwhelmed me, I didn't care if she had a dozen. With a sweet kiss goodnight she said I should call her.

I did, and we planned our first date.

I wanted a perfect place to take her, and lots of folks recommended The Patio as romantic and good. The little French restaurant met my expectations, but Judy more so. I came from a world of "Dees guys," and "What's fer dinner." Her accent came from a different planet.

"Pleaz pahz the glayus."

I concentrated so hard on understanding her I was missing out on being with her, so I did something radical. I stopped listening. I nodded in agreement to everything she said and focused on how beautiful her eyes were when the candlelight flickered in them.

If there was something like love at first sight, I caught it. But I wasn't capable of genuine love. Mine was self-serving and only interested in me.

I had to make her fall in love with me, so I sent her a huge bouquet of flowers every day. I didn't tell her about my wife.

Shirley chose a place in the Buckhead area of Atlanta, and we moved. But I still saw Judy every moment I could.

At Christmas and New Year's, I took Judy and her darling little girls to Aspen for two weeks of skiing. We went on weeklong cruises and traveled at least once a month. Sometimes Dennis brought a girl and sometimes Johnny brought his mistress. Shirley knew of my intimacy with the mob, so I often used it as my excuse for disappearances.

"It's business. You know I can't tell you more." I think she enjoyed the money and the good life so much, it didn't matter I wasn't around. Can't say I blame her. I wasn't a nice person to be around. Combine ego and selfishness with a bad temper...

Judy fell in love with me. Not the real me, but the actor. I played hard at being the perfect companion, and we talked of marriage. I sent her to look for homes. Sometimes she glimpsed my dark side. I grew terribly suspicious and jealous over the smallest things. Since I couldn't be trusted, why should she?

Then one day the inevitable happened. Shirley found out about Judy and called her. Judy was horrified, and she tried to break it off, but I begged and pleaded.

"I'll leave her soon. We'll get married. I love you."

So selfish, I was a little glad when Shirley contracted breast cancer. I used it with Judy as an excuse why I couldn't leave my wife just yet. While I wanted to marry Judy, I wasn't ready to change my life.

The Atlanta office exploded with sales. Almost overnight it more than doubled the Chicago office. Dennis bought a Rolls Royce while I humbly chose a convertible Mercedes. Because of Dennis' multiple DUI's, we invested in a limousine and a chauffeur. We purchased a racehorse at a Keeneland Farms auction for over a hundred thousand dollars. We prophetically named him Fly-by-Night. Life looked good, from the outside.

Why did I feel so empty inside? I had money and power. But, the hollow longing in my soul wouldn't go away. I figured I didn't have enough, so I started plans to open a restaurant with Dennis.

Ross wanted no part of it. We gave him one of our Chicago operations and severed our partnership with him so we could forge ahead.

We planned on a unique concept at that time. TGIF was one of the most popular bars and restaurants in Atlanta, so we decided to do a Mexican version. We settled on the name Carlos McGee's.

The restaurant started well. Everyone loved our frozen drinks and the great mariachi band. Our first two weeks grossed twenty-seven thousand each. Since over sixty percent was liquor, it was clear we had a winner. An assistant manager's idea hurled us to a new level of success, and towards becoming what Fortune Magazine later named one the fifty most popular bars in the country.

"Our band won't be able to play next week. Apparently they had a previous obligation they didn't us about. I know this great band and would love to hire them."

"Better call them soon. We don't want to be without an act."

"There's just one problem. They're a fusion band."

"A what?"

"Fusion. It's kind of progressive rock. I think the young crowd will love them." The assistant manager seemed confident.

Not quite our business model, but maybe he knew something I didn't. Under the pressure of no alternative, I agreed. We increased our take by six thousand that week and signed the band to three more weeks. Within a month we pulled in sixty thousand per week, and the lines to get in stretched for blocks.

Carlos McGee's became so popular, Willy Nelson wore our T-shirt's at some of his concerts. I suppose he liked our theme, "A Sunny Place for Shady People." Very fitting.

Chapter 24
James Bond and the New Deal

"And out of that hopeless attempt has come nearly all that we call human history—money, poverty, ambition, war, prostitution, classes, empires, slavery—the long terrible story of man trying to find something other than God which will make him happy."
C.S. Lewis, Mere Christianity

We soon opened another Chicago toner operation and a very successful one in Baltimore. Rizzo came to Atlanta often, but I usually met with Johnny in Chicago. When Ciccone did fly in, it was often for mysterious reasons.

"Hi Jim, I'll be arriving tomorrow. Okay if I stay at your place?"

Whenever Johnny asked to stay with me and not at a hotel, I knew it wasn't my company he sought. But since I separated from Shirley, I didn't mind.

The attorney arrived, rented a car, and drove to my house. We had a drink, but said very little. We headed out for dinner to an Italian restaurant near the Fox Theatre with a private parking area in the back, hidden from the street. Someone met him there and they left. I ordered a drink and carryout. I left after dark. Tinted windows made it difficult to see inside. Before I exited the car, I closed the garage door. Johnny returned a day or two later, ready for his flight back to Chicago. I knew his stay was an alibi. For what, I rarely knew.

Sometimes I picked him up from one of the two small private airports in the area. He never said where he had been, and I didn't ask. Friends, sure, but friendship in Johnny's world was granted with caution—and nosiness would get it revoked. I paid ten thousand a month for Johnny's legal retainer and brought his firm at least another two hundred thousand a year in fees. That went up after the Baltimore raid.

Dennis and I were meeting with Johnny and Tony at the Ritz Carlton when the call came.

"Jim, I'm glad I tracked you down. There are FBI agents all over the place." It was Mike Smith, the manager I moved from Atlanta to open the operation. "Armed agents poured out of the back of a semi and others were dropped on the roof by a helicopter. It was like a James Bond movie."

I had no words. I handed the phone to Ciccone.

John listened and finally gave instructions. "Okay, that's a good sign. Since they didn't arrest anyone it was just a fishing expedition. Tell everyone to go home. Say you'll be closed tomorrow and to come back the next day."

Johnny told Dennis and Tony what happened. He summarized the raid as, "Another stupid waste of time and money by the feds."

The search warrant mentioned possible drugs being shipped from our warehouse, but clearly they were after Johnny.

"...An illegal enterprise of the Chicago Mafia." They not only thought we distributed dope, but that Dennis and I fronted for the mob.

Fear blended with a touch of pride. This could hurt revenue from the Baltimore office more than it might uncover criminal issues. I didn't think they had anything on us, especially since they were searching for drugs.

The warrant exhibited how little the authorities understood the Chicago Outfit's business. First, and foremost, they hated drugs.

"People don't care if there's gambling and prostitution. But, no one likes drugs. The mob will take a piece sometimes, but they won't get close to it." At least that's how Tony explained it.

The FBI didn't quite get my relationship with Johnny and the mob. Johnny later tried to convince me to let some others front my toner businesses.

"I know some guys. They'll take a little salary and you'll be a consultant. You come in, open them up, train everyone, and keep making money." I was giving that plan serious consideration, including the "Dennis doesn't have to know." My partner was becoming a liability. He rarely worked, and stayed drunk most the time.

I actually had more dealings with Tony than Johnny. When we were ready to plan a second Carlos McGee's he flew into Atlanta with a proposal.

"You guys can do Johnny and me a favor." We were sitting in my high-rise office overlooking the interstate. I went to our liquor cabinet and poured us both a drink. Dennis already had one. I sat back and watched the clouds through the glass walls. I knew being asked a "favor" by Johnny meant it was illegal.

"What is it?"

"Use our company to build the next restaurant." I didn't even know they had a construction company.

"But, we use Troy to do our buildings."

"Let's talk later." We kept equipment at our office and my house that could detect if we were bugged, but we tried to not discuss anything improper at either place. That night at the Buckhead steakhouse, Tony and I sat in the bar waiting for Dennis. We always sat on the far side right below the caricature of Dennis and his Rolls Royce grill on the bar's wall. He and his car were regulars.

"Before he gets here, let me tell you what we want. We have a Las Vegas company called Stardust Construction."

"Is it tied into the casino with that name?"

"Loosely, but that's not important. We have a way to make a little money, and it won't cost you a thing." The bar was getting crowded, but the noise level would make it difficult to be overhead.

"How much do you plan to spend on the building?"

"Seven hundred thou."

"Spend nine hundred and you each get sixty thousand cash."

"Tony, I don't think I need an accounting degree to figure that's not a good deal for us."

"Listen, if you give yourself a bonus of one hundred grand, how much do you take home after taxes?"

"About sixty."

"So you break even in the deal, plus you don't have to worry about the IRS accusing you of making excessive compensation. Since I'm your accountant, assume what you would be doing is legal, and I'll take care of the taxes." He gave me a smile and a wink.

"Like I said, it's favor. I need you to sell Dennis on this. You understand we help each other out, but he's always looking for a deal." He was right about that. Dennis' greatest asset may have been his negotiation skills. He was ruthless.

"Will you use Troy?"

"Yes, he'll work for Stardust while he builds it."

I saw no harm in it, and Dennis agreed. A few weeks later Tony showed up with a briefcase full of hundreds. We split it up, and never discussed it again. These were the type of deals Johnny liked—arm's length.

I never thought of any parallels with my dad's life on the run and the life I was creating for myself. I looked at my father as a small-time crook. I considered myself a bright businessman willing to straddle the legal line to make a buck. Ethics and integrity were for suckers.

Chapter 25
Counterfeit Happiness

*"For all that is in the world—the desires of the flesh and
the desires of the eyes and pride in possessions—is not
from the Father but is from the world." 1 John 2:16*

As I grew more successful, my relationship with Johnny
and the Chicago Outfit flourished. However, the way a
mob boss stays out of prison is to live an ambiguous life.
Concealment and Johnny went hand-in-hand. My times
with him were often like smoke and mirrors. For
instance, the time he asked me to help him with a
clandestine meeting with other mob leaders.

I gave Johnny and Tony a tour of my newest purchase.

"We bought this farm to be a weekend retreat close
enough to Atlanta to get there in an hour, yet isolated
enough to feel like we're away. " I walked them past the
beautiful maze-like boxwood shrubs into the grand old
house being renovated by our builder.

"We're adding a swimming pool and riding horses for
the stable."

"What about all those cows? Are you going to sell
them?" Tony was probably mentally figuring how he
could get a cut.

"We have three hundred head, one for each of our
acres. Cletus, Dennis' half-brother, is moving to the white
house on the edge of our property to work the farm. Most
of the equipment, like tractors, came with the purchase."

Both were impressed by our retreat. Judy and her
daughters enjoyed our get-away. The girls had a blast
riding horses and being daredevils on the three-wheel

motorcycles. Hayrides, fishing, and starlit nights—Johnny, though, saw another way the farm could be used.

It started with a phone call I received in my Atlanta office.

"Jim?"

"Yes?"

"Call me," and then nothing but a dial tone.

I yelled at Jeannine, "I'll be right back," and headed to the elevators. I drove the Mercedes to the nearby Sheraton. I knew Johnny would be at one of three possible pay phones in downtown Chicago.

I arrived at the hotel and went to a row of phones in the back. If someone came close enough to hear me, I'd say, "I love the weather down here."" If someone approached him, I'd hear, "I hate Chicago in the winter time." We would then make small talk until the threat passed.

"Hi Johnny, what's up?"

"Is your farm available for rent in two weekends?"

"It can be. Do you have someone you think wants to rent it?"

"Maybe, I've got to fly to D.C. for business. Can you meet me there?"

"When?"

"Tomorrow."

"I don't know. I have some meetings with my Carlos McGee's staff."

"How about we hook up at the Atlanta airport? I'll take Delta, which means a connection there. I'll call back with some possible times." We were able to settle on meeting at a Delta Crown room early the following afternoon.

As I entered the club, a big man in an out of date overcoat, tapped me on my shoulder. "Are you Jim Hall?"

"Uh, yes."

"The Jim Hall who owns National Toner Warehouse?" What in the...? I thought about not answering, but I couldn't see the harm.

"Yes."

"Good, all I had was a description. I've already asked six other guys. Mr. Ciccone sent me." No real surprise, there. Never was with him.

"There's been a change of plans. Please follow me."

I obeyed and we were soon on a Hartsfield Airport underground train heading away from the terminal. We exited at the International Concourse, and I followed him up the escalator. He pointed down the wing to the right.

"Head down that way. I'll stay here." About halfway down I spotted Johnny standing next to an empty booth at one of the gates.

"I thought you were going to D.C. Are you heading overseas instead?"

"No, just thought these concourses would be a bit emptier this time a day. Come, sit down." We settled on the metal chairs with fake-leather seats. He sat directly across me.

"Sorry for the escort. You may not have spotted them, but there were a couple others further back making sure you weren't followed."

"What's up? I thought this was just about a rental of the farm."

"It is, but this is a most serious and confidential rental. No one must know. Not Dennis, not even Judy. There will be people coming from all over the country, and they will want assurances they won't be bothered." A couple passed by toting some baggage and items purchased at the Duty Free Shop, so I waited.

"That might be tough. What about Cletus and his family? They live there."

"They are about to win a wonderful trip to Florida for that weekend. I expect you'll have a call from him when you return to your office requesting the weekend off."

Smart. "Do you want me to stock it with food? We only have four bedrooms, how many will be staying?"

"We'll take care of the food, and I've rented two very nice motor homes for extra rooms." Johnny stood to signal his departure.

"What do you need me to do?"

"Tony will leave instructions on where to leave a key, and don't go there from Thursday until Monday. Now, I've got a plane to catch." He lifted his brown leather briefcase and was off.

I never knew what happened that weekend, or who attended the meeting. Some Internet research implies that a summit of Mafia bosses took place around that time. However, it was supposedly held in Florida. Since the place looked spotless after that weekend, I'm not even sure if anyone arrived. It might have been another ruse. I suppose I'll never know, but I'll always remember Johnny's final words as he left me at the airport.

"Jim, this is a favor for my dad. I'm sure you know what that means."

I understood. He also took the word *favor* literally. I never received a dime for the rental.

Johnny's desire to stay unnoticed was especially evident when he invited me to a heavyweight boxing championship fight.

"Bring Dennis and Jeannine."

"Why Jeannine?" I was a bit surprised he wanted my executive assistant with us.

"I've got someone I'd like her to meet."

We met Tony, Johnny, and a man they called Michael at the restaurant close to the Horizon Arena near O' Hare Airport. Michael seemed more interested in Jeannine than our meal or conversation.

"I didn't know you were into boxing, Johnny," I mentioned over dessert.

"I am when I own one of the boxers."

"One fighting tonight?"

Johnny nodded. "Main card."

The main event was between James "Quick" Tillis and Mike Weaver for the heavyweight championship of the world. In a world of huge gambling on sporting events, getting an edge was vital.

There was no better edge than a fixed match.

We entered the arena and headed to the front row. Johnny grabbed my arm.

"You want to meet Angelo Dundee?"

"You bet." He was the famous manager of champion boxers, including Muhammad Ali.

After quick introductions we headed back to our seats, but Johnny stopped dead in his tracks.

"No one told me this would be televised." ESPN was a relatively new sports network. "Go tell Tony and Mike to come back here. I need to talk with them."

I followed his instructions and returned to my seat. That evening Dennis, Jeannine, and I watched three matches as close to the ring as possible. The entire night, afraid of being televised, the others stood back in the shadows and never returned to their seats.

Michael asked Jeannine out for a date, and they went the next night. When we returned to Atlanta we learned she was the last person to see him alive. That is, except for the person who killed him and stuffed him into a car trunk.

Whenever a mob hit happened I blocked it from my mind. Its reality didn't agree with my perception. There is a glamorous allure to the mafia. Power, money, and mystery have been strong attractions for centuries. On some levels the mafia delivered all that. It also brought sadness, pain, and misery. I chose to see the glamour.

Maybe the man that Jeannine dated wasn't all that nice. Maybe my ex-partner Mario did cheat us. But in each of their lives loved ones cared. Innocent parents, brothers, children who were affected by their choices and the consequences that followed. When Mike's body was found, my mind placed it in the "try not to think about it" files. However, sometimes late at night the facts appeared and I had to wonder just how far I'd fallen.

Dennis and I went to Vegas often. Tony went at least once a month. However, Johnny always turned down our invitations to join our gambling trips.

At one of our monthly dinners I asked Tony about it.

"His dad is banned from entering a Nevada casino. Since their names are the same, it can be embarrassing at check-in."

I remembered a board meeting on the U.S. Virgin Island of St. Thomas. When we flew home, Jonny was detained because of his name. He had to spend an extra day there. He was freed, but they would have deported his dad back to Italy.

"I didn't think any mob guys could still own casinos."

"They may not be listed, but they direct the official ones. For instance, The Teamsters Union owns the Stardust Casino, but Johnny's dad and the Chicago Outfit control them."

"I hear rumors a lot of money goes missing from the back rooms of casinos." Dinner over, I hoped the drinks had done their job to loosen Tony's lips. As usual they had.

"They call it skimming, and it's where the real money is made. Millions of dollars walk out of the Stardust straight into the pockets of the Family."

I thought for a moment. "I suppose it happens back in the count room, where they tally the daily take. They simply grab a handful of dollars and put in sacks."

He smiled and took another sip. "Nah that worked in the old days, but the gaming commission put rules in place that stopped that."

"So, how's it done?"

A few drinks more and Tony told me. "Kid, it's all about the coins."

"The coins? They steal rolls of coins?"

Tony, now sensing he'd said too much, "Let's just say the Stardust has some unusual ways of controlling coin boxes from the slots. And there are lots of coins."

He changed the subject and I knew not to pry. Later, I learned much more about the Chicago family and its role in casino skimming. A big, dangerous business and it eventually brought Johnny's dad and the head of the Teamsters Union down.

There was only one time Johnny traveled with us to Vegas, and it was at his request. I was at the Sheraton answering one of his secret calls.

"How about a little trip?"

"Where?"

"Vegas?"

"Johnny, I just got back in the office from Christmas vacation in Aspen. I've got a lot of catching up to do."

"C'mon, Tony and some of the guys are coming. Grab Dennis and we'll party. I've got a special reason."

"What's that?"

"I want you to meet Frank Sinatra."

Sinatra!

Johnny continued, "We'll go to his show and then go party with him later. It's his birthday." I'm invited to Frank Sinatra's birthday party?

"When?"

"Monday, the sixth."

We arrived a day before Johnny and Tony. I needed some exercise and went for a run. Las Vegas in the daylight could make the happiest person weep. At night, the city came alive with lights, but in the glaring desert sun, it looked sad. A couple cars, a delivery truck, and a city bus passed me as I jogged the concrete strip.

The rest of the day Dennis and I gambled, drank, lounged in the sun, and saw a show. Around three a.m. I figured I'd better get some sleep and headed to my room. The bedroom of my suite, like all Vegas bedrooms, was darker than black. The massive wall-sized curtains against the suite's windowed walls blocked any light from peeking in from the strip. Seemed like a wise design decision in a city known for night lights and bright days. I was exhausted, but sleep wouldn't cooperate. I waited for something. If only I knew what.

I turned on the light. It was impossible to sleep in that town anyway. As I exited MGM Grand's elevators, bells rang and coins clanged on metal plates. The smell of smoke from the cigarettes and cigars almost gagged me.

Later that afternoon, Dennis and I were the only ones at the high-minimum limit blackjack table. At one time, I was up to six tall stacks of hundred dollar chips and two of five hundred. I should have stopped then, but didn't. I wanted to win more. With me, it was always about pushing the envelope. I lost it all.

I changed into my best silk suit and headed down to dinner. As I stepped into the exclusive restaurant, I saw Johnny surrounded by six guys. Dennis, Tony, and Ronnie the Greek, but I didn't know the other three. I walked into the huge room, centered with a large chandelier hanging from the ceiling. Below the crystal lights stood a long portable bar between two huge round tables. A lavish mirror surrounded by an ornate gold frame hung behind the bar. A marble block offered a squadron of liquor and wine bottles, arranged like good soldiers, to be used in the evening's drinking battles. That's where everyone clustered.

I walked toward the group and the strangers stopped talking and stared at me. Johnny grabbed my right hand, and put his left arm around me. The three guys relaxed and returned to their conversation. As we embraced, he whispered, "I was with you last night. What show did we see?" Alibi time.

"Joan Rivers."

"Come on. Let me introduce you to a couple guys." The three were introduced by first name only. They were from Cleveland. I knew better than to ask their last name or what they did for a living.

The Maître d', with arms spread wide, walked up to Johnny, "*Buena Sera, Senor Ciccone.*"

"*Buena Sera, Senor Costello. Come stai?*"

They talked to each other for a few moments more in Italian, most of which I didn't catch. I did hear him say something about Johnny's dad and Johnny responded, "*Vero, vero. Trazie.*" True, true. Thank you.

"*Prego, prego,*" the Maître d's hands flapping like a mother hen's, guided us to the table on his left.

Once seated, a waiter filled our wine glasses. Johnny rose and made the toast, "*Cento anni di salute e felicita!*" Cheers, a hundred years of health and happiness. In unison, with glasses raised we responded, "*Salute!*"

The waiters brought out platters of food and placed them in the middle of our massive table. Lobsters, steaks, pastas, and antipasti covered all but our dinnerware.

Tony leaned over, "This is the way the early mafia leaders, the Mustache Pete's, would eat when they all got together."

Ronnie laughingly whispered, "It's a La Cosa Nostra smorgasbord." The food continued and the wine flowed.

Johnny sat on the other end of the table, mostly speaking with the strangers. A couple times he'd motion to one or two of them and they'd head to the other end of the restaurant for a more private conversation.

Toward the end of the meal, the waiters brought out platters of fruit and cakes and filled the table across from us. Then, with much drama, they splashed liqueurs on top of the dessert creation. The Maître d' appeared with a small torch and lit the center.

Ronnie yelled, "*Opa!*" We all laughed as waiters wheel out different flavors of ice cream to top our flaming desserts.

Self-indulgent. Important. Decadent. Just the way I liked it.

The meal was comped by the hotel, but not the tips. So as we stood to leave for Caesar's Palace, Tony put out his hand to collect money. We each contributed two hundred and headed for the waiting limousine.

Caesars Palace buzzed. We entered Cleopatra's Barge and looked down on the milling crowds. Everywhere I looked, little old ladies grinned as they posed with toga-clad waitresses and gladiators for souvenir picture mementos of their trip.

Once seated in the luxurious floating lounge, someone in a tux approached Johnny and whispered. Johnny stopped smiling. He motioned me over.

"Sorry, no Sinatra tonight."

"Why not?'

"His mother was in a plane crash in Palm Springs. Paul Anka loaned him his jet and is performing for him tonight."

Dennis shrugged. "I like Paul Anka more anyways."

Johnny gasped and the other faces looked like a nun's after hearing blaspheme. To them, Sinatra was like a god.

We headed to the showroom and were escorted to our front row booths. Anka did a great job and at the finish of his rendition of *My Way* he changed the lyrics from "And I did it my way" to "... Johnny's way." As he sang, he pointed to our booth.

We stayed at our tables and waited for the star to join us. The room cleared out and Paul came over, spoke with Johnny, shook all our hands and left. The party was canceled. Paul Anka wasn't the partying type and most importantly, he wasn't Sinatra.

That night sleep again played its hiding game. Lying in the king-sized bed, in the dark oversized suite, I couldn't help but remember how I hated feeling isolated as a child.

Yet, I never felt as alone.

Chapter 26
Presidential Power

"They are darkened in their understanding, alienated from the life of God because of the ignorance that is in them, due to their hardness of heart." Ephesians 4:18

I appreciated the warm limo that chilly November evening. Cold even by Chicago standards. I opened the bar and poured myself a drink. I relaxed and turned the TV on for a long rush-hour drive from my house in Oak Lawn to downtown. I flipped through blurry channels and finally settled on the local news.

Tony Rizzo and I planned at least one meal together each month. I never told Dennis about them. Johnny had never thought too much of my partner, and I was being groomed for something. I just didn't know what. Tony was often used as Johnny's mouthpiece and a cautious way to get me more involved with the Outfit. Often these dinners were just small talk among friends. Sometimes they were more serious.

"You can wait at the bar. Have them add your tab to my dinner bill." I gave my chauffer his instructions and entered Gene and Georgetti's Restaurant. We ate there often and always at the same table, probably that area was regularly swept for bugs. Tony was already there, and looked way ahead of me in the drink department.

I never exactly knew Tony's role with the mob. He was obviously the accountant for many of them, and had a close relationship with Johnny. His brother ran many strip clubs and porno theatres, but I wasn't sure how deep he was involved. Vagueness—the Outfit's best friend.

"Hi partner, how you doing?" A big guy at six-foot-six and well over three hundred pounds, he first reminded me of Luca Brasi in the original Godfather movie. In reality, he was more a gentle giant.

"Fine, Tony. How long you been here?"

"About three drinks long." He looked down at his glass. "And it looks like I'm about ready for the fourth."

It was election night and the place was packed. The restaurant was a favorite for both politicians and mobsters, something hard to differentiate. The TV in the bar showed the returns and every now and then an explosion of applause leaped into the dining room.

"I sure hope we keep Carter, not that actor Reagan." Tony's words slurred some.

"What about the local elections?"

"They're all in the bag. They always are around here."

Everyone knew the mob in Chicago controlled the Democrats, and thus most of the state's political power. I also had good reason to believe they were hoping to have some influence in the White House with Carter reelected. My suspicion stemmed from a banquet six weeks prior.

Dennis and I each received the same invitation.

"You and your guest are cordially invited to the annual Italian American Hall of Fame Banquet. This year's inductee: Tommy Lasorda." It was to be held at the main banquet room of a Hyatt Regency Hotel.

Johnny was the chairman of the Hall of Fame and had asked we make a contribution earlier that year. We sent fifty thousand dollars in Carlos McGee's name, and they placed a recognition plaque on one of its walls.

"Fifty grand and all we get is a plate on the wall and free dinner." Dennis never did like the idea of sending the contribution. He made the same complaint when I made a twenty-five thousand gift to a local theatre group.

"Dennis, if you are successful it's expected you'll give to some causes. Whether it's public recognition, or future favors just consider it an investment.

He shrugged and said he was heading down to the Buckhead Carlos McGees for drinks. No surprise, he practically lived there.

The evening of the banquet Judy looked spectacular in the new Lynx coat I'd bought her. Our round table included Tony and his date, Ronnie a friendly Greek man I understood to be a former cop turned hit man, Johnny's mistress, and some faces I vaguely recognized from Johnny's restaurant. Johnny, his father, and their wives sat at the main table with Tommy Lasorda.

The meal went as expected until a man in a dark suit approached the Greek at our table. He whispered in Ronnie's ear.

Ronnie rose. "Excuse me, going to the washroom."

Soon, the whispers seemed to spread to all the tables. One by one, men rapidly exited from each table.

"Tony, what's up?"

"I think I know, but I'm not sure."

Soon there were no more than a handful of men remaining in the huge room. It seemed most left their dates to hit the toilet at the same time. Johnny went to the podium to speak.

"We are extremely proud of our country and are most pleased to have a wonderful president in office. He not only loves the Italian people, but also is sympathetic to the unfair way we are portrayed in the movies and media. Tonight, with much pride, I introduce the president of the United States."

He motioned for us all to rise as the band played "Hail to the Chief." A group of men flanked a thin man shaking hands and waving to the crowds. I looked at Judy and laughed. "It's one of those imposters." I had to admit the act was convincing.

When they reached the podium the man began to speak. "My fellow Americans." He took a long pause and flashed a grin of huge white teeth. "And Italians are some of the greatest Americans." The crowd rose in thunderous applause. If this was an act, the guy was very good.

Judy leaned over. "It's him. It's Jimmy Carter."

Wow, it was. He gave a short speech, had some pictures taken with Johnny and his dad, and left. I was flabbergasted. I couldn't imagine the president getting that close to the head of the Chicago Outfit, let alone being photographed with him. A few moments after the presidential entourage departed all the missing men returned to their seats. I leaned over to the Greek.

"You missed it. President Carter was here."

"Oh really, wish I could have seen that."

Tony whispered, "They all left once they knew for sure the president had arrived. The Secret Service made it clear no one with guns could be in the room."

Right. "Did you know he was going to be here?"

"I knew they were trying to cut a deal with the president's people. I guess they did."

"What kind of deal?"

"He's behind in the polls and desperately needs all the votes he can get. We promised to try and get him elected. He's promised to be friendly to our needs and concerns. Not like that jerk Kennedy."

The memory of that evening disturbed me because I somehow expected more from Jimmy Carter. He was supposed to be this great Christian, even a Sunday School Teacher. Judy tried to get me to go with her to church at times. Just like the president, it was Southern Baptist. Carter had to know about the mafia influence when he showed up at that banquet. His willingness to be in bed with the mob disappointed me and added fuel to my doubts about God.

At our dinner at Gene and Giorgetti's, the election-night conversation moved back to Tony's observation at the Hall of Fame Banquet.

"You mentioned at the banquet that Carter would be a friendly ally in the White House. But what did JFK do to rile you up?"

A grenade of curse words exploded at our table. "Worse mistake we ever made. I'm glad they killed the

S.O.B." This wasn't the first time I witnessed astonishing anger when President Kennedy's name was mentioned. It seemed everyone connected with the Outfit hated him.

I let the "they killed" slide. When Tony drank, he loved to talk. If he wanted to add more, it wouldn't take any prodding. Our discussion traveled from politics to football. The Bears beat the Packers, and there was plenty to talk about. About midway into our second bottle of Chianti we heard more applause from the bar.

"Let me go see how Carter's doing." Tony said.

"While you're at the bar, make sure my driver's still sober enough to drive."

When Tony returned he dropped his huge frame into his leather seat and said, "It's still too close to call. But, the network declared Teddy Kennedy a huge winner in his Senate race." The cursing returned. "The jerk kills a girl, wins in a landslide. I hate that family."

I asked the obvious, "Why, and who do you think killed President Kennedy?"

Between bites of steak and sips of wine, Tony told me what he knew. "I don't know all the details, but I can tell you one thing, that Oswald punk wasn't smart enough to plan the killing."

"Are you saying he didn't shoot the president?"

"Nah, as far as I know he pulled the trigger. But, someone put him up to it. Whenever I ask who, I usually get silence."

"Who do you think?"

"Sam Giancana."

The same man who sent his driver for me years before, killed the president? I leaned forward and topped Tony's glass off.

"What makes you think he was responsible?'

"I was in a room with him and some other connected guys when someone mentioned they doubted Oswald did it. Giancana simply smiled and said, "He may have been no smarter than a one-year old, but he was an excellent shot."

"Besides, I can't think of anyone who had more reason to see Kennedy dead."

"How's that?" The drinks were beginning to slow my words and brain.

"You got to go back to when Giancana dated that Exner broad."

I knew the mafia chief had been dating the famous singer Phyllis McGuire, but had never heard about Exner.

"Sinatra introduced her to Sam and they became a hot item. She later admitted to an affair with Kennedy. Probably a little jealousy. Sam wanted nothing to do with the then senator. When Joe Kennedy called Mayor Daley asking support of Jack for president, the mayor told him it would depend on Giancana's approval."

Tony reached in his coat pocket and took out his cigar case. Like magic our waiter took out a lighter and lit it.

"Shall I bring our dessert cart over?"

"Yeah, a bottle of Sambuca with some seeds too."

"Where was I? Oh yeah, Sam was a bit ticked the Kennedy kid had been with his girlfriend. Joe Kennedy, the daddy, was a former bootlegger and had many dealings with Sam's friends. So Joe contacts his old buddies and they arrange for a meeting, and a deal was struck."

"A deal?"

"Sam, and his friends, would help get Kennedy elected, but they wanted two things in return." He stopped, teasing me.

"What?" I had to fight the urge to lean forward lest I look too eager.

The cart arrived and we chose our desserts. The waiter poured the Sambuca and we each reached for three seeds, coffee beans, to be added to our drinks. Johnny introduced the anise-based liqueur. "You drop three beans in for good luck."

When the waiter left Tony continued, "For some time the FBI didn't care much about the mob. They concentrated more on the communists, but Apalachin, New York changed that." The late 1950's raid on almost a hundred American Mafioso leaders had been a huge news story.

"If Kennedy got elected, he had the power to turn down the heat from the FBI. That was the first condition. The second was to get Castro out of Cuba. Giancana, Meyer Lansky, and Santo Trafficante all own casinos and clubs in Havana. That is, until Castro nationalized them."

"Joe Kennedy agreed his son would honor the two requests. Sinatra and his Hollywood pals did tons of fundraisers to help bring in money. Much of it was mob money. I heard they raised more than fifteen million."

I vaguely remembered old film clips of Sinatra and his rat pack entertaining John Kennedy. Tony poured us both another shot of Sambuca, dropped three beans in each glass, and took out his gold Dunhill lighter. His thumb flicked a flame, and he lit the liqueur. We brought the glasses to our noses to inhale the licorice odor. They soon clinked together in a toast.

"Salute!"

"So the mob sent a lot of money Kennedy's way?"

"Not only that, they did what they could to fix the election. There were a lot of people who didn't want a Catholic president. The mob made sure the unions supported him big time. He never would've won West Virginia without their help."

"Daley stuffed the Cook County ballots on election day. Good thing too, because Kennedy only won the state by about eight thousand votes. There's no doubt the mob did its part." Usually about this time at our monthly meals Tony would bring up anything new he wanted me to know. Tonight, though, he was on a roll presenting his conspiracy theory.

"Now we all know Jack makes his brother Bobby the Attorney General. And the punk kid goes on a rampage against the mob. Sam has a meet with Joe Kennedy, and the old man says to give it time. Well, before long there were all sorts of Congressional hearings. Everyone was livid. Then the president double-crosses us by not helping with the Bay of Pigs invasion and Castro stays in power. Like I said, I don't know all the details. Bottom line, no one, not even a president double-crosses the mob and gets away with it."

The time Calabrese and I fixed the books at the Indy 500 flashed through my brain. Hidden deep behind the glitter and excesses of the mob lived a shadowy warning—enter at your own risk.

Our dinner finished that night with the news that President Carter lost. Maybe God thought it was best for him to leave the temptations of politics. As far as the murder of John F. Kennedy, I think it's possible the mob played a part. Part of the culture so long, nothing they did surprised me. Like much of the country I cried when I learned Kennedy had died. Now, my heart had hardened so much it didn't bother me that the mob might have been responsible for a presidential election.

Chapter 27
Shades of Gray

"You belong to your father, the devil, and you want to carry out your father's desires. He was a murderer from the beginning, not holding to the truth, for there is no truth in him. When he lies, he speaks his native language, for he is a liar and the father of lies."
John 8:44

Shirley and I divorced in 1982, and I married Judy soon after.

Nobody every impacted my heart as much as Judy. Yet, my love for her was still self-seeking. She knew the feds were after us, but I always assured her everything would be okay. I really believed it would be. And she trusted me.

Dennis and I always knew our toner sales tactics were not exactly honest, but we never expected the raid on our Baltimore office. After the raid we considered closing, but the money flow was too enticing.

Johnny sent one of his law partners to Baltimore to convince the staff to sell as usual. They were told their sales tactics were legal, "But in a gray area."

Dennis and I consulted some Atlanta attorneys' opinions. They agreed the initial sale seemed legal, but the reorder presentation probably wasn't. Dennis didn't care. He flew to Baltimore to make sure nothing slowed the reorder money down. I thought the whole thing would go away, until the indictments.

All the Maryland office managers were indicted for wire fraud. Dennis, Johnny, and I were listed as unindicted co-conspirators. Johnny explained we were believed to be involved in the scheme, but there wasn't enough evidence to indict us.

Johnny and his stable of Italian lawyers represented my employees. The company paid all expenses. The plan? Vigorously defend them in court, and make sure we weren't implicated. Johnny tried his best to get the case transferred to the Chicago Federal District Court.

"We control all the courts here, even the federal level."

The Assistant U.S. Attorney and Chief Federal Judge of the Baltimore District opposed all our arguments. It seemed my guys were headed for trial, and then the prosecution threw a curve ball. She motioned that all defendants have separate counsel. Johnny had each attorney assigned to two defendants. The fees increased, and Johnny was short one trusted staff attorney. Before he could bring one in from another area, the prosecutor had the court appoint a Baltimore area lawyer to one of them. Within in a day, the guy copped a plea.

I hardly knew him, so I doubted he could point a finger at me. But, there was a reason the feds had a ninety-five percent conviction record. Once someone took a deal, other defendants lined up to get theirs. The pressure to plead out, and hopefully get no jail time is enormous. But it's a trading game. They don't offer major sentence reductions unless they get something in return. In this case the offer carried only if the defendants could help the prosecution nail the real targets—us.

As the defendants asked for new court-appointed attorneys we fired them all, but kept the office open. Johnny's idea presented maverick employees that went too far. I, however, noticed a difference in Johnny. He seemed more guarded in conversation, and no longer found excuses to get together.

I went to Dennis with my worry. "Johnny is more concerned with covering himself than us. We need some impartial advice on what to do." Dennis agreed.

We searched for the best attorney in the Baltimore and Washington D.C. area. We tried to meet with Robert Bennett in D.C., but he was in the middle of a trial and recommended Judah Best, also in the Capitol. Dennis and I flew out to meet with him.

The offices of Steptoe and Johnson on Connecticut Avenue were as plush as the number of associates in their firm. The large conference room overlooked the busy street. Dennis and I nursed our coffee cups as we watched Judah read the indictment paperwork.

"I don't get it." His eyes raised above the Ben Franklin glasses balanced on the tip of his nose. He was near the end of the stack of stapled pages we presented him. "This doesn't look like something the federal courts care about. It should be a civil FTC case. Are you two involved in something else?"

"No." We answered in unison.

"I just don't get it. You have any dealings with people whose names end with a vowel?"

"Well, Johnny Ciccone is our attorney and a board advisor." Judah took his glasses off.

"Do you guys know who his father is?"

We nodded like little kids caught stealing.

"I've worked some with Johnny on Teamster issues. If he has been close to you guys, then we know why the feds are interested. What they want are you two. If they get you, maybe they get Ciccone. So, do you want to cut a deal or fight this?"

"Why should we cut a deal? We've always been told what we do may be unethical, but legal. It's in the gray area." Dennis seemed hot at the suggestion.

I cringed at what Dennis said. I'd tried to believe I was a good person. I hid the truth from myself. I'd become my dad.

"And who told you that?"

"Ciccone."

"Your gray just turned black. He'll never testify. Guys like him never do."

"Johnny is a friend, I think he will." I really believed what I was saying. I looked out the massive windows of the opulent meeting room and saw that it was now dark out. I heaved a sigh. Appropriate.

"Here's my suggestion. You go see him. Have him give you an affidavit on how he advised you. If you get that, you might just beat this."

"Should we close the Baltimore office down?" Deep inside I felt it would be best, but Dennis hated to see that source of income go away.

"I'd keep it operating. We may use it as a bargaining chip later."

I felt upbeat and certain Johnny would cover for us. I called Tony from my Watergate hotel room. "Tony, Dennis and I are in Washington. We met with Judah Best, an attorney Johnny knows. He says we can escape future indictments with Johnny's statement. Can you set up a meeting with him tomorrow?"

"I'll see what I can do. I'll get back with you." Tony called a short while later and said he'd pick us up at the airport. Dennis and I had a great steak dinner and felt things were looking up.

It was a cold clear Chicago morning when Tony pulled up in his white Lincoln. The trunk popped open and we threw our bags in. "What time are we seeing Johnny?" I hopped in the front, Dennis the rear.

"We're heading straight there." We small talked some before I noticed we weren't heading downtown to Johnny's office. I didn't say anything until we turned to hotel row near the airport.

"What's up? Where we heading?"

"To a nearby hotel, Johnny figured he'd meet us there." We pulled into a Sheraton parking lot and followed Tony to the health club near its lobby. Tony told an attendant that we were with the Rothschild party, and we were waved in without signing anything. When I glanced at Dennis he looked as confused as I felt.

"Why are we here?"

"Johnny has a cold. He said for you two to meet him in the steam bath."

The steam bath? I couldn't help but think of some old gangster movie. I then noticed some very big men standing nearby like giant sentries. If either of us were wired they'd be our escorts out. Dennis and I undressed, grabbed some towels, and opened the door. The cloud of steam made it difficult to see. I made out three figures sitting on the top bench. My eyes adjusted and I could tell that Johnny was in the middle flanked by two men, both had towels and unfolded newspapers on their laps.

"See you later guys." Johnny dismissed the men, but I clearly saw the outline of a gun under one of their papers. I wasn't sure if I was meant to see it, but I knew our relationship had drastically altered.

I didn't know about Dennis, but by the time we sat down I was already sweating. And it had nothing to do with the steam. Johnny guardedly agreed to get us a statement and testify for us if there was a trial. Dennis and I, ecstatic over the news, rapidly showered and left. When we had dinner with Tony that night I patiently waited for him to have enough drinks to loosen his tongue.

"So Tony, what do you think? When will Johnny give us the statement?"

"I shouldn't talk about this, but my guess is there will be no statement. He probably meant it when he said it, but I'm sure he's talked to his dad since then. The first rule of self-protection is to never put anything in writing. The second is to never testify in a courtroom if you can avoid it. If there's a trial he'll be in some place no subpoena could ever reach him. It's not about you guys. He likes you. It's just smart business."

"I don't get it. How can it hurt him?"

"Let's say it's a crime. The feds would say he's been advising you to continue with the scheme so he could keep making the hundreds of thousands you pay him. He's in a no-win situation."

"What if we're indicted?"

"That's a long way off. Lots of things can happen before then. Johnny says your D.C. attorney is one of the best. The guy was able to keep Spiro Agnew out of prison. No small feat. Hire him, and he'll find a way to keep you out of prison."

The realization that Johnny wouldn't help cut deep inside me. Friendships were expendable in the mafia. I had chosen my direction in life, and it led straight to Johnny and the mob. I was being used. Much like I treated the many girls I dated over the years. More than hurt, I was angry. Not so much at Ciccone, but myself. *How could I be so stupid?*

At a tremendous financial cost we did as Tony advised. Judah knew every trick in the book, but it seemed the federal prosecutor and judge wouldn't budge. All of our Baltimore employees pleaded guilty and agreed to testify against us. Dennis, Johnny, and I were all informed we were official targets. A year after retaining him, Judah called me with more bad news.

"It looks like indictments are only a few months away, and they're going for RICO." I'd heard the term applied in mafia movies. All I remembered was the "R" for Racketeering.

"But, we're not a mafia organization."

"The RICO act is very broad. Basically, if you make money from something illegal, everything you invest that money in is part of the scheme. This means your Carlos McGee's investments are at risk. You face higher minimum time in prison and forfeiture of everything you own, even your home."

When I informed Dennis how grave this was getting all he said was, "Let me see if I can find a way to fix this."

A few days later Dennis asked me to fly with him to Chicago. "There may be a solution to our problems. We're meeting with Randy Luppa to discuss it." Randy, an attorney on Johnny's staff, had been assigned to two of my Baltimore guys until the feds split them up. I'd heard his father was connected, but wasn't sure.

Our company apartment was attached to the building that housed the famous Pump Room restaurant. Dennis seemed upbeat and happy over dinner. I didn't know what he had up his sleeve, but I was certain the feds were not going away. The next morning I heard Dennis' plan, one I will never forget.

"This is where we're eating breakfast?" Why would Dennis set up this meeting at such a dump?

"It was his idea. He picked the spot." Dennis looked on top of the world. I knew he had something up his sleeve.

The place gave the term greasy spoon a bad name—and smell. Randy sat at the counter on some backless round stool flanked by two others obviously reserved for us. I looked at Dennis and whispered, "How are we going to have a meeting sitting up there?" He just smiled and took the seat to the right of the attorney.

Ashtrays, most still packed with stubs, lined the counter. I was handed a laminated menu, but I'd rather drink the water in Tijuana than take a chance eating the food. "I'll just have coffee," I told the waitress.

Both Randy and Dennis had no reservations. They ate huge platefuls of eggs without a word.

"Let's go for a walk." Randy flipped some money on the counter and we followed him. He was short, and a little younger than me. His beige silk suit jacket ruffled in the cool April winds of Chicago.

"Here's the deal. If the prosecutor is gone, they'll just assign another. The biggest problem is the judge. We need a judge who'll agree to change the venue to Chicago. Since your home office and many of your businesses are in Illinois it makes sense in a RICO case. The judge on your case won't go with it. But even if a new judge were brought in, the current U.S. Assistant Attorney would strongly fight the change. It seems they are both major liabilities. My suggestion is they both go, but it would be difficult."

"Gone" and "go" jumped out at me. We turned unto a block with a ridiculous amount of construction noise.

Randy drew us close to him. "We know where they both live, but taking out both of them would create a huge firestorm. Imagine a Baltimore federal judge and an assistant U.S. attorney both getting hit? Not only would the press be all over it, but it wouldn't sound like a coincidence. You have to figure they'd check what cases they were working on. It could easily be traced back to you. It would also get the other families upset over the heat something like this would produce. I've talked with Ronny and he thinks he can work something out when they're together at some legal function."

What? Murder them? It was like I was having an out of body experience.

We walked across the street and stopped outside the window of a not yet open laundry. "If a tragic accident happens, then your problems are over. However, there may be some peripheral damage. It's hard to be exact about accidents."

The pounding jackhammer was no more intense than the beating of my heart. Murder was Dennis' plan. Peripheral damage meant bystanders might also die. I couldn't believe Dennis seriously considered this. Somehow I misunderstood or Dennis must have been drunk when he launched the inquiry.

But his question made it clear how involved he was. "What's it going to cost?"

"Seven-fifty for the entire operation. That includes expenses. Two-fifty for the broad and five hundred for the judge."

I don't know what else was discussed. My brain stopped functioning and I worried my heart would follow. On our drive to the airport Dennis was talking, but the same words repeated in my mind.

Is this how far you've fallen? Is this how far?

When we arrived in Atlanta our chauffer met us in front of the baggage claim. As we waited for our luggage, my head cleared. I grabbed Dennis by his arm and yanked him where we couldn't be heard. "There is no way I'm going to be involved in this." I expected some angry push back, but Dennis remained calm and content.

"I agree. The price is too steep. Johnny should pick up a third, or no deal." He was thinking about negotiating murders. For years he was as close as a brother. At that moment I wanted to disown him.

A few weeks later Judah Best requested a meeting at his office. "It looks like you both will be indicted next week. I may be able to beat the RICO part, but you guys need to prepare for a trial. However, the government put a deal on the table and I'm obligated to tell you." I wasn't sure why we were in their basement computer room. Usually we met with a slew of attorneys, but Judah and his associate Patricia Riley were the only ones with us.

"You testify against Johnny, and any other mobster you have information on, and you get money and witness protection."

Once again I felt trapped in a mafia movie.

Dennis jumped in with the questions. "How much money? Explain this protection program, how it works. Can we keep our businesses?"

"The offer is one million dollars each. They are talking with the IRS on how to make it tax-free. You would be given a new identity, and moved to an unknown location. And no, all your businesses would be confiscated."

Dennis complained, "Not enough! The restaurants alone are worth much more."

My thoughts were on two things. First, there's no way Judy would leave her mother and family in north Georgia and disappear. And second, I wasn't sure anyone could protect us against the mob if I took the stand against Johnny. "Mr. Best, I will never testify against Johnny."

"Then, you might lose everything."

"What kind of deal would they offer for a guilty plea, but no testimony?"

Dennis jumped up. "I did nothing wrong! There's no way I'm pleading guilty."

"Boys, at times like this I like to separate my clients for a brief discussion. Pat, would you take Jim to the other side of the room."

We passed huge IBM computers that stood over five feet tall. I supposed Judah chose this as our meeting place so no one could hear us over almost deafening noise.

"Jim, it seems you're leaning in a different direction than Dennis?" She was tall and lanky with a Katharine Hepburn appeal.

"Pat, I just don't know. Some things have happened recently that have me questioning my entire life. I know I don't want to risk losing everything. Prison would be tough enough, but my wife and little girls homeless is another." Pat motioned towards a tiny office nearby. I followed her and sat on a tiny wooden chair. She leaned on the metal desk and said something that set everything in motion.

"Jim, I've been in many meetings with you, grown to like you. Can I ask you a personal question?"

"Sure."

"You have lots of money and grownup's toys. Are they the most important things in your life?"

The question hit me hard. "No, maybe they were. My family is more important."

"That's good, but it's possible you've added them to your shelf of toys. Why were you willing to do almost anything for financial success?"

Tears dampened my eyes. I couldn't answer her.

"Are you happy with your life?"

"Sometimes."

"Jim, that's the point. No matter how much you have, it's never enough. The happiness things bring is always temporary. I don't want to influence your decision, but don't make it based on money. Follow your heart."

"Find out what they would offer me for a plea, with no testimony." Where did that come from?

"Wait here."

I sat in the tiny office trying to concentrate on what she'd said. How can I follow my heart when it's lost? Fear swept through me like a cold wind. I didn't want to be isolated from Dennis, but his willingness to murder drove a barrier between us so wide I knew no bridge could bring us back together again. I thought of my dad living his outlaw life running from the law. If I took the witness protection offer I'd be following in his footsteps. But I'd have a different more ruthless pursuer.

When Pat returned she had Judah with her.

I stayed in the chair because I was afraid my legs wouldn't do their job.

"I told Dennis to take a cab back to the hotel, but he refused to leave without you. He's waiting upstairs in our lobby. Here's the offer. You plead guilty to one count of wire fraud. They will recommend five years. We will present a case for less. Pat is excellent in presentencing strategy. If you make the deal it pretty much saves Dennis from being indicted for RICO. If they don't nail you for it, they can't go after your partner."

"I want to call my wife." The call was quick. Judy wanted me to do what was best and honest. She trusted me. I didn't deserve her. I looked up at Pat. "Will I really have to do jail time?"

"It depends on how hard the prosecutor pushes, the case we present and the judge's mood. I am going to try hard for community service, not prison time."

"Let's do it." A part of me couldn't believe I was agreeing to this, another was relieved.

Judah lifted the phone receiver. While he talked I noticed a small metal nameplate on the edge of the desk in the office we borrowed. *Robert Briscoe, I bet you will never know I just agreed to be named a felon in your little office.*

"They accepted it. Tomorrow you make your plea and the judge will set a sentencing date."

"Tomorrow? That seems so fast?"

"It's how they do it. They don't want you to change your mind."

When the elevator door opened I saw Dennis holding his huge mobile phone. He waved and finished his call. "Let's get out of here and get a drink."

I told him of my deal in the cab and he exploded. I didn't know that many curse words existed. He finally calmed down after I explained he wouldn't face the RICO charges.

The next day Pat accompanied me to the courtroom where the judge, the assistant U.S. attorney, and a court stenographer waited. Dream-like, I pleaded guilty, and the sentencing was set for August fifteenth. The hearing sped by so fast I hardly had time to worry. A federal marshal took me to a room for a mug shot and fingerprints. In a little less than an hour I'd become a convicted criminal.

Before I flew home, I stopped in Chicago to talk with Tony at the airport. "Tony, tell Johnny I turned down a deal to talk about him. Tell everyone I would never say anything about them in anyway."

"I'll tell him. If you stay true to your word, no harm will come to you."

For the three months before my sentencing I did very little. I had to sell all my interests back to Dennis, so I had no job. Pat interviewed people and hired a special consulting firm to help prepare her case. The March of Dimes agreed I could work for them pro-bono as my community service.

August fourteenth, Judy and I flew to D.C. hoping for the best, fearful of the worst.

Chapter 28
Judgment Day

"...your sin will find you out." Numbers 32:23

Insecurity is like a virus. Unnoticeable. You don't know it's there. Then it multiplies. And multiplies. After a while I knew I was infected, but I didn't know with what. Then it multiplied again. Once this powerful parasite invaded my soul, I believed I could cure it. The emphasis was on the "I." I gave it doses of money, power, and booze, anything that temporally deadened the pain. As I grew more successful, I adopted an air of arrogance.

Sentencing morning, my swagger was gone.

10:00 a.m., August 25, 1982
United States District Court for the District of
Baltimore, Maryland

"All rise!" the bailiff commanded.

Frank A. Kaufman, the federal district chief judge entered the courtroom.

I placed my hands on the desk and forced my quaking legs to stand. Sweat, like a block of ice in a sauna, rained down my pants. Could that grandfatherly man in the flowing black robe really be the man the Chicago mafia and I had plotted to murder? Did he know how close we almost came to success?

"Hi, Judah. What you been up to? Been at the club much lately?"

My attorney stood up and smiled. "No, Judge. I'm afraid my golf game is going south. What about you, been hitting the ball straight?"

On trial, scared out of mind, and they were talking about golf. Lovely.

I sat between Pat and Judah.

The assistant U.S. attorney stood at her table and addressed the judge. She listed a litany of reasons why I was a danger to society. Her goal—the maximum.

She rolled out a huge board covered with photos of men's faces. "This is a chart I received from the Federal Organized Crime Task Force." The name Chicago was tacked to the top.

Judah jumped up.

"I object. How is this relevant to today's proceedings?"

Not waiting for the Judge's response, she continued, "A task force made up of FBI, IRS, Postal Inspection, and other CID agents have spent years investigating the Chicago Mafia's enterprises. As you can see, Mr. Hall's picture is prominently displayed toward the top."

I could see Johnny's father tagged as the don and Johnny below him as the consigliere. A line below him connected to an unfamiliar picture of me. There was a large question mark next to my name.

My attorney shook his head. "Your Honor, the fact that my client may know, or have legal business with possible mob members is irrelevant. I believe the question mark tells us all we need to know."

"The learned counsel makes a good argument. Motion sustained."

Seeing my image on a criminal organizational chart was unreal. Like a role in a mafia movie.

Judah started his case with an endorsement audiotape from a partially paralyzed and legally blind young man I had befriended and helped. He then presented letters from friends and employees. "Judge, these, and other affidavits, show how Mr. Hall has benefited society."

U.S. assistant attorney general replied, "Your honor, he probably did these so called good deeds to get time off his sentence. He had to know some day he'd be here, or some other courtroom."

Judah responded, "He's happily married with three young girls at home that need him."

"He's only been married a few months. For all we know he did this knowing he'd be sitting here today. He thought it might buy sympathy."

Ouch.

The banter went back and forth. The harder the prosecutor pushed, hope for community service vanished. She pointed a finger at me and snarled like a dog. "He doesn't deserve a break."

"Would the defendant like to say anything?"

I'd prepared for the judge's words, but in my fear the memorized words disappeared.

"I'm so sorry, your honor. If you release me to serve the community, I promise to make a positive contribution to society." My voice cracked and tears streaked my face. Fear was too weak a word.

"Is there anything else counselors? If not, I'm prepared to make my decision." No one said a word.

"Will the defendant please rise?"

My attorneys stood with me.

"Mr. Best, you and your staff did a marvelous job in presenting reasons why the five years requested by the government should be reduced."

Hope rose.

Looking at the file my defense team submitted, he said, "Yes, it's probably the most professional presentencing briefs I've ever seen. However, there are now federal guidelines that suggest an even stiffer penalty."

No!

"The presentence report from the U.S. probation officer does indicate the defendant wouldn't be a risk to society."

Yes!

"However, like I said, the federal guidelines for an offense like this recommends a much longer sentence."

I was at his mercy.

"On the other hand, they are just guidelines, and I have the discretion to hand down whatever sentence I deem fair."

The rollercoaster of emotions churned in my stomach.

"James Hall, you have pleaded guilty to one count of wire fraud. I sentence you to a term of three years and six months in a prison selected by the Federal Bureau of Prisons."

Prison.

Chapter 29
Divine Interventions

"I urge, then, first of all, that petitions, prayers,
intercession and thanksgiving be made for all people."
1 Timothy 2:1

Within moments of hearing my sentence, three emotions piled on top of each other. Anger came first. *This isn't fair. I didn't deserve this.* Deep down I never expected to be sent to prison. I was ready for community service, a fine, and probation. *Real criminals, those that rob with guns, get lesser sentences.* Then fear enveloped me. *What will happen when I get in? Will my wife leave me?* But worse than worry, resignation grabbed my spirit. I wanted to be alone in my self-pity.

The press had other plans.

The morning after my sentencing, I opened my front door to retrieve my newspaper. A mélange of television vans, cameras, and microphones greeted me. News people, each louder than the next, shouted a string of questions.

"Mr. Hall, will you make a statement?"

"Are you a member of the mafia?"

"Were you offered a deal?"

I quickly retreated back inside and opened the Atlanta Journal and Constitution. The front page screamed, "Owner of Carlos McGee's sentenced to Prison." Well, I once wanted fame, looked like I got it.

I had three months to mentally adjust to the inevitable. The first month I pretended it didn't happen. I went to my restaurants. Some treated me like a celebrity. Dennis stayed away from me, as did Tony, and Johnny. Most friends showed great support, but I never felt so alone.

Judy was a rock. She managed to convince me to go to a few church services. I found some of the services appealing, but I really went to please her. Charles Stanley was a good speaker, but my Catholic roots struggled with being in a Baptist church. Although I fought the idea of becoming "born again," I heard the words of the Bible when I attended. I didn't know then about their power in my life, but my wife easily swerved back toward her Christian beliefs thanks to her mother's influence.

Blanche, Judy's mother, had been widowed for many years. Whenever we traveled, even before our marriage, she babysat the girls. She lived in Cleveland, Georgia about an hour and a half away. In some ways she reminded me of my grandparents. Maybe it was because she lived in a small house in the middle of farmland. Most likely it was because Blanche seemed content with her life and non-judgmental of others, especially me. She must have agonized over her daughter dating a non-Christian, yet she always treated me like a son.

Her inner peace amazed me. I had money, fine things, and power. However, despite her simple lifestyle Blanche had more influence. Everyone was drawn to her. I couldn't understand that kind of joy.

Rather than berate her daughter or treat me unkindly, she did the best thing possible—she prayed.

I traveled to Washington, D.C. for my last meeting with Judah Best. "I've been able to get you into the federal prison at Eglin, Florida. At least you'll have nice weather. Before Chuck Colson went to prison I told him to make the best of a bad thing. He apparently did. You do the same. Get in shape physically and mentally. Be ready to start a new life. Now about our bill..."

Dennis and I had paid millions to Steptoe and Johnson. I no longer had the company's money, so Judah worked out a payment plan.

Before leaving, I met with Pat Riley for some last minute advice. As it turned out, it was one of the most important moments of my life.

"Jim, I was really hoping this wouldn't happen. I've done some work with Prison Fellowship. Maybe they can help you while you are incarcerated."

I knew she was a Christian, but she never beat a drum about it.

"What can I bring in?"

"You can bring toiletries, but no straight edge razors. You're also allowed to bring in one book, the Bible."

In fact, I could have brought any book in. For years I wondered if Pat was lying, justifying it as a better good. Maybe it was more of a strong recommendation like, "If you bring a book in, it should be the Bible." In reflection, I believe her words were an integral part of a bigger purpose linked to the greatest chance and most important decision of my life.

When I told Judy about the Bible being the only book I could carry in, she quickly offered hers. But I remembered another one nearby. "I think I have one on a shelf. It was a Christmas present from someone who only worked for me part of a day." I searched the bookshelf. "Here it is. A Good News Bible. Is that different than yours?"

"It's more of a paraphrase. It'll probably be good for you because it's easier to read and understand."

Even through all my years in Catholic schools and the seminary, I never opened a Bible on my own. I remembered my grandparent's nightly readings and the one Aunt Mary gave me. Where had that Bible ended up? I opened the book to see it signed with the inscription, "You'll love the ending."

I had a faint memory of a nice young man who quit during my sales training because he couldn't lie to get a sale. I thought it strange someone who only worked for me for a few hours would bother sending a Christmas present. Like Pat Riley, I believe he was part of a higher plan. He couldn't know exactly why, only that he had to do it.

I moved in a fog. Like I was leaving for a long vacation and should be packing a big suitcase, or boxes, or something. But there was nothing more to pack.

Susie and José Porto, good friends, joined us in Destin, Florida for my last weekend as a free man. Perfect weather. I tried to not think of what I faced. My last night with Judy seemed otherworldly. *Could this really be happening? When will I wake up from this bad dream?*

Monday morning came.

Time to go to prison.

Chapter 30
Freedom

*"Because he lives, I can face tomorrow.
Because he lives, all fear is gone."*
Bill and Gloria Gaither

The sign above its huge doors read, "Eglin FPC-Administration." Except for the heavy metal bars on the windows, it could have been any uninteresting federal building. It was six-forty in the morning.

Another twenty minutes of freedom.

I grabbed the rail and tried to walk up the short cement steps, but I couldn't move. The concrete had hardened my joints. Slowly my body obeyed. I pushed open the big doors to enter my new prison-home.

No one noticed me. I stepped up to what looked like an impenetrable drive-thru-teller's cage at a bank.

"Uh, I'm here to check in." *Did I just say that?*

Before I could think of a brighter way to declare I was there to be locked up, a blue-garbed guard gave me a card. "Here, put your full name on it. I'll then stamp your arrival time on it."

It was blank, except for one short line. I signed it, and he quickly whisked it away. He pushed it into a gray device on the wall. With a snap of a machine, I became prisoner 19355-037.

"Empty your pockets and place the contents in this envelope. Then, address it wherever you want it sent."

I obeyed as they examined my toiletries and confiscated a prescription bottle.

"But that's my blood-pressure medicine."

"You'll be given a physical tomorrow. If the doctor prescribes it, you'll get it back. Put your toiletries, paperwork, and reading materials into this box." It was a translucent case. "They will be examined, and if approved, will be in your locker next to your bunk."

I numbly followed his instructions.

"Now, follow me." He led me to a door I had heard about and feared. The examination room.

"When you get inside you'll see some boxes. There are labels in the boxes, and markers on the table nearby. Place your home address on them." His memorized words traveled slowly, like he spoke to someone mentally challenged. "When finished, strip all your clothes off. The only thing that remains is your shoes. No jewelry or watches, except a plain wedding band. I emphasize it must be a plain band with no stones. Place everything in the boxes, and seal them with the tape on the table."

"What about underwear and socks?" It seemed like a reasonable question, but the look in his face made it clear he considered me dumb for asking.

"Did I not say everything?"

I stood naked, except for my Gucci loafers, in a room the size of my closet and waited. The inner door opened and I moved into a room where two guards stood wearing rubber gloves. One pointed to a small shower stall to the right. The water was already running.

The next twenty minutes were some of the worst of my life.

I marched to the next phase of my humiliation wearing clean, but used underwear, white socks, and a white uniform stenciled with my prisoner identification number on the shirt.

One of the guards gave me my parting instructions, "Memorize your number. It's now your name. Head to the next door and sit outside."

The end of the corridor had four doors all labeled, *Counselor*. One of the doors opened and a balding man in a drab brown suit shouted out some numbers.

I glanced down at my shirt. Me. Feeling like a zombie, I entered a small grey room. The man sat on the other side of a metal table that filled most of the room. The examination had taken its toll on me, and I was still shaking. The idea of having a counselor seemed reassuring, like I'd have an advocate.

"Hi, I'm Mr. Wilson." He didn't offer his hand. "You have been assigned to me. I'm here to be your advisor. I can sum up my advice with this, Follow the rules, and do your time well. Now, go outside and wait."

That was it? That was my counsel? What were the rules? What were my rights?

There never was a set of printed rules. Most I learned from other prisoners, like don't walk on the grass. Some I learned the hard way, like when I was the only one in a TV room after watching a ball game. As I left I noticed the sign above the light switch, "Conserve energy. No lights on when room is empty." I flipped off the lights.

"What are you doing?" One of the correction officers glared at me.

"Sir, turning off the lights."

"Prisoners are not allowed to touch electrical mechanisms without permission. This can earn you a shot." Two nights in the hole for turning off a light?

"But sir, it says to conserve energy. I thought..."

"Thinking in prison can get you in trouble."

"But, what if I didn't conserve energy and left the light on?"

"You could be given a shot."

This kind of circular mentality was one way they controlled the inmates. Fortunately, the guard let my light switch conundrum slide. I bet he had a good laugh relating the incident to his fellow workers later.

Sitting outside the counselor's office I strived to move my thoughts to something hopeful. I still had optimism my forty-two months sentence would end up reduced because of good behavior. I'd heard of people doing only a third of their time. I would obey the rules.

Maybe do a year there and then a few months at a halfway house. I could handle that.

A young guard woke me from my daydream.

"Follow me."

I silently stepped behind him like a lamb, but I knew he was no kind shepherd.

He took me to the laundry room for bedding, a pair of work shoes, and two sets of underwear and socks.

"You'll make your bunk military style."

The beds at St. Mary's came to mind.

"Deposit your belongings in this foot locker." The box with my toiletries, Bible, and paperwork sat on top of the gray three-foot tall steel cabinet. "Change into your work shoes, and I'll return in a few minutes."

My bunkmate was missing, but it was clear I had the upper. That seemed the only positive of the day. My childhood fear that the top would crash down on me while sleeping hadn't totally left me.

Every able-bodied prisoner was required to have a job. Most started at seven in the morning and finished at three-thirty. Lunch at eleven and dinner at four. The first two weeks in prison, new inmates were given temporary assignments before being placed in a permanent job. My temporary tasks included kitchen duty, digging ditches, and raking grass. If you're going to fall hard, cleaning prison commodes is as low as you go. My first job duty— cleaning toilets.

Looking down at an especially gross task I almost laughed. All these years of wanting to be loved, to feel special, and this is where I ended up. Insecurity and dung make curious partners. In a daze I worked my job. When others took a lunch break I just sat down in the corner of a bathroom and cried. I deserved punishment, but that didn't make my heart feel less deserted.

I joined a flood of prisoners returning from road crews and various other jobs at quitting time. Trancelike I made my way to my bunk and met the man I'd share sleeping quarters with. His ponytail hung down to his massive shoulders and arms. Many of his numerous tattoos gave homage to gangs, various women, and his mother.

"You a newbie?"

"Yeah, I'm Jim Hall."

"I'm Bruce Simpson. What are you in for? I'm here for distribution."

Gosh, that surprised me, I sarcastically thought. I told him my crime, and my hope to be out within a year. That's when terrible became worse.

"I bet you had a group of fancy attorneys. Well, they know nothing. This is the federal prison system, not the state. No one gets out early or easy." He sat on his bunk to exchange his heavy work shoes for some sneakers. "The feds never let anyone out without doing two-third of their time. Then, the sentencing guidelines dictate whether you do more. What level is your crime listed at?"

"I opened my locker and lifted a page out. "It says it's a level five crime."

"Level five? What'd you do, kidnap the Pope? Man, you ain't going anywhere. You will do the max." He laughed as he walked away.

In prison misery didn't just love company, it insisted on it.

I vaguely remembered someone saying the crime was listed at a big money figure. That, combined with the mafia ties must have made me an especially undesirable prisoner. That's why Judah Best thought he had a victory when I wasn't sentenced to a longer sentence. My life went from horrible to hopeless. I would do the max.

I had no appetite, no desire to mingle with others. I just wanted to lie down and die. I climbed up and curled into a ball on my bed. I still had my clothes on, including my shoes. I wanted to blame my dad for how I ended up, but I knew I'd made my own choices. He didn't write my life story. I thought about my grandparents, my Aunt Mary, and Judy's mother. They all lived simple and almost unattractive lives, but they never seemed unhappy. They had something I didn't.

Something hard scraped against my thigh. I reached down. My Bible. *How'd this get here?* I must have put it up here when I pulled out the sentencing report. I tucked it under my pillow.

My spirit broken, I resigned myself to doing nothing. Within ten minutes boredom clashed with misery. *Maybe I'll go for a walk.* But I didn't want to be around anyone. Feeling dirty from my labor, I jumped down, undressed, quickly cleaned up, and returned with nothing else to do than get back in my bunk. There were still five hours before lights out. I reached under my pillow and opened the hardbound book. I read, and read, and read.

I started in the Gospels. I knew many of the stories, but few of the words. Some passages jumped out at me. "Do not store up riches for yourselves here on earth, where moths and rust destroy, and robbers break in and steal. Instead, store up riches for yourselves in heaven, where moths and rust cannot destroy, and robbers cannot break in and steal. For your heart will always be where your riches are."

"I am the gate. Those who come in by me will be saved; they will come in and go out and find pasture. The thief comes only in order to steal, kill, and destroy. I have come in order that you might have life—life in all its fullness."

This hit me hard. I had spent most my life stealing, and in many ways destroying. I knew I had chosen the wrong path.

Some other parts, written like letters, made it clear I'd been a sinner, but Jesus came to forgive my sins. Paul wrote so much about peace and joy, something I had been desperately searching for. Finishing the New Testament I felt confused. I got it, but I didn't. I was crammed with questions, but no one to ask.

Somehow, I knew the answers could be found in that Bible. Darkness set in and the overhead lights hurt my eyes. Yet, I felt compelled to keep reading.

My bunkmate returned and said something to me, but I ignored him. It was no time for negativity.

"Count!"

Everyone jumped in front of their beds to be counted by the guards. There were many counts during the day.

I finished in Psalms before the florescent lights dimmed. Three passages squeezed my heart.

Psalm 146, "Praise the Lord! Praise the Lord, my soul! I will praise him as long as I live; I will sing to my God all my life. Don't put your trust in human leaders; no human being can save you. When they die, they return to the dust; on that day all their plans come to an end."

I spent a lifetime worshiping the created things of the world and not the Creator.

"Happy are those who have the God of Jacob to help them and who depend on the Lord their God, the Creator of heaven, earth, and sea, and all that is in them. He always keeps his promises; he judges in favor of the oppressed and gives food to the hungry."

Had I ever truly felt happiness? My aloneness no longer surprised me. Then the next line sent my tears flowing.

"The Lord sets the prisoners free..."

The Bible fell from my hands and I lost my place. I reopened it randomly to Psalm 65.

"God, who lives in his sacred Temple, cares for orphans and protects widows. He gives the lonely a home to live in and leads prisoners out into happy freedom, but rebels will have to live in a desolate land."

This can't be a coincidence.

My brain exploded with the realization that I may have been physically in a penitentiary, but my soul had been in prison most my life. My fingers found Psalm 27, and it shouted into my heart.

"My father and mother may abandon me, but the Lord will take care of me. Teach me, Lord, what you want me to do, and lead me along a safe path."

"Lights out!"

Darkness. Afraid, I took that Bible and squeezed it like a child hugs his teddy bear. My weeping turned to anguished tears as I cried out to the Lord.

Father, I was abandoned so many times. I feel so alone, so afraid. Please help me. I am so sorry, please forgive me. Tell me what you want.

I clutched the Bible so tight against my chest I thought it would rip through the skin and puncture my heart. Then I heard a voice. It may not have been audible, but I was certain it was.

"My son, my son. I am your Father. I love you so much I gave up my only Son for you. I will never abandon you, just come."

–and I did!

I fell into the most peaceful sleep I'd ever had. When I awoke the next morning I couldn't wait for the day to begin. I may have been in prison, but I was free at last.

Chapter 31
A New Day, a New Life

*"But in a cross I found a doorway, and a hand that held
a key. And when the chains fell at my feet, for the first
time I could see. This is how it feels to be free."*
David Allen Clark, Sean Craig, Don Koch

The freedom of my soul didn't translate to my physical
body. I didn't know how my time in prison would go. My
first full day there I called my wife collect and told her
what happened to me the night before.

She asked me some questions and finally shouted,
"You were born again. I'm so happy."

I could hear the relief in her voice. The joy.

Why hadn't I been able to give her that joy in the past?
She didn't want the things I'd always thought would make
her happiest. Her treasures were eternal. A new wave of
love for my wife swept over me as I realized how she must
have prayed for me after God drew her back.

"But, Jim, this is just the beginning. I'm sure they
have a chaplain there, get with him and share your story.
I'll send you some books to read and help you learn."

Each Friday Judy drove six hours to the prison and
stayed nearby for weekend visitation. I desperately
needed that time with her. She also faithfully sent me
many study guides and Christian books. Instead of a
desire for things of this world, I now had a hunger for
His Word—and I had plenty of time to read it.

Being a new Christian didn't take away the
loneliness and fear of the unknown. More than
anything I wanted to get out as soon as possible. I

desperately wanted a miracle. "God, I now believe in you, so please zap me out of here." I hadn't yet matured in my faith. I didn't realize that God is a God of miracles, but they come in ways and at the times He decides for reasons we don't always know.

The calming of my spirit affected my body. I no longer needed blood pressure medication. My pressures were actually a bit low.

The next major blessing the Lord sent happened about a week after arrival.

An older inmate approached me while I raked in the yard. "Hi, I'm John Wilson. I was the one who gave you the education test earlier this week. I'm glad I ran into you." I remembered taking a very easy test with all the other new prisoners. "I'm a short-timer now, and will be gone next week. You aced the test, how would you like my job?"

"What's your job?"

"I'm the education clerk."

He arranged for me to meet with Dr. Applegate, the head of the education department. A few days later I sat at my own desk with the best job and the nicest boss in the entire prison.

There are no coincidences with God. I didn't know it then, but this job would be a big part of His answering my prayer for another blessing—a BIG miracle.

There were about seven hundred at a facility designed for only four hundred. While overcrowded, I never feared other inmates. The prison ran a very tight ship, and there was an abundance of guards.

I found new friends. About five or six of us would meet each day in our tiny chapel for a Bible study. My best friend was a muscle-bound man nicknamed Yogi. We spent much of our time together playing Hearts and discussing the Bible. I often thought of him as my Peter, partially because of his size, but also because he was a fisherman. That's how he got in trouble.

Yogi once shared his story, "I had a charter boat at Marathon, Florida. Things were going a little slow when someone I knew offered me twenty thousand dollars to pick up a load of marijuana. I fell for the temptation. My buddy Al and I picked up fifty huge bales of it."

"We were making our way back to our rendezvous spot in Florida when Al said he thought he saw something in the water coming at us fast. I grabbed my binoculars and squinted to see what it was. Al was panicking, asking what I could see.

"It looked like...Yep, Coast Guard. We were doomed."

Many inmates were like Yogi, good people who did something stupid. Fortunately, the more dangerous criminals were sent to a higher-level prison.

Dennis, my ex-partner, and Kemp Henry, a minor partner in the Atlanta operation, were indicted shortly after my incarceration. Pat Riley informed me that due to conflict of interest her firm no longer could handle my case. She recommended a former U.S. prosecutor, and I retained him.

A few weeks after I arrived at camp the public address system announced my name, "Number 19355-037 report immediately to Control." Control was a glass booth, almost like a bank teller's window, connected to the administration building. My mind raced. What did I do wrong? Their never-printed rules kept me in that half-panicked state.

Like the time a hack, what we called the guards, had stopped by my bunk for a chat. He was a young Christian who often stopped by to discuss some scripture. I opened my locker. I took out a jar that once housed peanuts, but now contained sunflower seeds. I offered him some.

"Why are there sunflower seeds in this?"

"They come in bags, so I put them in this old peanut jar to keep them fresh, and keep bugs away."

"I am supposed to give you a shot for this. The rules state you can't store anything in something other than its original container."

The last thing I wanted was a citation on my record. "I didn't know that. No one ever gave the rules." Although he was always friendly with me, who knew when he might turn on me?

"We don't give inmates the rules because they may look for ways around them." Typical government logic. Fortunately, he let the incident pass, but not until I emptied the seeds from the jar.

Control told me the new lawyer had called and he wanted me to call back. Attorney calls were the only calls not monitored, and all had to be made under strict guidelines. A gray metal desk with matching chair sat in the middle of a small room.

"Hi Jim, this is Dan. I have been talking with Pat Riley. She says some nice things about you. In all my years I've never seen a fellow attorney more interested in helping a client. She really believes in your change. Thank you for hiring me, and the check." Judy had sent a retainer. The meter was always ticking with my lawyers. "How are you doing?"

"As good as can be expected considering where I am. What happened with my sentence appeal?" In the federal court system a judge could modify the sentence he doles out within one year. Usually, within the first seven days of sentencing there's an automatic appeal submitted by the defendant's attorneys. I learned it was almost impossible to get a reduction, and routinely rejected. However, it was my only hope.

"I got the paperwork from Pat's office, but the judge is sitting on it. Kauffman is the senior federal judge for the district. He generally sits on things like this until the last minute."

I wished I had brought something to write with. I had many questions. "Does he have a formal hearing? Will I need to be there?"

"There almost never is a public hearing. It's extremely rare a prisoner is allowed to be present." I couldn't help but be discouraged. Judy and I concentrated prayers that the judge might look favorably at our petition and grant some cut in time. But the more I learned the system, the more I learned that this was close to impossible.

"One of the reasons I wanted to talk with you is the feds called. Would you reconsider their original offer of testifying against Ciccone?"

"No way. Why ask now?"

"A change of attorney might mean a change of mind. They also figure you might be anxious to get out."

"Well, my answer is still no." I had no choice.

I didn't speak with my lawyer again until January when Dr. Applegate buzzed the intercom at my desk.

"Jim, head over to the admin building. You've got a call." News of deaths and other catastrophes were all delivered there. It wasn't unusual to see big, tough guys weep as they returned from there. I rushed over and learned it was again from Dan.

"Jim, they want you to testify at your partner's trial."

Dennis' trial? "Why? I can't imagine I can give them anything of value. Besides, the prosecutor hates me. I see no good in it." I had no reason to help her.

"She's no longer with the department. They hired a new guy. This is his first case. He doesn't want to take a risk. You'd be a safety valve."

My mind raced.

Then he said something that would begin a chain of events only God could have orchestrated. "They want you up here to interview you."

"When? I don't want to be in their transfer system." Prisoners needed for a trial often stayed at many different jails and prisons along the route to the city the courtroom was at. He'd be picked up in chains and bused to a jail in a series of moves until they reached the destination. The process took four to six weeks. They often slept on floors because of overcrowding, and sometimes were housed with some of the most hardened inmates. I heard horror stories about things that were done to some of them.

I shuddered at the memory of Terry Cumbie, my first friend in prison. He was summoned to trial this way, and when he returned he had lost his smile. His eyes reflected that something bad happened to him. He would never talk about the experience, but I was sure he was abused.

"I think they're anxious to talk with you as soon as possible." Could I get something out of this? I doubt if they'd need me at the trial, but the fact that they wanted to talk with me gave me an idea. "What if I got a three day pass, a furlough? One day to travel to Baltimore, one for the meeting and then another for traveling back?"

"Let me talk with the prosecutor."

I tacked on another condition. "I want to be able to have my wife to stay with me while I'm up there."

My attorney laughed. "It can't hurt to ask." The idea of two nights with Judy gave me a smile so wide it almost tickled my earlobes.

The next few days I couldn't wait for the lawyers call back. I called him collect at least twice a day. Each time they hadn't answered yet, until the fourth day and ninth call. "They said if you paid your own expenses, they'd request a three night furlough."

"Did you say three nights?" *Please, please!*

"Yes, they might need you here more than just a day."

It's hard to describe my emotions. Things like that didn't happen, especially in the federal prison system.

But someone didn't like it.

The warden, or as he liked to call himself, the superintendent, received paperwork requesting my furlough, but denied it. My attorney called to tell me that the judge would have to step in and help. Two days later Dan gave me the news, "The prosecutor asked Judge Kaufman to request the pass, and he did. Your warden turned him down."

My heart sank.

"Federal judges aren't used to hearing people say no to them, so he changed the request to an order. If the warden tries to block it, he can be arrested."

Wow! I didn't want to be in the middle of some sort of power play, but I was glad the judge had come through.

The next day I was given some paperwork that said a furlough was granted, the rules and guidelines were spelled out. On the morning I was to leave, I was sent to a room with discarded clothes spread around. I found an old gray pair of pants and a yellow polyester shirt that fit. With long hair and a mustache I might have been mistaken for Sonny Bono. My only coat was prison-furnished, so it stayed behind. I knew Judy would bring some clothes, so I didn't care how I looked.

I sat in the back seat of the taxi and thought of how good God is. I may end up in prison for years, but at least I'd been given the gift of a short time alone with my wife. At the airport I hit a snag. All I had was my paperwork. Judy had used a credit card to reserve me a seat.

"Sir we need some form of identification." They were not about to let this strangely dressed person claim the reserved seat without an ID. And, of course, that had been sent home with my clothes.

What could I do? Had I gotten that close to a few moments of freedom only to be turned away? I stepped away from the line and went to a corner to pray, "God you've got to help me."

Why hadn't I at least shown them my paperwork?
Pride.

I didn't want the people in line, or the airline crew to know I was a convict–I was embarrassed. Even then. But I wasn't going to let my pride keep me from my wife.

I moved back to the line. "I'm sorry but I'm a convict out on a pass. All the prison gave me was this paperwork. You can call them if you want."

The gate agent looked a little startled and waved at someone wearing a red coat. They had a quick conversation, and the supervisor motioned me to the side.

"Huh, I'm not sure..." He stared at the papers and shook his head.

"Please, I'm not sure what will happen if I miss this flight. I'm on my way to see my wife."

He gave me a sympathetic look and nodded. "I can't imagine anyone making up that story. I'll go get you your ticket."

I met first with my attorney at his office before the assistant US attorney arrived. During my interview I made it clear that even with a subpoena I would not testify against the mob. I also was emphatic that I was now a Christian and could not sway my testimony, not even to receive a reduced sentence.

The time with my wife was wonderful.

A few days after my return to prison I spoke with Dan. He seemed excited, "From what I heard there was nothing you could say that could substantially help their case. Depending on the questions, you might even hurt it. However, this new prosecutor really wants to win it, so he would like to bring you in as one of his potential witnesses." This immediately set alarm bells off in my brain. "Where would I be housed?"

"Probably the local jail."

"Is there an alternative? Jails are even worse than prisons. Also, remember what I said about transfers? This entire thing makes me nervous. At least I have a good job here. I feel safe, and Judy can drive down every week." My stomach soured at the thought of how bad this could go.

"Let me talk with the young guy. He seems like an agreeable sort. Plus, he doesn't want a hostile witness."

"Daniel, I can't be hostile. I'm a Christian, I can only tell the truth." I had spent so many years living a life of deceit. I refused to go back to it, even if it hurt me.

"The transfer may not be a problem. Seems you did fine with the other pass. I can't see that as a stumbling block. Where they keep you is another matter."

"I know, but you've got to fight for me."

"I'll do what I can."

Later that day I shared my plight during our Bible study. They all knew the negatives to temporary trial transfers. Bill Hinton, probably the most mature Christian in our group asked, "How should we pray?"

"What do you mean?"

"It's obvious we should pray that you get another furlough. Although I'm a little envious you got the first pass." He laughed at what was probably a true feeling. "What exactly do you want God to do concerning where you are incarcerated while in Baltimore? It's easier to give God the glory when there is no doubt He has answered your prayer. We are supposed to think it through, search our hearts, and then be specific."

That had never occurred to me. I stopped and silently pleaded, "God what should I be asking for?"

"Besides the furlough, I'd like one of two things to happen. Either ending up in a very safe cell for such a short time it wouldn't interfere with my job here, or place me in a halfway house." My friend looked me deep in my eyes. "Good, but it sounds like you are hedging a bit. Our God is bigger than compromise. What is your specific prayer?"

Could I say it to these men? "That I get my pass and stay at a halfway house." I knew deep down that this would be beyond my wildest dreams. But my faith still had some growing to do. If I believed God could do it, I should pray and believe. If He answered differently, I could accept He knew best.

The next day I spoke with my attorney.

"You are one lucky guy." Dan whistled. "It seems they want easy access to you. Not only are you getting the furlough, but you'll stay at a halfway house."

I knew it had nothing to do with luck. I filed it in my miracle file. It wouldn't be the last.

Chapter 32
Miracles

"Miracles are a retelling in small letters of the very same story which is written across the whole world in letters too large for some of us to see." — C.S. Lewis

Sometimes answered prayer doesn't look like we want it to. The Volunteers of America Halfway House was in an old industrial area about three miles east of the Inner Harbor in Baltimore. It was a huge old warehouse run by nuns. I was assigned a bunk surrounded by fifty other inmate beds. The clothes Judy sent were locked in a locker across from my bed where I kept some money until someone broke in and stole it while I slept.

Layers were my friends, as I spent my nights in a hooded sweat suit because the light blanket couldn't keep the February cold away. Each day all the inhabitants left for their jobs or to look for one. There was no place to jog or get exercise. I was there only a few days before I wished I could return to my prison.

My first Sunday I was allowed to leave for a few hours to go to church. I was excited to be attending my first church as a new Christian, but where would I go? I took a bus into the city central where many stately old churches stood. I stopped outside one that had a plaque inscribed with some of the names of former members. Woodrow Wilson and George Peabody were two names I recognized. It was a beautiful church, but I never heard the name of Christ mentioned once.

The service included a lady reading a poem and the message was about "following our path toward truth." It wasn't until I spoke with Judy later that day did I learn that The First Unitarian Church of Baltimore wasn't exactly the best choice for me. I think that day taught me of the importance of being mentored as a new Christian. It was so easy to fall prey to many different religious ideas that are far from the real path toward truth.

My fourth day in Baltimore, I took the bus to meet with the prosecutor. My new freedom seemed strange. I'd grown accustomed to the prison life. There was a tendency for inmates to focus on the world inside fences and walls. It was almost like there was no realm except there. I found it difficult to adjust when I was first able to freely move on the streets. I almost wanted someone to tell me what to do.

Bob McDonald was the new assistant US attorney. With his Ivy League looks and Harvard Degree above his desk, he reminded me of Bobby Kennedy. I told him of my boredom at the halfway house.

"Well, why don't you come here during the day? You can sit at one of the desks and read or write."

"Thanks." It had to be better than staying in that cold warehouse. "I'll send the paperwork to the nuns approving a weekday pass for you." This meant I could leave at eight, but must return by seven-thirty. I found my new freedom exciting, but that also grew quite tedious.

Sitting in a federal prosecutor's office, with no real job made my days seem as long as they were in prison.

One day Bob invited me into his office. "I'm catching some heat because we didn't indict Ciccone. The members of the Federal Organized Crime Task Force want to interview you. I set it up for this afternoon."

They could interview me all they wanted to, but it wouldn't change anything.

We took an elevator down to a different floor in the federal building. There were a number of agents from various arms of law enforcement in a large Spartan conference room. The questions came hard and fast, but I would not implicate Johnny or any other mobster.

"I'll see to it the IRS goes after you." The US postal inspector took the hardest approach in the interrogation. His threat frightened me, but I'd already endured a major audit that required me to pay forty thousand dollars more.

"I'm still not saying anything about that."

He then tried to put words in my mouth about Dennis and Kemp. "I bet you can remember talking with them about breaking the law. How you all knew what you did was illegal. If you can remember a conversation like that, I'm sure I can put in a good word for you. Maybe I can get a few months knocked off your sentence."

I knew what he wanted, and the temptation was there. "No sir, as a matter of fact we often remarked how we were in the gray area of the law. That at worse it was a civil matter." I wasn't going to take the bait.

The postal inspector erupted. I thought he was going to hit me. "You liar, if you think you're going to sabotage this case..."

Bob McDonald jumped up and calmly said, "I believe he's telling the truth."

The postal inspector took a chair and pouted silently the remainder of our time together.

I sensed a change in my relationship with the assistant US Attorney that day. The man whose job was to keep me in prison, and put my partners there, had softened. He treated me like a man, and not a criminal.

Many times he'd stop and ask me about what I was reading. I didn't know if he was a Christian, but he acted like one. When he announced the trial would be delayed at least two more months, I tossed him the obvious question.

"What's that mean for me?"

"Normally, I'd just send you back to your Florida prison. My department is picking up the tab on the cost of keeping you up here."

Ah. I hadn't thought of that. "However, your warden is a pain. I don't want to have to go through hassles with him again. You could continue sitting here I suppose."

God what to do? Months of sitting here doing nothing would drive me batty. "Do you think I could spend my afternoons at the gym? There's a big one nearby, they even have pickup basketball games at noon."

"No, that would give a bad impression to my bosses. You are still a convicted criminal doing time."

I had never forgotten that.

"Besides, it might look like we were trying to give you special treatment. That could hurt your testimony."

God, please help me here. My mind tried to grab at something he would buy. *Maybe work at a job. Nah, no one would hire me under these circumstances.* "What if I could do some charity work, be a volunteer? It would be like a job. At least I'd be doing some good."

He smiled. "I like it. You have something in mind?"

I was clueless. "Let me investigate some ideas and get back with you. Okay if I make some local calls from the desk?" With his approval I called the Red Cross, Goodwill, and others listed in the yellow pages. My early calls ran into dead ends. When I later told Judy of my idea, she said she'd ask her pastor if he had any Baltimore connections. The next day she gave me the number of Mark Hodge, the Baptist Home Mission Board representative in the area. Mark agreed to pick me up at the federal building and spend some time with me.

We sat on a bench outside while I shared my testimony with Mark and my desire to be of service for at least the next two months. "Jim, your story is compelling but I really don't know if I can help you. Maybe if you were a carpenter or skilled with tools I could find you something."

I was the total opposite of a handyman.

"The Southern Baptist arm in this area is getting shorter. Let's drive out to Seventh Baptist Church. They do a lot of great mission work there." He led me to his vehicle and motioned to the passenger seat.

I opened the car door and shuffled empty paper cups and napkins to the side with my foot as I climbed in.

"It used to be a very large congregation, but the neighborhood has changed. Those not living on the street are living in poverty. The church is down to about fifty regular attendees. Almost all of them live in the suburbs and travel in for services and to help with their ministry."

As we pulled up I viewed a beautiful old stone and brick church. Mark pointed to the connected apartments across from it. "They own the row houses on this block. They use them as a sort of halfway house for those leaving mental institutions. They house up to thirty people, help them adjust, and hopefully get them placed into jobs."

I started to leave the car and Mark stopped me. "Let's say a prayer first." He bowed his head, "Father, Jim is a new member of your family. Please find him the perfect opportunity to grow in his faith as he learns the importance of mission work."

I felt a bit ashamed that I didn't suggest praying. "Sorry, Mark, I should have thought of that."

Mark smiled. "It's a good habit, and the more you pray the more it comes automatically. Someone once told me good habits start out as hopes. I'm hoping something good happens today."

Dr. Dorr was a tall, thin, soft-spoken man. I was drawn to his gentle spirit. After sharing my testimony he said pretty much what Mark had said earlier, "Your conversion is inspiring, but I don't know where we could actively put you to use. I'd hate to waste you. Let me show you around." We toured the church that once held almost two thousand attendees, but now never reached more than a one hundred. After stopping by the communal kitchen below one of the row houses, Dr. Dorr pointed at the last building on the block. "That's our Thrift Shop." The sign above its windows said "Seventh Baptist Boutique."

"Let me introduce you to Mildred Boughan. She's a remarkable lady. She retired as the highest-ranking woman employee with the C&P Telephone Company.

She told me she would move back to Virginia if I didn't keep her busy. That was almost ten years ago. She manages the housing here, is the church treasurer and runs the thrift shop. At seventy-five she'll outwork anyone half her age. She has never asked for a day off all these years. She is an unbelievable jewel."

We walked up the stoop and entered a room crammed with every used item possible. Mildred was behind a long glass counter. She looked much younger than her age. "Mildred, this is Jim Hall, and I think you remember Mark."

"Hi, Mark. It's nice to meet you, Jim." She walked around the counter and shook my hand.

"Mildred, why don't you show Jim around?"

I followed her as she talked. "The room behind this is our clothing area." Racks after racks lined the walls. There were coats, suits, dresses and shirts flowing like cramped flags from the ceiling down. Boxes of shoes, socks and other clothing packed into every free space. "Around the corner we keep housing items. Mostly small ones like lamps, chairs, and tables. And where you came in is where we display most electronic items and anything else that we feel will go fast." The three large rooms had enough merchandise for a space four times its size.

A bell rang as the door opened and a street person came in holding a portable radio to his ear.

Mildred seemed to know him. "Terry," she reached under the counter, "I've saved this for you." It was a pocket protector with some pencils sticking out of it. He reached in his pants pocket and removed a nickel. Mildred took it and he proudly placed his new purchase in the left pocket of his tattered blue shirt. He turned and left without ever taking the radio from his ear.

Mildred looked at us, "I'm not sure if his name is Terry. He never talks. I just started called him that a few years ago. He seems to like whatever I sell him." I'd never been in a thrift shop, although most the items in it were nicer than what my family had when I was a child.

"Why sell it to them? Why not give the stuff away?"

Dr. Dorr replied, "It keeps their dignity. When people receive nothing but handouts they eventually lose self-worth. It makes it that much harder to make a comeback from their bad situation."

"Are most of your clientele like this Terry?"

Mildred nodded. "Half of the people coming here are street people. Most of them have some mental problems. Terry always keeps that transistor radio to his ears, but its batteries died many years ago. The other customers are just people down in their luck. We also charge a little for each item to help pay the utilities. It's just enough to break even." She said that with a smile and a wink at the pastor.

"Well, Mildred, Jim here has quite a story. I'd like him to share it with you." We all sat on some old rockers in the furniture room as I shared.

"So Jim is here looking for something to do the next two or three months." Dr. Dorr added. "I told him I couldn't think of anything. You always have everything under control."

Tears streamed down Mildred's face. Dr. Dorr looked at Mark and raised his shoulders. "What did I do?" He placed his hand on Mildred's arm. "I didn't mean to upset you."

She lifted a small delicate hanky from inside her sleeve. "Dr. Dorr, my sister is very ill, and I have been praying for a way to go take care of her for a few months. I didn't want to tell you because you would have tried to make me go. I couldn't do that unless I had someone responsible here to take care of all this while I was gone."

It was like a gush of air retreated from our lungs all at once. We knew we had just witnessed the awesome power and grace of God. Mark fell to his knees. Dr. Dorr hugged Mildred, and I joined them all in tears of joy and gratitude. Both Mildred's and my prayers were answered in a way that no one could doubt God had been at work.

The next few months I spent six days a week at this wonderful church. Dr. Dorr mentored and counseled me with a gentle wisdom that only God could give. Until my time there, I always had a bit of a prejudice against street people. I used to think, "Why don't they just get a job?" But the precious people I met were mainly mentally incapable or tragically too damaged to do much better than they were doing.

One day a mother came in with little kids needing school clothes. She looked so proud when she took out the five dollars to purchase the three stuffed bags.

I thought of my mother and her life on the run. My father had died a couple years before I was sentenced. My mother now lived in a condo in Atlanta where I moved her shortly after my dad's death. I called her that night.

My experiences working with the apartments helped me see mental illness in an entirely different light, and to appreciate ministries that do their best to help the needy.

Most mornings I met with the church's volunteers and we'd pray. Then, we'd greet the renters with sweet rolls, coffee, and various breakfast items. It was always exciting when news came that someone landed a job, or they were ready to move on to their own place. I'd thought I'd gotten some bad breaks when I was young. I could have had it so much worse.

Spring teased, but winter didn't want to leave. Each morning I'd take the bus from the halfway house, join in prayer and breakfast, and then open the shop. During the cold days it wasn't unusual for three or more regulars to spend their entire day sitting on rockers. Judy came to visit, and although I had to return to the warehouse at night, it was wonderful to share what I was doing during the day.

One morning three were sitting on the rockers.

"That really tall girl seems to have a crush on you," Judy teased. She nodded at the not-very attractive Bernadette sitting on the middle chair.

"Take a good look at her...notice anything different?"

"She's got an Adam's apple!" Judy tried not to gawk.

Bernadette was a transvestite living on the streets,

afraid of the shelters. One of the wonderful things I learned during my time there was God loves everyone. Our role as believers was to be His hands and feet and minister to everyone just as He would have done while on earth.

Mildred's sister died in early April and she returned in time to attend my first sermon. I had shared my testimony at an earlier service, but this was to be my goodbye message to the many I had grown to love so much at Seventh Baptist. Many of the street people, and those staying in the apartments that I had the privilege of serving, joined the rest of the congregation at my humbling attempt to speak in God's house.

The next day the trial began.

I was stationed at the usual desk near the prosecutor's office. Late that afternoon I was summoned to the courtroom. In many ways this was almost as difficult as facing a judge myself. I really liked the younger Kemp, and considered Dennis like a brother. Since my plea he'd had little to do with me. He even tried to stop the money due me from the sale of the restaurants, but I didn't want to harm him.

Bob McDonald asked some expected questions and finished with me in thirty minutes. About all I said was related to the areas of the business we were involved in, how much mark-up we had, and that the written sales pitches they had entered as evidence were in fact what was used.

Kemp's advocate, a well-known Atlanta attorney, was the first to ask me his questions. "Would you say you were in charge of the business?"

"Yes."

"If Mr. Henry wanted to change anything in how you did business, would he be allowed to?"

"No."

"No further questions for this witness." He sat down and I sighed with relief. That was it, only two questions.

It was now Dennis' lawyer's turn. I had never heard of him, but was sure he was the best money could buy. Before long I changed my mind about that.

He started with a strange line of questioning, "Wouldn't you say Dennis drinks quite a bit?"

"Yes."

"Wouldn't you say he was drunk many times you talked business?"

"Yes." He continued to paint a picture of Dennis as this hopeless clown of a drunk. Each question made Dennis into a lush. He continued along this vein until we dismissed for the day. Before I left the building the US postal inspector came up to me, "You trying to get them off?" He was furious. "You could have added something to help nail Henry. Instead you made it sound like he was a choirboy."

"I was answering honestly."

"Well, I'll see to it you rot in prison."

Bob McDonald saw what was going on and jogged over to us. "Please, I want to be the only one who talks with my witnesses during a trial."

The angry bully grimaced and then left. Bob grabbed me by the arm, "Let me buy you dinner."

Bob looked at me. "Jim, I admire your honesty. I do believe something has happened to you, and you are a changed man. When you were sworn in you were asked to not just tell the truth, but the 'whole truth and nothing but the truth,' what do you think that means?"

The waitress brought our sodas. I took a sip through the straw and said, "I've never thought about it. I guess it means don't lie."

"It's more than that. The key is the word 'whole.' If you omit something or if you know the truth is not coming out, you must make it true. For instance, what if I asked you in court 'weren't you born on Monday, August third?'"

"Well, my birthday is August third, but I was born on a Sunday."

"That's the point. You could technically answer no, but would it be the whole truth?"

His words hit me harder than I'm sure he thought. I had spent a lifetime of not telling the truth. I had held on to the idea that the gray area was only stretching the truth, but with God there is no gray.

"I suppose I'd have to correct the mistake."

He smiled, "That's all I am asking of you tomorrow. Let the entire truth be presented. You swore on a Bible, and I truly trust you will do the right thing."

I don't remember what other small talk we shared. He did ask me about my volunteer work, but my mind stayed on the lesson I learned—truth can be more important than the facts.

The next day Dennis' attorney continued with his defense. Nothing changed, he was trying to make him look like nothing more than a drunken pawn. The questions seemed repetitive and continued to come, and then court was recessed for lunch. My attorney joined me for our quick meal.

"Judge Kaufmann has agreed to a sentencing hearing in three days. I will ask for a one-year reduction, the prosecutor will fight it and then we'll see. I sent word down to your prison in Florida to send any reports about your conduct there to the judge. There isn't anything that can hurt you, is there?"

"No, I was a good boy. So do you think I can get a reduced sentence?"

"My guess is three months, six if we are really lucky. The good news, you can attend the hearing. You probably won't be asked anything, but ask your wife to fly up here. It can't hurt having her there to support you."

That afternoon the defense continued repeating the same questions so often the judge finally jumped in, "Okay, we all get it. You are saying your client was too drunk to know what was going on. Let's speed this up. If that's your question, ask it. And he did.

My answer was the whole truth. "Dennis, especially the last few years, drank a lot. He was drunk a lot, but he wasn't drunk all the time. I was in charge, but he knew what our business was and did." With that I was dismissed.

The verdict came swiftly. Kemp Henry was innocent on all counts, but Dennis was declared guilty. I wept that night knowing I'd hurt someone I loved, but pain is sometimes the price of honesty.

The Wednesday before my hearing the people at Seventh Baptist prayed over me and wished me well. The next day I anxiously took the bus to the courtroom. It was a beautiful May morning. I tried to read the newspaper during the voyage, but my thoughts went to how I had been waiting for this day, and now it frightened me. I remembered the many times in the past young Bobo took buses, many times to escape his circumstances. It seemed I was doing that again.

Judy was waiting for me in the lobby. We hugged and she said a prayer. She took her place in the empty pews behind my table. My attorney read through his notes. I sat and looked at Bob McDonald at the opposing table across from us. I hoped he'd notice me and give a thumb's up, or at least smile. Instead, he wrote notes on a yellow pad.

I tried to silently pray, but sometimes fear blocks the words. All I managed was the repeated mantra. *God, help me.*

My attorney made a plea about how I'd changed and how I deserved a break. He'd already told me his argument would have little merit. "Legally, a judge should only consider whether he made a mistake in his original sentence or the federal prosecutor makes the reduction request based on help given." Bob McDonald was not making any recommendation for a reduction. The fact he was present indicated he was there to do his job—object.

The judge surprised us all when he raised a big manila envelope, "Have you two had a chance to see what I got from Mr. Hall's prison?"

They both answered no. "Well, I've got to say in all my years on the bench I've never experienced this."

Was the warden angry at being pushed into my furloughs and now getting back at me?

The judge continued. "I've got a letter signed by the head of their education department, the chaplain, two guards, and one of the prison counselors."

My hopes went up at the mention of Dr. Applegate.

"I can't remember ever receiving a packet like this from prison officials."

Dear God, let it be good. Please.

"I'll give you the gist, and then give you both time to read the whole thing. He placed a small pair of glasses on his nose. "It says Mr. Hall, in his short stay, became president of both the Toastmasters and the Rotary." He took a sip from a coffee cup, "Didn't even know they had a Rotary."

My heart raced. I'd done those things only because no one else would agree to.

"He apparently was active with the chapel and part of a Bible study. Now, all these things are good, but not all that remarkable. What impressed me most was the special education program he began for the illiterate inmates. He did this on his own time and with his own funds."

Oh that? Sure, as education clerk I learned many inmates were functionally and literally illiterate. I'd test them and they had no idea what the words said. One night as I lay in bed, my heart was grieved for a new elderly inmate who had whispered, "I can't read the questions on the test." There was a need I could fill, so I did. I didn't see it as that big of a deal. In fact, I didn't know if I'd mentioned it to Judy.

As the judge spoke there was a commotion behind me. I turned to see people filing in—lots of them. The judge stopped his dissertation, took his glasses off, and directed his next remark at the crowd. "Excuse me. It's very unusual to have an audience for a hearing like this."

They're all from Seventh Baptist!

"Is there a leader?"

Dr. Dorr stood up. He walked up in way I can only describe as gentlemanly.

"Judge, I am Dr. Robert Dorr. I am pastor of Seventh Baptist Church, and these are my members."

"Welcome, Pastor. So why are you all here?"

"To be honest I don't know. Jim Hall has been a volunteer and a wonderful member of my church these past few months. I got a call last night from a deacon who said we should all get together and pray during today's hearing time. I wasn't sure how many would take the day off work, but this is the crowd." He gestured at those who'd gathered with him. "Someone suggested we come here to show our support. We piled in our cars, and here we are."

They loved me. Tears slid to my lips.

Judge Kaufmann looked moved. "Thank you, Pastor. You may sit down." He looked over at the assistant U.S. attorney. "I'm just thinking out loud, but I welcome your opinion. First, I read something I've never before experienced, a letter from prison authorities asking for mercy for an inmate. Then this group of people came in." He stopped. It looked like he was considering his words.

I was energized, but my attorney whispered, "Don't get too excited. He's just thinking out loud."

The judge continued, "I don't believe Mr. Hall would commit another crime, and I think he probably would be a fine citizen once released. What if and this is a big if, what if instead of just reducing his sentence, we released him?"

Things were happening so big and fast I hardly caught what he was saying. I knew the prosecutor would now argue against it. It was his job.

Bob McDonald rose. "Your Honor, I cannot say that would not be justice served."

What? Was that a double negative?

"Mr. Hall?" The judge was now looking at me.

I was still trying to discern what the prosecutor said.

My attorney stood with me and whispered, "It's time to get excited."

"The order of this course is that your sentence be changed to five years on parole. You are free to go."

Free to go? Free to go!

Tears, hugging, and cheering filled the courtroom. The noise buzzed in my head and joined together to form the sound of one word.

Free.

Chapter 33
An Offer You Can't Refuse

*"Not surprisingly, the place we're most likely to
experience testing is exactly where we struggle most to
trust God."*
— *Bruce Wilkinson, The Dream Giver*

September 1995

"If you take the job, I'll give you a million dollar bonus."
Okay heart, slow down.

I knew Nabeel Esfahani wanted me, but not this bad.
Dave Deans, a wealthy computer executive, one of the
few from my past I could still call friend, had introduced
me to his Iranian-born neighbor a few weeks before.

Maybe one of the biggest tests for a new Christian is
what to do about old friends. Most from my past thought
I'd either faked my conversion, or it would soon pass. As I
became more committed to my faith and church, they
became less devoted to me. Thankfully, God graciously
replaced each dropped friend with new Christian ones.
Dave always seemed amazed at how much I'd changed, and
remained one of the few in the retained friends column.

Nabeel needed some business advice, so Dave
recommended me. I agreed to do some sales and marketing
consulting for Nabeel's new start-up endeavor. I could only
offer a few hours per week because I worked fulltime for
Walk Thru the Bible Ministries.

A week before I received Nabeel's amazing offer, I
stood in his walnut-paneled boardroom making a
presentation to him and a board member of one of his

investment companies. Nabeel was partnering with a company that owned many of the cruise lines I was familiar with. His new travel organization had already sold blocks of shares to them.

"I think your marketing campaign should emphasize your ties with the cruise lines." As I continued my talk, Nabeel often leaned over and whispered in the board member's ear. If heads bobbing up and down were any indication, they were in agreement with my findings.

"Gentlemen, are there any questions?" I settled into a lush leather chair directly across them. The questions came fast, and their obvious excitement pumped me to new heights. I jumped up and starting drawing a diagram on the marking board when Nabeel lifted his right hand.

He bounced up. "It's him! Armaan, I think we've found our man." I hadn't known Nabeel long, but I already knew he was easily excited.

Armaan, a dark, dignified, white-haired man, softly asked, "What makes you say that?"

"Because not only does he get what we are doing, he's the perfect combination of what we need." Nabeel's eyes went wide as he moved behind me and placed his hands on my shoulder. "Jim, we have been looking for a new president for this company. There are many bright gentlemen like you, and most can do a good job. However, you bring two things hard to find, integrity and you're deeply religious, like us."

I was stunned silent by the moment. I knew Nabeel was a Muslim, although not a strict one. My assumption was Armaan wasn't a Christian either. "You work for a ministry and are deeply committed to God. We are also religious, but we know that many in your country look at Iranians with caution. You are white, smart, and trustworthy. I am convinced God has brought you to us at this time."

One part of me wanted to explain the difference in religion and Christianity, another wanted to hear the offer.

Nabeel explained the job, the extensive international travel, "...first class, of course," and the large compensation package, an excitement surged within me that I hadn't known for quite a while.

"Talk with your wife, but I am sure you are the man."

The allure of travel and the challenges that came with such an important position were enormous. That night, when I told my wife about the offer, I expected her to be excited. However, her eyes revealed a sense of caution.

"You love your work at Walk Thru the Bible. It's allowed you to work with wonderful Christian churches and leaders. It's opened the door to your two big inner-city Bible studies in Atlanta, and frankly it's helped you grow spiritually. Let's pray about it, and see what God tells us."

"How can we tell? What if the offer is gone?" There was no denying that my emotions were in favor of taking the job.

"Let's not get ahead of God. You're supposed to share your testimony at Jere's church in a couple weeks. I think he would be a good advisor. You should also meet with Bruce about this."

Jere Wilson was the senior pastor of The First Baptist Church, Henderson, Texas. He and his wife were close friends of ours. Bruce Wilkinson was the founder and president of Walk Thru. He was one of the reasons I committed to ministry work.

I agreed to wait, but Nabeel was more persistent than I expected. He called me first thing every morning. "Did you decide? I need you!" After a few days his message changed. "Stop by during your lunch hour. I have something to show you."

When I arrived at his office he smiled and rose from his leather chair and took a chair next to mine. He was always meticulously attired, so much so I usually overdressed when I knew I'd be meeting him. He reached for a stack of textured papers on his antique oak desk. He waved them in the air.

"You know what I've got here?" He continued before I could answer, although I had no idea. "It's why you can't say no." He carefully leafed through the papers.

"These are copies of shares for our startup. Each is worth a million dollars." He placed all except two back on his desk. Investors have purchased those, but these two are still available. One is designated for me as the new chairman." He placed one on his desk and waved the other in front of my face. The other is yours if you become our new president."

"If you take the job, I'll give you a million dollars as a bonus."

I felt like a hungry fish facing a plump worm. I wanted to grab at the bait so bad it hurt. My response surprised me. "Nabeel, your offer is amazing, and I'm quite humbled. I'm flying out this weekend to be with a dear friend. I'll try to give you my answer when I return." I desperately wanted to accept his offer, but something held me back.

When I returned to my office I asked for a meeting with Bruce. I knew Bruce to be a godly man of integrity and wisdom. When I entered I sat on a brown Naugahyde chair and looked across his large, but inexpensive desk. I couldn't help but notice how much more humble his setting was compared to Nabeel's.

"Bruce, I have a dilemma." I explained the offer.

"Well, you have some major incentive to take this position. I'm not sure how to advise you." He took out a sheet of paper and drew a line down the middle. "On the left list all the reasons you feel you should stay with Walk Thru. On the right, list the reasons why you should take the other job."

He patiently waited the five minutes it took me to complete the task. I handed the page back.

"Hmm, hmm." His head slowly moved up and down as he considered my replies. He grabbed a pen and wrote on the page, sealed it in an envelope and placed it in a desk drawer. "I've written down what I think you will do. I'll share it with you after you've made your decision."

I still had no idea what to do.

That weekend I shared my testimony at my friend's church in Texas. I also asked for advice from Jere and his wife Joyce, but left still uncertain. He leaned towards taking the offer, but she felt I was called for ministry.

That week Nabeel phoned often, but I still couldn't decide. Judy and I prayed, but it seemed like we were getting conflicting answers.

I said, "I think God would have me take it."

My wife responded, "Are you sure? I have a strong check in my spirit." She questioned working for and with so many Muslims.

I rationalized, "What a great opportunity to help bring them to Christ."

"Or they could move you away from Him."

Our conversations teetered and tottered like that all week. The one thing we could both agree on was the prayer, "God, please give us a sign."

Sunday we decided to go hear Andy Stanley. He began preaching at Dunwoody Baptist shortly after he left the north campus of his father's church. Not to interfere with their normal services, Andy held his in the afternoon. We had already been to our church, but felt the nudge to get more of the Word in us.

The crowd was big, but the moment he started it was as if he was only speaking to me. "Matthew 6:24 says 'No one can serve two masters. Either you will hate the one and love the other, or you will be devoted to one and despise the other.' In other words, you can't serve both God and money."

My heart soaked up the truth like a sponge.

"Greed is almost impossible for us to see in the mirror. The key to breaking the power of greed is to live as if God is your master and not money."

His message continued to pierce my soul. When Judy and I left the church we said nothing. In the parking lot we looked at each other and tears overcame us—we knew the answer.

The next day I called Nabeel to decline his generous offer, and made an appointment to see Bruce.

"I said no to the offer."

Bruce smiled and slid open a drawer. Taking a silver letter opener he slit open the envelope. "Jim, I looked at your rationale for taking the job. The only reason to leave the ministry was because of money. Here's what I wrote."

He turned the paper, and I could see "Stronghold: Money," was printed in large letters across the page. Below it was, "He will choose God as His master." It was as if he and Andy Stanley met with God and planned this trial for me.

"Jim, God called you. I'm glad you listened."

Epilogue

My Aunt Mary and grandparents all went to be with the Lord before I came to Christ. Special Mildred from Seventh Baptist, and Bill Hinton, my mentor in prison, are also both walking the streets of gold. While I was writing the last few chapters of this book, sweet Blanche was rewarded with one of the greatest mansions in heaven.

Both Tony Rizzo and Frank Calabrese are dead. Frank spent many years in prison and eventually entered into federal protective custody after revealing many family secrets. Johnny Ciccone Sr., went to prison for skimming money from a Las Vegas casino, he passed away shortly after his release. His son is retired and was never convicted of any offense.

Bob McDonald is now a judge and Pat Riley became an important part of the US Attorney's office in Washington, and recently won the Rosenberg award for excellence in government service. I think the service she gave to me and God surpasses her wonderful service to society.

My ex-partner Dennis spent about four years in prison. We are no longer in touch, but it's my understanding that he eventually went back to the same toner and office supply business we used to run. I know this story paints a negative picture of him, but that was not my intention. In many ways you might say I was a negative influence on him. It's my prayer he someday joins the family of Christ.

I would love to say life was perfect after I came home. God had a plan for me, but it was according to His timing and my level of spiritual maturity. God wants us to grow spiritually, but doesn't force it. I have struggled at times, over the years, as my old past wages war with my new true identity as a believer.

I am thankful my wife was already involved in a church that openly welcomed me. Recently I asked someone from that church what they thought when I showed up.

He said, "I knew you just got out of prison so I did keep an eye on you. But I prayed God would let me treat you well."

He did, and Duane Armstrong and his sweet wife Carla are still some of our best friends.

Christian growth is a voyage. It takes a while for the baggage of the past to be discarded. I had no idea what God's plan for me was. I worked, stayed active in my church, and watched my stepdaughters grow into beautiful and delightful ladies. I was devoted to Judy, but still trying to learn what unselfish love was.

I knew God didn't bring so many obvious miracles into my life without a purpose. I thought being a Sunday school teacher may be the answer, but I often wondered if He had something more in mind. In 1993 the Lord pointed me in the direction He had all along intended for me.

I was doing some marketing consulting for Walk Thru the Bible Ministry, and Judy and I were invited to a donor retreat. Calvin Edwards, the executive vice president of the ministry had been trying to recruit me to work for them, and he felt this weekend would help me decide. I was just happy to aid such a great ministry.

Judy and I were invited to be at the dinner table with the president of the ministry Dr. Bruce Wilkinson, and his wife Darlene. At one point, while someone was giving announcements from a podium, Bruce turned to me, "So are you going to join us? Your extensive business background would be a tremendous asset for us."

Before I could answer Dr. Wilkinson was introduced as the next speaker. He thanked everyone for coming and then pointed towards me. "I'd like you to welcome one of our newest employees, Jim Hall."

No way.

I looked over at Judy and she was crying.

"I always dreamed I'd be married to a preacher. I guess this is pretty close."

I was cooked. I couldn't let her down. I didn't think I was worthy, but I accepted. My life has never been the same. I worked with that great ministry for fifteen years, and continue my full time work in Christian ministry. Dr. Wilkinson and the many other Christian leaders that I've had the privilege to meet have greatly helped me grow and learn. Without their encouraging words this book may not have been written.

When I have the opportunity to share my story I often say that what really pleases God most is often the opposite of what we think. "When I grew up I didn't know what it was like not to be in church. I became a Christian when I was little. I had a little rebellion in college, but have been an active member of my church and a supporter of His causes most of my life. I guess you'd say that's a boring testimony." Not to God. I wish my life had been so uninteresting.

Jesus said, "Let the children come unto me." He is delighted with the little "Bobos" of the world who find Him early in life and walk faithfully with Him. He equally welcomes those like Zaccheaus, the thief on the cross, and Saul, the murderer of Christians who became the Apostle Paul. His arms are open anyone of any age no matter what they have done, as long as they are willing to change their course and come to Him. Every life is precious to Him.

I'm blessed to be married to the most wonderful woman. In many ways Judy has become her mother. She is kind, loving, wise, and humble. In fact, she'll probably be embarrassed I wrote that. We have eight beautiful grandchildren, all within driving distance. I continue sharing my story of all God has done.

I am currently writing my first fiction story entitled *Belladonna*. It's an historical suspense novel loosely based on the mafia, the teamsters and the biggest art theft in US history. Much of it is set in Italy, a country my wife and I have grown to love.

The family of my youth hasn't totally recovered from our scars. I have never been as close to them as I'd like. This reminds me why I spent years writing and rewriting this book. We all need God's miracles, both big and small.

The good news: He wants us to experience them, too.

If you'd like to see some pictures from my past and present, they are included on the e-version of this book, and are available on my website www.jaldenhall.com.

J. Alden (Jim) Hall was a successful businessman for many years before committing to full-time Christian Ministry in 1992. Jim's businesses were diverse and included the popular Carlos McGee's restaurant chain. His involvement and close connections with members of the Chicago Mafia brought his name and businesses up before a special "Organized Crime Task Force" (OCTF). He  became a target of the OCTF, and in 1982 was sentenced to 3 ½ years in federal prison. It was there that his life changed.

After his release, Jim owned a sales and marketing consulting business when Bruce Wilkinson, the founder of Walk Thru the Bible Ministries, persuaded him to work with his organization. For fifteen years Jim led their Seminar Division and when he left was Vice President of Seminars and Training, as well as Interim Vice President of Publishing.

He is a marketing and business consultant and a popular speaker in both Christian and non-Christian settings. Jim is active with his church and leads two large monthly Bible studies in Atlanta. He lives in the Atlanta suburbs with his wife Judy and is within driving distance of their three daughters and eight grandchildren.

Powerline365
Plugging Parents of Teens into the Source

Powerline365 is a high-voltage, multi-format daily devotional to help parents raise Christian teens without losing connection.

Tap into the power you need to lead your teens into a vibrant personal relationship with Jesus. Many teens, even those from Christian homes, fail to connect with Him on a personal level. They search for identity as the enemy pelts them with temptations and doubts. As parents, we're left reeling, wondering where we went wrong.

Powerline365 offers daily insight to ground you in truth as you plug into the Source. It's time for you to power-parent from a place of confidence and surrender, believing God's Word is true, and His promises will never go unfulfilled.

Try it completely FREE for 30 days by visiting www.powerline365.com.

And I am certain that God, who began the good work within [your teenager], will continue his work until it is finally finished on the day when Christ Jesus returns. Phil. 1:6, NLT

30+ inspiring experts write issue-focused columns for parents of teens. Learn how to set boundaries, how to guard against peer pressure, and how to keep your teens solid in the faith. We cover hot-button issues like teen pregnancy and eating disorders, parenting choices and lifestyle questions...and much, much more. Visit www.choose-now.com.

Choose NOW Publishing

Family struggles, hot-button issues, sound biblical support...that's what you'll find in CNP publications. Books written from a Christian worldview will leave you challenged and inspired. Parenting & self-help books, devotionals, Bible studies, and audio resources...CNP provides tools for Christian parents and families. Visit www.choosenowpublishing.com.

Choose NOW Radio

Parent Talk supports parents of teens and tweens on the battleground of peer-pressure, hot-button issues, choices, and insecurities. With expert guests and newsworthy content, Parent Talk confidently prepares parents for and guides them through the turbulent teen years. Visit www.choosenowradio.com or iTunes.

Choose NOW Speaker Team

Talented and anointed speakers are available to minister at your events on a wide range of topics, all focused on reaching people right where their real life is happening, making Jesus known to them in a new way. If you need help with your choice of a Christian keynote speaker, or you'd like more information about our team or about the work of Choose NOW Ministries, please visit www.choose-now.com.

CPSIA information can be obtained at www.ICGtesting.com
Printed in the USA
LVOW12s0217100914

403054LV00005B/19/P